CAN SOCIAL WORK SURVIVE?

To CLP and RFL

Colin Brewer & June Lait

CAN
SOCIAL WORK
SURVIVE?

Temple Smith • London

First published in Great Britain in 1980
by Maurice Temple Smith Ltd
37 Great Russell St, London WC1

ISBN 0 85117 188 5

Printed in Great Britain by
Billing & Sons Ltd.
Guildford, London, Worcester and Oxford

Contents

BASW	— British Association of Social Workers
CCETSW	— Central Council for Education and Training in Social Work
CQSW	— Certificate of Qualification in Social Work
CSS	— Certificate of Social Service
DHSS	— Department of Health and Social Security
MOH	— Medical Officer of Health

Introduction

It may seem a strange principle to enunciate as the very first requirement in a hospital that it should do the sick no harm. Florence Nightingale, *Notes on Hospitals. (1863)*

Social work is one of the helping professions and the good intentions and sincerity of its practitioners can hardly be doubted. Like doctors, social workers want to do good (though both doctors and social workers also have to earn a living), and the satisfaction to be derived from social work, as from the practice of medicine, is often proportionate to the extent to which practitioners can feel — rightly or wrongly — that they have actually done some good. Doing good is not, of course, the exclusive preserve of professionals — in the sense of those who are paid for doing it — and there is certainly no lack of unpaid volunteers for social work. However, it is an unfortunate fact of life that not everything done in the name of helping or doing good is actually helpful to those on the receiving end, however satisfying it may be to the helpers. As Florence Nightingale realised, good intentions are not enough.

Doctors generally believe that the help they can provide in their particular field is an improvement on what can be provided by the average unqualified citizen. Social workers generally take the same view, which is why — like doctors — they increasingly require those entering their ranks to undergo special training and pass examinations, and why they generally expect their pay to reflect the possession of allegedly useful special skills, as it does in most fields. It cannot be assumed, however, that such training actually confers specific skills on its recipients which enable them to do their job more effectively than the untrained. We make the point in this book that for all their elaborate training, it is only since comparatively recent times that doctors have probably done more good than harm, and there are still areas of medical practice which are of very questionable value.

We start, therefore, from the premise that social workers, like doctors, can do harm and that even when they do no positive harm, they do not necessarily do any positive good. When one of us advanced this idea previously, he incensed the social work establishment, and was accused of 'impertinence' by a leading British social worker, while the assistant secretary of the British Association of Social Workers went further and said: 'He should have his head examined. Of course social workers don't do harm.' We do not propose to trade insults, and merely remark that it is customary to be a little suspicious of those who are judges in their own cause, and that there is no obligation to accept that a particular service is beneficial just because those who provide it tell us that it is. Faith and conviction can be attractive qualities, but they can also be incompatible with objectivity.

We hope that no reader will imagine that we are against the existence of organisations intended to provide help for those who find life a struggle. We believe that modern western societies can and should enable all their citizens to have at least the basic material necessities of life, and while we think that priority should be given to providing these necessities, we are not against private or public attempts to gild this basic utilitarian lily, though naturally enough we prefer successful attempts to unsuccessful ones, especially if the failures are also expensive. All western industrial societies have evolved institutions for assisting their less fortunate members. Ours is an imperfect world, and we recognise that these institutions have had some serious imperfections, though we think that they have at least sometimes learned from their mistakes and that they do gradually reflect improvements in living standards and consequent changes in what a society regards as basic necessities. Historically, social workers have been closely involved with the operation and evolution of these institutions. As valued but essentially subordinate employees of the traditional health and welfare agencies, social workers have made a contribution the usefulness of which we do not seek to question. What we do question in this book is the idea that social workers can do more than carry out the practical work of these agencies. We therefore question the status of social work as an independent profession.

In Britain, the Social Services Act 1970, following the recommendations of the Seebohm Committee (Seebohm 1968) created Social Services Departments to undertake the functions previously performed by children's, welfare and public health departments of local authorities. The legislation was based on the idea of 'a community based and family oriented service which will be available to all'—a phrase used, but not defined, by the Seebohm Committee (Seebohm 1968, para 2)—and reflected the conviction of some of the Committee's members that, given adequate resources and suitable organisations from which to operate, social workers could enhance the quality of life for all citizens, as well as more effectively help 'the neglected flotsam and jetsam of society'.

In ten years of operation, the social services departments have come under increasing criticism. Sensational cases of child abuse (Maria Colwell and Steven Mears, notably) have raised doubts about the ability of the new departments to guard the interests of the helpless. Neglected old people dying alone have also been cited in criticism. Social workers have replied by saying that society is using them as scapegoats for its own shortcomings.

It is our conclusion that much of the disarray apparent in social services departments is due to the over-ambitious and loosely-formulated aims of the services, and to the unrealistic training offered to social workers. We believe that cooperation between doctors and social workers is very important and has not been enhanced by the creation of free-standing social services departments. We seek to explain, by examining the origins of the relationship between doctors and social workers, how the present unhappy situation has arisen (Chapters 1 and 2) and to look at the operation of the departments since the Social Services Act (Chapter 3). In Chapter 4 we summarise a previously unpublished survey of the work of a typical department which shows, among other things, the unfortunate effects of reorganisation on the care of the mentally ill. Chapter 5 further examines the functions of social workers and emphasises the importance attached to quasi-psychotherapeutic activities and the influence of psychodynamic ideas.

Some aspects of radical social work are examined in Chapter 6 since we believe that its wilder exponents both contribute to the lamentable diffuseness of the aims of social work and antagonise other professions on whose cooperation social work depends. Private practice in social work is discussed (Chapter 7), partly because those who advocate it are at the other end of the theoretical spectrum from the radicals, partly because of what it tells us about the nature of social work, and partly because we think it may be one of the ways in which social work will develop, if it is to develop at all.

We have already mentioned the idea that some activities designated as 'helpful' can actually do harm. In Chapter 8, we develop this theme and, in the context of how to assess the effectiveness of intervention, whether by doctors or social workers, describe some of the factors which can make objective assessment difficult, especially those which can lead to unwarranted enthusiasm about a particular technique. This is followed in Chapter 9 by a review of published studies concerned with the effectiveness of social work of various kinds. It reveals, in general, a highly discouraging picture, and in Chapter 10 we suggest reasons for the apparent ineffectiveness of much social work. We suggest ways in which effectiveness might be improved, although we also present disturbing evidence that many social workers do not appear to have much interest in whether or not what they do is effective.

In our final chapter, we conclude that social work is currently in such a muddle and is so confused about its functions (and while we have concentrated on British social work, we think this may be true of other countries too) that the situation merits an urgent and energetic enquiry. We know that the British Association of Social Workers also feels that an enquiry is indicated; but because of the evidence we have presented that social workers are at least as prone to conspiracies against the laity (in the words of George Bernard Shaw) as other professions are, and that they are as certain of their value as they are reluctant to put that value to the test, we feel strongly that social workers should not have a prominent role on any investigating body.

While we do not want to anticipate the findings of such an enquiry, we have made a few suggestions about how the undoubted and—in our view—highly praiseworthy desire of social workers to increase the sum of human happiness might be more effectively harnessed. We anticipate that many social workers will not agree with them, but if the reaction to some of our previous publications in this field is any guide, we feel confident that disagreement will be far from universal. At all events, we make these suggestions, as we have written this book, in the belief that without some very radical—and doubtless rather painful—changes, social work in its present form is in serious danger both from the increasing disillusionment of those who practise it, and from the increasing irritation and derision of those who pay for it.

1

Beginnings: Social work, medicine and training until Seebohm

Training and the Charity Organisation Society. Doctors and almoners. Training for the practitioner, not the client? Psychiatric social work and the American influence. Effect of the National Health Service on almoners and psychiatric social workers. Mental Welfare Officers and Duly Authorised Officers. Seebohm and medicine. Social work and general practice.

In England, social work for which training was thought necessary goes back to the Charity Organisation Society, which very early in its existence began to train its workers.* Mainly occupied in giving material aid to people judged to be morally superior to those with whom the Poor Law dealt, Charity Organisation Society workers were initially instructed in financial matters and record keeping. Gradually, however, training came to include instruction about human behaviour and social functioning (Smith 1953), it being hoped that an understanding of these aspects would enable decisions about deserving and undeserving recipients of aid to be made on a basis of sound theory rather than individual prejudice. It is likely that then, as now, theory burgeoned to meet a demand, rather than, as is fortunately inevitable in the natural sciences, by the advancement of hypotheses which stand until overset under experimental testing by better ones.

Most of the jobs undertaken by trained social workers between

---

*Its pioneering efforts were not the very first. That honour goes to the National Children's Home, which in 1860 instituted in-service training for its workers and throughout its long and honourable history has continued to pioneer and innovate. The Reverend W. Pennefather founded the Mildmay Institute for the training of deaconesses in 1864, influenced by Pastor Fliedmer of Kaisenwerth. (see Heasman 1962).

the wars involved close collaboration with doctors, either as almoners in hospitals or as psychiatric social workers in mental hospitals and child guidance clinics. Many untrained and a very few trained social workers also worked with doctors in the Health and Welfare services of local authorities. To study the history of medical social work (a title present practitioners prefer to almoning) is instructive on several counts. Almoning began at a time when hospitals outside the Poor Law were privately financed, and was itself a creation of the Charity Organisation Society. Most social services were pioneered by volunteers and it is tempting (though probably unjustifiable within the compass of a book with small pretensions to historical insight) to assert that services shown by volunteers to be useful are either subsidised or taken over by the state when voluntary finance runs out. Medical social work does not substantiate this assertion. From the first Lady Almoner, Mary Stewart, appointed to the Royal Free Hospital in 1895, until salaried employees of local authorities began to be appointed after the Public Health Act of 1936, almoning attracted ladies of independent means. The Association of Almoners must be one of the few bodies which, finding itself with a surplus of funds, was able to halve its subscription and start a library with the residue (Bell 1961, p. 109). Prosperity was not simply a result of having prosperous recruits, but of generous funding from outside charitable bodies, notably the Northcote Trust. Well-connected ladies appear to have been able to extract funds from hard-headed businessmen for very unlikely purposes, and some would say that social work today has been profoundly affected by Dame Eileen Younghusband's ability to do this, notably with the Carnegie Trust.

It is the present writers' contention that this ability did, and possibly does, permit aspiring professions to indulge in activities whose primary purpose is the satisfaction of the professionals rather than of those they serve. It would be unjustifiable, nay churlish, to assert that the early almoners were not motivated by a desire to serve, but service had to be given in a form acceptable to middle-class ladies whose fathers, brothers, and in a few daring cases, husbands, were in professional occupations. Benevolence in a hospital setting, avoiding the physical labour of nursing, was one of the earliest respectable jobs available to women, and it was perhaps inevitable that they should seek to mould it on professional lines, irrespective of whether the functions undertaken were in any real sense professional. From the desire to be regarded as professionals grew the desire to *reject* activities that were unprofessional, even though it was precisely these activities that benefited the public and the doctors with whom almoners worked. Training developed, it would seen, to meet professional aspirations as much as to meet the needs of clients. Not being subject to any stark market test, almoners could and did assert the need for training at university level, training with grandiose objectives like understanding humanity and society rather than detecting fraud and dispensing charitable funds. Having been introduced in training to such elevated concepts, some almoners resented the humdrum reality of the work they actually did, a resentment some social workers still feel. (See Chapter 3).

The history of almoning reveals another potent factor in the development of social work: a desire initially for regard by, but later for parity with, doctors. The first lady almoner was not welcomed with open arms by the doctors at the Royal Free Hospital. Moberly Bell describes the situation (Bell 1961, pp. 27-8):

> Mary Stewart had for some years been working as Secretary to the North St. Pancras Committee of the Charity Organisation Society. She belonged to that generation of Victorian women to whom the opportunity of education had appeared as a glorious adventure. She had come under the influence of Miss Buss of the North London Collegiate School, and not content to live a life of refined penury as a daughter in the home, she had trained under the COS as a social worker. She came to the Royal Free Hospital therefore with much knowledge of the conditions of the poor and the problems she would be called upon to face. The most difficult of these problems she had probably not anticipated—this was the suspicion and hostility with which most of the medical staff regarded her. Her work had been carefully defined. She was to prevent the abuse of the hospital by those who could afford to pay, to refer those in need of relief to the Poor Law and to recommend all who could afford to do so to join a Provident Dispensary. The doctors, however, made it perfectly clear that the ultimate authority to select or reject applicants was in their hands and not hers. The medical staff certainly wanted the chaos of the out-patient department reduced to order; the doctors resented the time wasted on trivial cases, on patients who wandered from hospital to hospital getting a bottle of medicine here and advice there and profiting by neither; they had clearly no time themselves to discriminate by inquiry into social conditions; something certainly ought to be done. But, to have a woman, not really under their control, in a quasi-official capacity—this was too disconcerting and very much to be deprecated.

This almost instinctive hostility of doctors and surgeons was not peculiar to the Royal Free Hospital.

Miss Stewart's salary was paid not by the hospital but by the
Charity Organisation Society, and at the end of a three-month
probationary period the hospital chose not to renew the appointment unless the COS continued to pay. For six months Miss
Stewart was relegated to COS headquarters, but eventually an
arrangement was made whereby the COS paid half her salary and
the hospital the other half, and she resumed her work. The idea of
almoning by COS ladies was not, however, quick to catch on. When
C. S. Loch, secretary of the COS, wrote to *The Times* in the sum-
mer of 1898 eulogising the work being done at the Royal Free, a
Governor of St Mary's Paddington pointed out that they too had
an investigation officer. 'He was a retired policeman, with an intimate knowledge of the district; he was present when all applicants
arrived and was able with long experience to assess their situation
with some shrewdness.' (One supposes he did not suffer from delusions of grandeur about his status *vis-à-vis* the medical staff,
probably genuflecting as they passed, a gesture obviously inappropriate in a lady almoner.)

By 1903 seven London hospitals had lady almoners. Miss Mudd
at St George's had ventured outside her financial and policing
functions, advising penurious expectant mothers in matters of diet
and encouraging tuberculosis patients to live in huts at the bottom
of their gardens. E. Moberly Bell reports that the Almoners Committee of St George's was unimpressed, even censorious, complaining that 'a department, preventing abuse and furthering con-
valescent treatment and sanatorium treatment has practically
become, without authority, a health visiting society; the almoners
department has taken up a branch of Health Education and Preventive Work entirely unknown to the Committee'. Miss Bell,
whose stance is that of a feminist and an admirer of almoners,
comments:

> Here was a pretty state of affairs! A woman giving advice (how-
> ever good) without asking the doctors. This was intolerable. It
> is a pity that Ethel Mudd was never able to do for St George's
> all the work her great intelligence might have accomplished.
> Success in the field of medical social service depends on
> co-operation and mutual understanding between doctor
> and social workers, and at St George's this had never been
> established.

It did not occur to Miss Bell that the objections to Miss Mudd's self-imposed advisory functions might have been based on her lack of competence to undertake them rather than on considerations of status and prejudice against women. Health visitors, after all, were also women, and they were considered suitable for these activities because of their training. (Almoners did, however, take an active part in the treatment of tuberculosis at a later stage, largely because they gained financial backing from the Northcote Trust.)

The development of almoning and of training for it proceeded slowly, without notable enthusiasm from the medical profession. When in 1920 voluntary hospitals were empowered to charge patients according to their means, almoners had an anxious time deciding whether they should undertake the job of assessing the contributions, since, in common with many social workers today (Parsloe 1978), they considered money likely to sully their relationship with clients, the development of which they believed to be central. But they gallantly took the collar, and as Miss Bell comments, 'the Institute minuted the opinion that the almoner was the person most capable of assessing the contributions of patients with justice, and that therefore the work should be entrusted to her'. While we do not suppose doctors wanted to be bothered with mundane matters like assessment, it seems unlikely that their readiness to cooperate with almoners was enhanced by a statement of such Olympian confidence, not to say arrogance. It is tempting to quote Miss Bell further, for her book is a mine of information and supplies (inadvertently, it seems) much ammunition for those who believe the profession of almoning to have been pretentiously inflated, and to have afflicted the aspiring profession of social work with some of its worst defects.

Almoners are no more. The advent of a health service free at point of receipt abolished their financial functions at a stroke, leaving them free to develop the functions suggested by their new title, medical social workers. Although the Social Services Act 1970 did not transfer MSWs from the health service to local authorities, this was done when the health service was reorganised in 1974, and they now operate in settings which are frequently governed by the principle of 'genericism', i.e. all social workers undertaking all sorts of cases rather than specialising. However, most MSWs are still based in hospitals, and it would be interesting to explore whether relations between them and doctors have changed under the new arrangements. One very real problem is confidentiality. Some doctors are even more reluctant to share confidential information about patients with a local authority employee than they were when the MSW, though not medically trained, was at least an employee of the hospital board with whom the doctor was contracted. But the principal problem still seems to be doctors' uncertainty about what service other than a purely administrative one the MSW can offer, and the inability MSWs share with other social workers to make this service comprehensible. The old problems of status do not seem to have gone away, either. While neither of us is uncritical of doctors, who are as likely as social workers to lay claim to expertise they aspire to rather than possess, we do know that part of a doctor's status comes from recognisable effectiveness in some activities. We can see no comparable attainment in social work, and find more than a little baffling comments like the following by Miss E.M.R. Clarkson, who has extensive experience in lecturing to doctors in the USA, Canada, the UK, and also in social work training at senior level:

> Sometimes patients are referred from other social workers in the community, but the greatest number of referrals are likely to come from doctors and nurses who in the course of their daily work with patients, are likely to learn what is troubling them. A good referral pre-supposes knowledge of what social workers do: sometimes doctors and nurses may use social workers incorrectly, thinking on the one hand that they can only make practical arrangements, and on the other that they are a type of psychotherapist. The real job of the medical social worker lies somewhere between these two—in the area of linking up supportive help with practical considerations. Increasingly now medical social workers are employed as teachers in medical schools, lecturing to medical students on the social factors of illness which they should be aware of in order to treat their patients properly, and helping them to learn how to make appropriate referrals. (Clarkson 1974, pp. 5-6)

Miss Clarkson does not, unfortunately, go on to elaborate on the 'somewhere between these two'; nor make clear what she means by 'supportive help', so that one is left unsure as to what are 'appropriate' referrals. Possibly the ones MSWs like and consider 'professional'?.

Social workers claim that their training endows them with skill in making relationships. We are indebted to a consultant surgeon, who wishes to remain anonymous, for permission to reprint the following correspondence between him and the medical social worker employed in his hospital, from which it would seem that at least some social workers have yet some way to go in the matter of relationships.

To: Consultant Surgeons and Orthopaedic Surgeons

Dear ZM

As you may know I provide a social work service to ZM ward and I would like to extend my activities to offer at least a welfare service to the parents of children admitted for surgery, or indeed to the children themselves. Not that all cases will need the attention of a social worker but certain parents see this as a crisis situation and can suffer a state of shock as a result. This is fairly common with first time admissions to hospital and the over anxious or attention seeking parent or child.

I am normally on duty within the hospital and could meet parents if you wish when admission is first discussed at out patients. We could then offer any support advice or practical help that may be required in the days leading to hospital admission and while on the ward.

The ward staff are very happy to arrange ward visits and to cooperate in any activity that would make things less distressing for the family concerned.

The paediatric unit will eventually be producing an instructive booklet for parents explaining the procedures, how the ward is run etc. and I have access to some simpler booklets designed for younger children which deal with the whole range of ward events with a fairly light-hearted presentation. I hope that you will agree this is a very useful service to offer some children and their parents and that it would serve to reduce some of the tension associated with a stay in hospital.

Principal Social Worker

To Principal Social Worker

Dear ZM

Thank you for your letter, telling me that the admission of some children to hospital can be an occasion of stress for their parents. I note also that you find that such stress falls more heavily on the over-anxious.

I shall bear your offer in mind, and will ask for your help through the usual channels if need arises.

In the main, however, I shall continue to rely on my own efforts, and that of the parents themselves, for the period before admission.

On and after admission, in addition, we naturally have the help of the nurses, who have the double asset of their nursing understanding, on the one hand, and their actually having the care of the children, on the other.

I should wish to study any instructive literature with some care before sanctioning its distribution to my child patients.

Yours sincerely,

Consultant Surgeon

If almoners were the Lady Bountifuls of the social work profession, psychiatric social workers have some claim to have been its intellectual storm troops. Unlike almoners, who in a sense 'just growed', PSWs were a deliberate invention, and were not appointed until after a special training course to produce them had been set up in the London School of Economics in 1929. It would be reassuring to report that this training was a response to some identified need in society to which those trained would respond. Rather it appears to have been the work of a few enthusiasts, fired by observation of American experiments in child guidance. American social workers were at this period heading for what K. Woodroofe (1962) terms 'the psychiatric deluge', a devotion to a psychoanalytic interpretation of behaviour loosely based on the writing of Freud. Training courses funded by philanthropists and demonstration clinics at which the new methods were displayed impressed an English magistrate, Mrs St Loe Strachey, so much that she determined to introduce them in Britain. The Commonwealth Fund offered help, and gave money to set up the course and scholarships to enable social workers to visit America. Several of these scholars subsequently became tutors at the LSE.

The detailed history of psychiatric social work is sensitively and accurately conveyed in Noel Timms' book (1964) to which the interested reader can refer. Two themes appear to run through the development of psychiatric social work. One is anxiety to define precisely the activity to which the label attaches. The other is a striving to ensure that psychiatric social workers neither are, nor are seen to be, subservient to the medical profession. Subsidiary to these, but to some extent dependent on them, is an effort to ensure employment for PSWs in settings where their skills may best be deployed, and to cultivate their image as an elite amongst social workers. Service to the public is the peg on which these ambitions are hung, but it is our contention that no real attempt was ever made to ascertain precisely what the need was to which the service sought to respond.

The problem of definition proved a tough one, and conferences of the Institute of Psychiatric Social Workers grappled with it unsuccessfully year after year. It is perhaps significant that even as late as 1935, nine years after the profession was born, there was debate about what it should be called. One of the present joint authors (JL) teaches in a department which has experienced similar heart-searching about what heading should appear on its writing paper, and which has in fact changed its name from the Department of Social Administration to the Department of Social Policy and Social Work. It is her belief that ambivalence about titles sometimes (though not of course invariably) denotes uncertainty about function, though such uncertainty appears not to inhibit the offering of instruction in whatever it is, a matter to which we shall return. Be that as it may, there was no uncertainty in the mind of one Dr W. Kimber, who, addressing the General Meeting of the Institute in 1935, boldly suggested the title 'psychiatric assistant'. It need hardly be said that this was not greeted with enthusiasm, though it may well have been an accurate description of many PSWs working in child guidance clinics and mental hospitals. Between the years 1936 and 1939, the Institute was concerned with the question whether its members should be registered as medical auxiliaries (for a full discussion see Timms 1964, pp. 169-71), a status which ensured advantageous conditions of service but also required compliance with a rule that an auxiliary should work only under the control and direction of a medical practitioner. Not surprisingly, auxiliary status was rejected.

A conference held in 1942 was once again preoccupied with problems of definition. *Faute de mieux*, because someone had to do it and they were around, some PSWs had been concerned with evacuation, more often than not in a very non-psychoanalytic if useful fashion, counting children as they boarded and dismounted from trains duly labelled, checking addresses and ensuring changes of underwear, for example. This had created what the profession styles an identity crisis in some PSWs and there was long debate about the propriety of allocating such mundane tasks to those whose expertise was with the psyche. One member sensibly remarked that it was odd they should still be wondering what they were or ought to be doing, and asked whether a useful approach might be to ask what were PSWs doing now that was different from the social work they did before training. A good question, that should be, but it seems rarely is, both asked and answered before the content of training is determined. We suggest asking it in our final chapters.

Opportunities for concern with status were legion in the fields in which PSWs were employed. Timms reveals (p. 78) that between 1947 and 1953 over 70 per cent of PSWs worked either in child guidance clinics or in hospitals. In both these settings they were under the general direction of a doctor, usually a psychiatrist. A few PSWs worked in clinics provided by local education authorities as part of the school psychological service, and here they were under the general oversight of an educational psychologist. (For a succinct account of the variety of administrative settings under which child guidance was provided, see Ryan (1967).) Others worked in clinics run jointly by health and education, and in some of these, with psychiatrist and educational psychologist disputing primacy, the position of the PSW must have been difficult. Nevertheless, child guidance was the preferred field for PSWs in pre-health-service days, but improved salaries in hospitals and in community work with the mentally handicapped after the National Health Service Act led to a shift in emphasis (see Timms 1964, Chapter 4).

The Younghusband Report (Younghusband 1959) suggested that PSWs were especially suited to act as advisers and consultants to other social workers, and they are substantially represented amongst social work teachers. E. Irvine, writing in Dame Eileen Younghusband's *Social Work in Britain 1950-1975* (Younghusband 1978, p. 189), reveals that, in 1969, 59 PSWs were teaching in universities and 48 in colleges of further education. They were also influential in central government, 6 working at the Department of Health & Social Security, one as deputy chief social worker, no less.

As already stated, the advent of the health service removed from almoners all concern with assessing cost and collecting fees, and the prospect of this development caused the two professions to confer about their respective functions, attempting to demarcate areas of competence. Timms (1964, p. 176) reports: 'The Almoners suggested as a distinguishing criterion the degree of maladjustment; if the general physician could deal with the patient, then the social work could be carried out by the almoner. The psychiatric social workers suggested as criteria the existence of physical illness, or of mainly psychological causes of illness. The first kind of case should go to the almoner, the second to the PSW.' The only element of reality in either of these criteria is the recognition of the central importance of medicine, and it is far from explicit.

Another identity crisis the PSW had to meet was concerned with the work of Duly Authorised Officers, who were to be Health Service employees under the National Health Service Act 1946. Could PSWs properly undertake these duties? In the *British Journal of*

Psychiatric Social Work, November 1949, A. LeMesurier opined that 'some of our profession feel that the D. A. Officers' duties are as remote from Psychiatric Social Work as are the duties of a constable on his beat'. Discussion on both these questions appears to have continued *sine die,* without resolution, and without noticeable effect on the course of the welfare state, or indeed on anything else except the taxpayer's pocket. Now that Seebohm has subsumed both PSWs and almoners under the concept of 'generic' social work these controversies have a slightly nostalgic dottiness, but at the time they seemed issues of the first importance to those involved.

The last group of workers whose emergence we study would not for most of their history call themselves social workers, nor would most of them have received training other than in-service. These are the Mental Welfare Officers employed in public health departments of local authorities under the direction of a Medical Officer of Health, sometimes with a Chief Mental Welfare Officer as a second in command. The mental health sections set up under the National Health Service Act 1948 were staffed principally by those who had worked in public assistance and had acted as Duly Authorised Officers under the Lunacy Acts, by Mental Welfare Officers who had previously worked for voluntary bodies, and by registered mental nurses. It is a staggering fact that duties so onerous as those carried by the Duly Authorised Officer had not been seen as needing formal training, involving as they did deprivation of liberty, and, some would say, clinical judgement of an advanced kind. But these officers unlike the almoners and PSWs, always operated within a firm legal framework, and would appear unquestioningly to have accepted the expertise of doctors with whom they worked.

Because of their status simply as employees of local government, their history is largely a matter of guesswork, since there are few proceedings of professional associations on which to draw, no separate identity to assert. Much of what we say must therefore be impressionistic, but both of us have worked closely with MWOs. It was our impression, and that of many colleagues, that these officers, in spite of, or possibly because of, an absence of formal training, were providing a sensitive, innovative, and above all efficient service based on a response to the client's need rather than their own. There did not seem to be the tension between them and the doctors so characteristic of the other two specialisms. Perhaps the precision and urgency of the functions undertaken left little time or energy for preoccupation with matters of status. This view might receive some support if, as seems to be the case, the Mental

Health Act 1959, which broadened and possibly obfuscated the functions of mental welfare officers, brought in its train claims for professional standing and dissatisfaction with the subservient position. Before the Act, numbers of PSWs in local authority mental welfare departments were small, but the increased scope for ill-defined activity occasioned by that benevolent but imprecise Act, the forerunner of many others of similar quality, attracted larger numbers.

Many criticisms have been levelled at the Seebohm Committee. It was imprecise, it failed to undertake research, it had made up its mind before it looked at the evidence, and so forth. In her book *Reforming the Welfare,* P. Hall (1976) adduces evidence tending to support many of these criticisms, but the aspect of the Seebohm Report that we wish to focus on in this chapter is its contribution to the social work/medical dialogue.

The first thing to note is the slenderness of medical representation on the Committee. Professor Morris was undoubtedly a most distinguished epidemiologist, but must have been hard put to it to represent the varying medical interests in face of the phalanx of social workers, or more precisely, social work teachers. The absence of an MOH (under the 1974 reorganisation restyled Community Physician) was an especial weakness.

Chapter XI of the Report, 'Social services for Mentally Subnormal and Mentally Ill People', asserts without any shred of evidence we can discover that 'only by breaking down the barriers between hospital and local authority, and *mobilising all the trained social workers in a single service* will there be a chance of deploying them where they are most needed'. A similar declaration of faith occurs in para. 348: 'We believe that the clearer definition of roles and responsibilities *which will result from* the establishment of social service departments should help' (our italics). Or again, para. 352, rejecting the evidence submitted by health committees and MOHs in favour of their retention of the mental health services: 'We think it would be a great mistake to exclude the mental health *social* services [an interesting creative insertion by the committee of the word 'social' without, of course, any clue as to its meaning] from the new department, not for administrative tidiness or to provide attractive careers for social workers, but because to include these services in the department appears to us most likely to serve the public need and to secure progress in ensuring social help for the mentally disordered and their families'. Dire consequences for the mentally disordered are predicted and totally unfounded statements about the state of mind of 'the community' (another word used as though it has precise meaning when it has little or none) are made in para. 354: 'Not to include these services in the social services department would mean further segregation for the mentally disordered when in fact the community is becoming ready for their further integration'. Seebohm concedes that the new departments will need expert medical advice, and remarks (para. 357) that 'in some areas public health doctors who have specialised in mental health may qualify for these posts'. The social work interest also ensured the inclusion in the Social Services Act 1970 of a provision that appointments of Directors of Social Service should be subject to the approval of the minister. Of especial significance in this context are paras. 616-636 of the Seebohm Report. It is possible to interpret much of the verbiage as a not very well disguised attempt to ensure that no MOHs were appointed to the new posts. The Committee do not go quite so far as to insist that Chief Officers should have social work training, but in para. 620 they say: 'No single profession in local government at present combines the ideal range of skills which will be required ... the objective should be to secure that most heads . . . . are people professionally qualified in social work (including those qualified in residential care) who have received training in management and administration at appropriate points in their careers, or administrators with qualifications in social work'.

It has not, for obvious reasons, been possible to obtain details of action taken by the minister to reject applicants without social work training, but it is well known that a great deal of in-fighting occurred, and that several local authorities were prevented from appointing their preferred candidates, several of whom were doctors.

In Chapter XXI the Seebohm Committee assess the implications of their recommendations for other services, and in para. 690 they mention with regret the failure of doctors to cooperate with social workers in the past. They refer to differences of opinion between doctors and social workers on what the latter's function is in hospital, and say: 'in the case of medical officers of health, mutual misunderstanding with social workers has gone so far as to be a significant factor in our overall thinking on the future shape of the social services'. We regard this as a serious understatement. In para. 694 the Committee refer to what they call 'contrasting developments in the two professions'. Medicine is 'ever refining its objectivity and technology, which increasingly is the basis of its authority and of the responsibility that it takes on behalf of the patient and society'. Social workers, on the other hand, attach much importance to 'the acquiring of personal insight and understanding'. The Committee consider that much of the difficulty over confidentiality is founded in doctors' poor training in 'the psychological and social factors in the management of illness and the prevention of chronic disability and dependency nor do they know how to get help from social agencies and to collaborate with social workers'. They believe, with an astonishing lack of humility, that the answer to these problems is to be found in part in altering medical training, a suggestion previously outlined by E. M. R. Clarkson (see below, p. 16). The Committee mention without comment that an irritant to many doctors is 'a lack of interest of many workers in the social services, and even among the academics, in evaluating the results of their work'. (It remains a profound irritant to the joint authors of this book.) Another factor in poor collaboration is 'the common assumption that the doctor must be the leader in any team of which he is a member, and such difficulties are reinforced by external indicators in pay etc.'. Seebohm does not go so far as to recommend equal pay!

These extracts from Cmnd. 3703 surely indicate that there was cause for concern by doctors about its recommendations, and it is an unsolved mystery why they were on the whole late and ill-organised in their opposition to it. (For comment on this see Hall (1976), especially pp. 85-7 and 93-7.) Preoccupation with the proposed reorganisation of local government but especially the National Health Service accounts for some of the apathy, but we lean to the view that organisations like the Society of Medical Officers of Health and the BMA simply did not believe so inept a document would be taken seriously. Whatever the explanation, the tardiness with which they organised opposition cost them—and, we believe, the general public—very dear. The incorporation of the mental health services into social services departments was perhaps the most controversial of Seebohm's decisions (and has had unfortunate results:see Chapter 5), and we have already referred to the assertions unsupported by evidence accompanying this recommendation. For dotty opacity Baroness Serota's remark when delivering the Fourth Younghusband Lecture at the National Institute for Social Work Training exceeds anything in Seebohm : 'The amalgamation of the medically orientated social work services with the non medically orientated social work services helps us to establish the principal of universality in those areas where social work is still somewhat tainted with stigma'. With supporters like this it is little wonder the Seebohm departments created by the Social Services Act 1970 have not been very successful in their dealings with the mentally ill. Such an assertion is difficult to substantiate, particularly when a term like 'successful' is not precisely defined, but some of the difficulties and defeats are sympathetically but incisively described by Eric Sainsbury, Professor of Social Administration at Sheffield (Sainsbury 1977, esp. pp. 52-5). He refers especially to the inadequate experience and over-diffuse training of many young social workers required to deal with the intricacies of the 1959 Mental Health Act and to understand the often bizarre behaviour of the mentally ill, contrasting them unfavourably with the former mental welfare officers. He also speaks of deteriorating relationships between doctors and social workers, occasioned by the replacement of small, accessible mental health sections of public health departments by the burgeoning bureaucracies of social services departments, and expresses anxiety about the 'anti-professional' movements in social work which he thinks alarm many doctors. Our Chapter on Radical Social Work refers to some of these movements.

2

A closer look at training

Dame Eileen Younghusband and social work training. Different but equal? Seebohm and training. Advent of the Central Council for Education and Training in Social Work (CCETSW). Certificate of qualification in Social Work. Certificate in Social Service. Residential work and its demands. The Birch Report; is there any such thing as social work? Should social work training be sited in universities? Selection of social workers for training. Course content. Universities v. CCETSW.

It is our contention that without a precise definition of the task for which training is deemed necessary it is impossible to devise effective training. An examination of the development of social work training reveals that many of those responsible for providing it do not share our view. The picture is so complex, the ambiguities so profound yet unacknowledged, that it is difficult to know where to start in an attempt to disentangle the themes underlying training. We have outlined in Chapter 1 the development of training for medical and psychiatric social work, and have suggested that the training provided met the desires of those teaching and receiving it, but was not necessarily relevant to any expressed need of the public. We also think that because of an unwillingness to question benevolence (or what advertised itself as benevolence) in too hostile a fashion, public agencies took on and funded existing training courses whose inception they would have been unlikely to consider.

Dame Eileen Younghusband, who has been styled by *New Society* the 'Grand Dame of Social Work', describes the situation in the 1950s and 60s thus:

By 1950 modern social work education (i.e. the application of theory in practice, learning how to make knowledge operational) had barely started, except in the mental health courses, and later only spread slowly. In the social work field as a whole in the 1950s, few people had any training, largely because no opportunities then existed apart from the small intake on social science university courses, the mental health, medical social work, child care, probation, and moral welfare training and various *ad hoc* specialised short courses, for instance for *NSPCC* inspectors or home teachers of the blind. The foundations of social work education had to be laid against many odds, and social work teachers faced conflicts in both the universities and the fieldwork agencies at a time when they themselves were struggling to discover a new identity.

The first stage was the long struggle to clarify the aims of the social science courses, i.e. whether they offered a good grounding in the social sciences, a pre-professional course, or the first stage of actual social work training. Fortunately the professionals lost the battle to make them more vocational. It was also fortunate that old university rigidities about vocational training changed, so that this began to be built on a foundation of social science, pre-professional courses.

In this second stage from about 1950, pressure was mounting for generic casework courses in the universities. This resulted in 'the Carnegie experiment'. . . .

The third stage began in 1961 with two-year, integrated — i.e. social studies and professional — courses in colleges of further education and university extramural departments. In time in employment these students achieved equal status with university students. As a result, the essential lesson began to be learnt that any professional course must aim at competence in practice, that knowledge must be both relevant and applied. At each stage, practice and teaching related to it were forced to go ahead of verified knowledge. (Younghusband 1978, p. 19).

How lightly Dame Eileen skates over so much thin ice, how magisterial her pronouncements on matters of the greatest complexity. (The word magisterial is not inappropriate. In an interview in *New Society* Dame Eileen revealed that when considering what career to undertake she was advised by the formidable Beatrice Webb to become a Relieving Officer under the Poor Law. This did not appeal, so she became a magistrate instead!) *Fortunately* the professionals lost the battle to make the courses more vocational, she tells us. Fortunately for whom? And what was so fortunate about an (alleged) change in 'old university rigidities about vocational training'? And whence came the pressure for generic courses?

And what actually does she mean, if anything? There is an un-accustomed, possibly unconscious, candour about the admission that 'at each stage, practice and teaching related to it were forced to go ahead of verified knowledge'. One of the authors remembers this phenomenon vividly when being 'trained' as a child care officer. 'All human life was there' in thirty lectures from a psychia-tric social worker who appeared never to question the most *outré* Freudian explanations of her and our remarkably conventional middle-class goings-on. The relevance to the author's subsequent experience of poverty-stricken families was tenuous in the extreme, as it was to the rearing of her two children. It was, however, delivered with the authority of a university teacher, and was difficult for the inexperienced to question (especially those lacking a sense of humour).

Dame Eileen modestly omits reference to her own central role in the setting up both of 'the Carnegie experiment' and of the 'two year, integrated courses'. Her role as tutor at the LSE is revealing-ly documented in Donnison's *Social Policy and Administration Revisited* (1975) (which those interested in observing experts at human relationships relating to each other should consider man-datory reading), but it is in the Younghusband Report (1959) that Dame Eileen makes explicit (if that is the correct term) her views about social work training. She sees it as necessary to have two, or rather two and a bit, grades of worker to correspond to the three grades of client. The university trained would deal with 'complex cases'; those who needed 'a competent social work service' would have the services of workers enjoying 'a new general training, relat-ed to, but outside the university'; and then the also rans, 'others who could be served by welfare assistants under the supervision of qualified social workers'. Democratic as always (within limits), Dame Eileen concedes that some of the welfare assistants 'would go on later to full training'. She does not commit herself on what any of these luminaries would actually be doing, but she knows, for she tells us what fields of study will equip than to do it:

(a) human behaviour—how people function in their physical, psychological and social aspects, with sufficient 'usable' knowledge about health and disease;
(b) social and economic circumstances, social structure and common social attitudes, especially towards handicap;
(c) the social services (including voluntary organisations), and the various forms of social care and treatment, and the principles and practice of administration;
(d) the principles and practice of social work (this would be

      primarily case-work, but later group work and community
      organisation should be added);
  (e) other optional skills, including Moon, Braille, handicrafts,
      and communication with the deaf.

If the reader finds this list unilluminating, he will be glad to know
that Dame Eileen had previously aided the Mackintosh Committee
(Mackintosh 1951) with the following definition of social work (p. 8):
'The Social Worker is concerned with remedying certain deficiencies which may exist in the relation between the individual and
his environment, and for this purpose is concerned with the total
individual in relation to the whole of his environment, in so far as
this is relevant to righting such deficiencies'.

It is both surprising and discouraging to us (since we hope in this
book to deflate some of the pompous pretensions of some social
workers) to recall that in the same year that the Younghusband
Report appeared, Barbara Wootton dealt hammer blows of such
force and precision against the profession that we are surprised it
survived. See for example her discourse on 'Clients and Casework'
(Wootton 1959), pp. 289-90). Having pointed out the inappropriate-
ness of the term 'client' she writes: 'Naturally the social worker's
"client", never having been in a position to pay any piper, must
make the best of any tune the caseworker choses to play . . . Outside the esoteric world of social work "caseworker" is not understood, nor can one easily imagine any social worker's "client"
saying "I must get hold of the services of a caseworker" as he might
say "I must find a doctor or a solicitor". In the mind of the uninitiat-
ed the professional label "caseworker" immediately provokes the
question—case of what? Other professions specify the nature of
their cases: in medicine general practitioners deal with cases of
illness, specialists with cases of particular diseases; judges and
magistrates deal with cases of fraud, burglary, homosexuality or
dangerous driving; but the caseworker deals with—cases of what?'
And much more in the same devastating vein.

Lady Wootton's book has run into at least five editions, but the
social workers have gone from strength to strength. A daunting
prospect.

Such was the influence of Dame Eileen that her recommendations were heeded, and social work courses were set up alongside the
existing university ones which had the effect of dividing the profession into officers and men, but in our opinion, in the absence of the
all important definition of function, left them an army without a
cause other than self-aggrandisement.

The next important pronouncement on training was made by

the Seebohm Committee. All the speculations and recommendations of this body appear to be fatally flawed by a failure to define
what they meant by the 'personal social services' or more precisely, what was common to the services they listed in para. 31, p. 17,
remarking that they took these services as 'a starting point' (see
discussion in Chapter 3). Saddled with terms of reference, 'to review
the organisation and responsibilities of the local authority personal
social services in England and Wales and to consider what changes
are desirable to secure an effective family service', failing to render
them precise, it is small wonder that the Committee's recommendations on training are themselves unfocused. Of course, there was a
demand for more of it, and a few sensible-sounding gestures were
made to the need for 'a good deal of interdisciplinary training' and
for training which enabled its holders 'to assess the effectiveness of
different ways of meeting needs' (Seebohm 1968, p. 164, para. 528).
We have found no evidence that either of these recommendations
was heeded, and indeed the committee gave no hints about how
they might be implemented.

The Report also conceded (p. 164, para. 529) that staff in residential establishments and even secretaries and telephonists
would carry heavy responsibilities in the new social services departments, and probably needed training, but devoted its attention
mainly to the training of fieldworkers. Para. 531. refers to 'the need
for staff trained in the principles and skills that are common to all
forms of social work with individuals and families' but does not
elucidate what these skills are. They include casework, of course,
but also (para. 545) social group work, social work with communities,
social planning and the administration of social work services. It
is our contention that without some indication of content, these
terms are just hopeful labels. The Committee's hope that some
universities will devote resources to the development of new courses
of training to prepare social workers to work with groups and with
the community and for advanced work with family problems, did
not seem unrealistic at the time the Committee was collecting evidence (if that is a fair description of its activities, which we doubt),
since these were the euphoric sixties when nothing seemed too
much to spend on universities and few doubts about value for money
were voiced. Indeed, between 1972 and 1975 the number of courses
offering the new qualification known as the Certificate of Qualification in Social Work (CQSW) had increased from 103 to 130, and the
number of certificates issued rose from 2,183 to 2,650 (CCETSW
1975a).

The Central Council for Education and Training in Social Work
(CCETSW) was set up in 1971 to replace the Central Training Coun-

cil in Child Care, the Council for Training in Social Work, and the Recruitment and Training Committee of the Advisory Council for Probation and After Care. The Seebohm Report suggested this amalgamation, on the grounds that the previous arrangements were 'educationally and professionally unsound' and involved 'an indefensible waste of scarce resources which should not continue' (paras 533-6). We have made an exhaustive study of the publications and activities of CCETSW and are not persuaded that matters are markedly different. In its second year of operation the Council's budget was £359.908 and it had twenty-four professional staff. In 1976-77, the last year for which figures were available, it spent £1,330,931; its central office employed twenty-eight professional staff, but it had offices in Bristol, Edinburgh, Leeds, Rugby, and London and the South East, employing thirty-four additional staff.

In its first triennial report CCETSW describes itself as 'an independent body with statutory authority to promote training in all fields of social work'. To this end it publishes a variety of papers, of varying quality. Many are concerned with attempts to define the activity for which the Council is busily promoting training, and assessing whether existing courses meet some (unspecified) end. Consultative document No. 3 (CCETSW 1977a) written by one of the assistant directors, Reg Wright, is perhaps not untypical. He tells us (p. 16) that 'social workers have a responsibility to individualise and personalise their clients', or (p. 12) that 'in the last analysis social work is concerned with greater personal and social fulfilment in any one generation and not with the complete sacrifice of fulfilment today for some long distant aim, however attractive the prospect. We have to examine carefully, however, what we mean by "fulfilment"—not all human potentials are desirable'. (Perhaps especially undesirable is the human potential to clothe vacuous thoughts in meaningless words.) Also typical is CCETSW Paper No. 10 (Central Council 1978b) which identifies a social worker's primary tasks as 'communication, assessment and organising change through the disciplined use of self' (p. 21).

But CCETSW doesn't just issue papers. One of its few tangible achievements has been to encourage the introduction of a form of training which entitles those who have undergone it to the award of a certificate in social service, henceforth CSS, as opposed to the Certificate of Qualification in Social work, hitherto CQSW. The present authors contend, on the basis of personal experience in the residential field (one as a consultant and the other as a housemother), that throughout the development of social services, those working in the residential sector have been and are called on to undertake duties of an exacting nature requiring advanced skills for their proper performance, beside which the task of 'fieldworkers' seems simple. It is the residential worker who has charge of the really difficult child for whom fostering is not possible, or who needs secure accommodation because he is a danger to himself and others. It is the residential worker who cares for incontinent and sometimes cantankerous rejected old people. Since the time when one of us was a housemother looking after twelve boys single-handed, twenty-four hours a day, and not having a day off because relief didn't turn up, conditions and hours have improved. But the residential worker cannot switch off at 5.30 if a child in his care is ill or unhappy, any more than a parent can. Yet, until recently, residential workers were not thought to need training (save in the voluntary sector, where even before the CSS, the National Children's Home pioneered realistic training for its workers), and the vast majority are still untrained. We are not sure that it matters, except to a society bedazzled by paper qualifications, and which pays those with a 'certificate', however bogus, more than those without, however effective.

Although CCETSW does not specify with clarity for whom CSS is designed, residential workers are the principal receivers, accounting (CCETSW 1977a) for 60 per cent. The CSS has proved a controversial innovation. Some workers see it as a second-grade qualification, since it does not involve full-time study of an extended kind; but Dame Eileen Younghusband remarks that it is in accord with her threefold vision of 1959 when seen in conjunction with the CQSW and various short courses leading to no formal qualification (Younghusband 1978, Vol. 2, p. 101). It shares with almost every other social work scheme an avoidance of description of the task for which the training is provided. There are constant references to the *need* for job analysis (see for example CCETSW 1975b, Paper 9.1, page 6, and CCETSW 1977b, Paper 9.3, page 10) and to the *need* for research, but while admitting these necessities the authors reveal the same compulsive eagerness to set up premature training schemes. The first CSS courses were instituted only in 1975 and we have little information about them. As late as 1977, contributors in *Social Work Today* were expressing concern and confusion about them (see Tilbury (1977) and report of the AGM of the Residential Care Association (1977)). We would guess that the major benefit accruing to staff in residential work would be the change of scene that day release offers, rather than the content of what is taught, and we very much hope that the mania for paper qualifications gripping the social services and other areas of public life does not occasion distress in people who have been doing jobs of great responsibility for years with success but who are incapable of 'academic' work.

CCETSW itself has proved an expensive and, arguably, superfluous body. Its power to validate postgraduate courses in universities has raised the hackles of many whose war-cry is academic freedom, while its intervention in local authority education provision has been viewed with scepticism by those who think CCETSW's high-powered staff have little contribution to make to modest in-service schemes they are already providing. It can commission research, but this function is also undertaken by the Personal Social Services Council, and one wonders whether both, or indeed, either, justify the amount of public money invested in them, especially in view of the continued if parlous existence of that bad joke, the Social Science Research Council (SSRC).

One of the most honest and perceptive comments on social work is to be found in the preface to the report of the DHSS Working Party on Manpower and Training for the Social Services (Birch 1976):

> Logically manpower planning can only be one part of a wider process of service and resource planning: statements of objectives and priorities should precede decisions about the types and numbers of staff to be employed. In practice it takes time to develop a coherent and systematic approach to the planning of newly reorganised and rapidly changing services. When the Working Party was established a relatively clear task seemed to exist, namely to improve the quality of an expanding service by committing sufficient resources to training, and estimating what this commitment should be.

The Birch Report, as it is commonly called, goes on to reveal its growing and crippling uncertainty about the objectives and priorities of the Personal Social Services (PSS), and stresses the need for research into them if the quality of manpower planning is to improve. Indeed, the members go so far as to ask 'whether or not there was a useful job to be done in the short term' (Birch 1976). We think they got the answer wrong, and the rest of the Report, though illuminated by flashes of insight and practicality, appears to us to be largely superfluous for the reasons the committee itself gave. We are in fact profoundly sceptical of the possibility of manpower planning in a free economy, but we see as expensive fairytale projections of numbers required and training appropriate for workers whose jobs a social worker said 'were impossible to describe in language both intelligible to lay people and acceptable to the

profession' (p. 79). It may be objected that our scepticism concerning, some believe hostility to, the personal social services
prevents us from seeing the strengths of the Birch Report, and
we are therefore grateful to Professor D. Nevitt, head of a department in the London School of Economics which comprises social
administration and social work, who told us that she eagerly read
the Birch Report for guidance about the social work task, and in
particular for guidance about subjects which would help undergraduates to qualify for professional training, and found it entirely
valueless for these purposes.

We do not know whence came the initiative for setting up the
Birch Working Party, but the terms of reference of the Working
Group on Numbers with their mixture of opacity and irrational
hope suggest that the social work profession was not far away.
They are, 'in the light of the number of staff needed in the UK for
the personal social services between now and 1984, to consider the
number and type of training places to be provided for them during
that period, and the implications for the resources of education
and service agencies, to take account as appropriate of the deliberations of Working Group on New Approaches to Services [their
capitals] and to report' (Birch 1976, p. 161).

The terms of reference of the main working party were wide
ranging: 'To consider the need for trained manpower in the personal social services in the light of the present state and prospec-
tive development of those services and of the resources which may be
made available and to recommend action to Ministers, to the providers of services and to the Central Council for Education and
Training in Social Work'. The membership of the committee ranged
widely too, many of its 47 members being civil servants or representatives of local authorities and not necessarily propagandists
for the social work cause. Unfortunately the working party does
not reveal its *modus operandi* and the sources of its evidence, so it
is tempting (but fruitless) to speculate which bits were written by
whom. We do not award our accolade to those members who on
page 3 proclaim: 'A substantial and continuing programme of
development in training for these services should be a *major
national priority*' (our italics), nor to those who somewhat gnomi-
cally assert that 'the qualifications required for top appointments
in the personal social services should be the same as those professionally required for posts within those services, with the addition
of appropriate management training. This means that while professional social work qualifications will continue to be of major
importance, the holders of other qualifications falling within this
definition should be regarded as eligible'. We like the working

party's forthright statement (p. 5), 'The personal social services should not be seen by the public and their elected representatives as solely responsible for meeting all the social needs of society [*sic*] but as one group among many with responsibilities in this field'. We find ourselves less admiring when on page 53 they attempt to be more specific.

> We consider there is a real risk that the public and their elected representatives will continue indefinitely to pile additional responsibilities onto the personal social services because they are seen vaguely as concerned with all the social needs of society. We think that a clearer perspective is required. It means that other agencies too must be seen, and must see themselves, *as partners in social care in the wider sense. It does not mean that the personal social services must become exclusive or boundary conscious,* or unwilling to undertake new and often co-operative enterprises at the margin of their field of responsibility (our italics).

We wonder what it does mean. We also agree with the working party's statement (p. 5) that 'All agencies which need to co-operate with the personal social services, but especially the public utilities, should be aware that the powers of social services and social work departments to provide assistance in the form of cash or kind are limited', and that (p. 53) 'bringing under the control of one organisation such a diversity of responsibility and provision, has perhaps made it even more difficult to state clearly the primary tasks of the personal social services'. We reiterate our and the working party's original view that to devise training and project numbers to engage in such unclear activities is a dubious exercise. Notwithstanding, the working party do it for 178 pages, at an expenditure of public money impossible to establish, but certainly excessive.

They grapple with the controversy, so beloved of the profession since Dame Eileen Younghusband introduced it, about which tasks need 'fully qualified' social workers, and which can be left to less elevated mortals (pp. 68-72). A CQSW holder should be involved in any circumstances which might involve loss of liberty (para. 5.22). This is a reasonably clear criterion, but then the working party wander off into the no-man's-land of 'complex assessment and/or treatment planning' (para. 5.23) (of what, they do not reveal), and end with the defeated complexity of para. 5.24, in which they struggle to define the situations which demand a qualified worker. They are, they tell us, 'difficult to describe briefly and coherently . . . Nonetheless such situations do frequently arise, although in present circumstances they may not always be recognised for lack of good assessment, or may not be able to be appropriately dealt with for lack of sufficient numbers of qualified social workers to do the job. CQSW holders should be available to clients whose needs can be met by the exercise of skill in social casework, social groupwork, or a combination of the two, whether in the home, in an institutional setting, or within a neighbourhood or community.

The working party tell us that they have had the opportunity to see the BASW document, *The Social Work Task*, before its publication, and indeed we think we see its malign influence in para. 5.17, p. 69, where they attempt a definition of social work.

Modern definitions of social work lay stress on its concern with interaction between people and their social environment. Qualified social workers would see themselves as having professional skills in linking individuals, families or groups with the available and appropriate resources, services and opportunities, while at the same time promoting effective and humane operation of such facilities. Professional social workers are also concerned to enhance the capacities of the particular client(s) to solve problems and to deal appropriately and effectively with situations. This direct involvement in and knowledge of social problems and the delivery of services, imposes on the professional social worker a responsibility to use his experience in contributing to the development and improvement of social policy. Social workers would not claim a monopoly of wisdom and expertise in all aspects of the work of the personal social services; they can however rightly claim to make a unique and vital contribution to the services by virtue of the particular cluster of concerns, knowledge and expertise which they acquire through their professional education.

This is surely a paraphrase of BASW's celebrated definition in *The Social Work Task* (BASW 1977). The language is perhaps a little more direct, the meaning equally tenebrous. What fun Barbara Wootton would have with 'enhancing the capacities of the particular client(s) to solve problems and deal appropriately and effectively with situations'. *What* problems, *what* situations, and how does one discern *appropriateness* and *effectiveness* when no objective is in sight?

From our study of the Younghusband, Seebohm and Birch reports we think three important issues of substance emerge. The first and overridingly important one is *definition of task,* and we have surely said enough to substantiate our view that neither Younghusband nor Seebohm were aware of or competent to tackle this central problem. Birch acknowledged, then ignored, and then ineffectually returned to it, but was not inhibited from making estimates, having the semblance of accuracy, of numbers required to perform this unspecified task, nor of sub-groups to perform equally unspecified sub-tasks. Two other issues interest the present authors. They are the location of social work training in universities, and the methods used to select students for training. In discussing each of these issues we are conscious that a concept of the task to be performed is as necessary here as it is in estimating numbers. We have slightly divergent views on the roles social workers should undertake, June Lait inclining to the view that their only functions are to attempt to remedy the shortcomings of other services, and to refer clients to existing services. She agrees with Baroness Wooton that the first function would be better performed by improving the other services, while the second would be unnecessary if existing services publicised their activities effectively. Colin Brewer, on the other hand, believes certain therapeutic activities can be undertaken adequately but not exclusively by social workers. Both are sceptical about the need for free-standing departments of social services to provide social work, and outline ideas for possible alternative structures in the final chapter.

One's views on the propriety of locating social work training in universities must depend on assumptions about the purpose of universities. This is no place to explore the ambiguities and uncertainties which characterise the development of the various sectors of higher education, nor to castigate the unfocused expansion of the sixties which in the authors' views distorted and obfuscated what had hitherto been fairly well understood, accepted, and quite possibly elitist functions. But it might be relevant to examine some of the general attitudes of universities to provision of training, as contrasted with education. The conflict between those who see their subjects as concerned with the examination and development of general concepts and the instilling of disciplined habits of thought, and those in the business of training, or imparting particular skills, can be seen in the introduction of social work courses to the LSE (Smith 1953). Of course, the conflict has a much longer history and is not confined to disputes in social studies. The nub of the matter appears to be that 'purists' fear the distortion of theory by pragmatists who seek to tailor it to meet the needs of practice. That this fear may have substance is illustrated by comments like the following: 'Theorists tend to succumb to the temptation to unload their theories *in toto* rather than use them to infuse a well planned curriculum appropriate to students' learning needs' (CCETSW 1977a; and c.f. Parsloe 1978). It is in social studies that this problem takes an acute form. The links between theory and practice in, say, chemistry and chemical engineering are less tenuous than those between, say, sociology and social casework. There are, moreover, experimental tests of validity that approach absoluteness in both chemistry and chemical engineering—indeed, invalid theories can be very dramatically and sometimes fatally refuted in both disciplines. Such tests put a term to bickering. In social studies (a term we prefer to the more pretentious 'social sciences'), the difficulty of validating or refuting any hypothesis can lead to perpetual deadlock, and to a state of hostility between competing schools never resolved by the sudden death methods prevailing in the numerate sciences. In *Enemies of Society,* Paul Johnson tells how non-scientific theories 'dodge refutation by reformulation, osmosis and imprecision' (Johnson 1977, pp. 156-7). He also refers to the instability of achievement in disciplines like sociology, where, he says, instead of a steady accumulation of new facts, there is a succession of 'leading schools each moving from manifesto to obscurity' contrasting it with what he calls the 'sinister stability' of the founding fathers. Another trenchant critic, S. Andreski (whose book *Social Sciences as Sorcery* deflates many of the improper pretensions of his own discipline, sociology), remarks that it and similarly ill-based disciplines 'have opened the gates of academic pastures to a large number of aspirants to the status of scientist who might have been perfectly useful citizens as post office managers or hospital almoners [*sic*] but, who have been tempted into charlatanry by a subject utterly beyond their mental powers (Andreski 1972, p. 204). Unfortunately the expansion of the sixties in universities was predominantly in subjects perceived by many as soft options. It is unsurprising, perhaps, that traditionalists suspicious (we think with reason) of the inadequacy of the knowledge base and the insecurity of the theoretical framework of many 'social scientific' subjects, were doubly alarmed when a 'training' based on a combination of themes for an undefined purpose with unpredictable outcome was introduced into their conservative ranks. We think that political considerations such as the initial funding by DHSS of many social work training courses may have caused some universities to accept activities whose intellectual foundations they would otherwise have rejected.

However that may be, it is remarkable that few academics, how-ever 'pure' their discipline, appear to feel that they or their institu-tion lose status by association with a medical school. Yet medicine is perhaps the most 'applied' of all disciplines, centrally concerned with imparting skills. Possibly the difference of esteem relates to the longer history and undoubted security of the theo-retical underpinning of medicine, grounded in physics, chemis-try and biology, and owes something too to the sophistication of the technology doctors employ. Or perhaps it is simply that doctors occasionally show themselves to be capable of attaining precisely defined objectives. Social workers would be hard put to it to demonstrate comparable precision of objective or attain-ment, except perhaps in fostering or adoption, or more negatively in removing children from bad homes or placing unwanted old people in institutions. The trouble with these activities, as ingre-dients in a quest for status or academic respectability, is that lay-men think, in our opinion often correctly, that they could under-take such tasks on a basis of common sense, whereas few would wish to undertake (or indeed undergo) a surgical operation by light of nature.

On balance, then, there would seem to be little intellectual justi-fication for sheltering social work training under the roof of an institution whose central purpose is (Newman 1923) 'to ensure the high protecting power of all knowledge and science, of fact and principle, of inquiry and discovery, of experiment and specula-tion; it maps out the territory of the intellect and sees that there is neither surrender nor encroachment on any side.' Universities may have little to gain save funds and numbers on the roll.

But that is only one side of the coin. Social work and the insecure disciplines on which it rests desperately need to acquaint them-selves with science and to adopt its habits of thought and scrupul-ous procedures. It has been the experience of one of the authors that when one is prepared publicly to debate the insecurity of one's discipline, colleagues from better founded subjects prove to be the most constructive and perceptive of critics. Physicists, chemists, engineers, mathematicians, metallurgists, geneticists, oceanographers, computer and management scientists are some-times consumers of social services, and their comments have a cutting edge seldom found amongst less sophisticated clients.

Interdisciplinary exchanges of this kind unfortunately seem uncommon. Andreski remarks that 'to acquire and maintain com-petence in any of the exact sciences demands so much time and effort that little time or energy remains for thinking about other matters; especially if they be of the kind that require the laborious

gathering and evaluating of masses of information, usually chaoti-
cally dispersed and often deliberately concealed and distorted'
(Andreski 1972, p. 200). A further barrier is then what Andreski calls
the smoke screen of jargon (ibid. Chapter 6) under which bogus
scientists hide the poverty of their thinking. Particularly inhibiting
to the fruitful exchange of ideas is the loose employment of words
with an exact scientific meaning like 'feedback', 'parameter',
'atimic', all of which are popular in so-called social scientific texts.
But the most substantial barrier is undoubtedly the inflated pretensions of some practitioners in social studies and the justifiable
anger of those whose hard-won expertise is devalued by association
with others whose chief attainment is verbosity. As Andreski puts it,
'No amount of plausible talking and posturing will make a bridge
stand if it has been incompetently designed, while ignorant dabbl-
ing with chemicals will soon lead to a fatal explosion. In contrast,
nothing will immediately blow up or fall down in consequence of a
politologist's or economist's inanity; while the harm caused by
his ignorance or dishonesty may not materialise until years later,
and will in any case be debatable and difficult to blame on a particular man' (Andreski 1972, p. 203). It is also galling to the competent researchers in many fields to see ill-designed research of the
kind we describe in Chapter 11 funded to the tune of £120,000 when
their own cannot be financed. The barriers to interdisciplinary
cooperation are indeed formidable, but in our view to cross them is
the only hope for worthwhile development in social studies, and
in social work training in particular. Because of this we hope universities will retain a small interest in these areas, and that practitioners will seize the opportunities as they are presented, realising how
much they are taking, how little giving so far.

It will be apparent to readers that since we doubt whether most
social workers have a clear purpose, and believe that social work
teachers are equally confused, we should not expect training selection procedures to have a clear focus either. CCETSW prescribes
desirable academic qualifications for various courses, but it appears that course tutors exercise a great deal of discretion. There
is at present an attempt by CCETSW to insist that all postgraduate
trainees must have a 'relevant' degree before they are admitted to
one-year as opposed to two-year courses, but the definition of a
'relevant' degree is likely to prove a tendentious matter, as is the
imposition on universities of what they will undoubtedly see as
restrictions on their freedom. One of the authors recently attended a course run by CCETSW at which teachers of professional
social work outlined to teachers of undergraduates what they considered constituted 'relevant' degrees. Unsurprisingly, there were

as many views expressed as individuals present. To some, no degree which did not include philosophy could possibly qualify the aspiring social worker to embark on professional training. For others economics was a *sine qua non*. Psychology and social administration had many supporters, others favoured history or sociology. One or two sages thought social science degrees were a distinct disadvantage, believing that arts degrees gave more emotional enrichment. One of the authors was in an unpopular minority in suggesting that only graduates in maths, physics or chemistry, with firsts or upper seconds, should be accepted for training, since to attract them one would need to put on courses with intellectual content. In the (likely) absence of qualified applicants, course tutors could occupy their time in defining objectives and preparing courses responsive to such objectives, or, failing that, obtaining work more suitable to their talents. Lait (1979a) expands this idea.

Many course tutors responsible for selection both require candidates to have experience in social work and ask practising social workers to help in interviewing. Some place great emphasis on the need for pre-training experience to have been in a 'good' placement, by which they appear to mean one in which the student has been encouraged to practise the sort of skills taught on professional courses (Payne 1977). June Lait is responsible for placing undergraduates in fieldwork placements in social service agencies, with the object of introducing them to problems with which social workers are confronted. To her a 'good' placement is one in which the student encounters the reality of referrals to the agency in all their disordered variety, and draws his own conclusions about the methods used in dealing with them. Many social work teachers think a 'good' placement is one which seeks to induct the student into the mores of professional social work as it is. We would, of course, question whether this is a desirable objective, and specifically whether it is the best way of responding to the client's need.

Since the first draft of this book was completed there have been developments concerning relevant degrees. CCETSW has published an account of a 'Workshop' (CCETSW 1978b) on the relationship of undergraduate education to the one-year CQSW course, incorporating the proceedings of the course previously mentioned. The following extract, arguing for the inclusion of psychology in undergraduate studies (p. 6), gives the flavour.

It was felt that the teaching of a psychological perspective has two particular characteristics. It takes the individual as the dimension to be explained, seeking to explicate individual variations in behaviour either across individuals in the same situation or in the same individual in different situations. In addition it gives students an appreciation of how problems feel from the client's point of view and also how it feels to be on the receiving end of help. This is in counter-balance to the more macro-cosmic views of other social science disciplines and is of equal importance. Secondly, a study of psychology gives students an understanding of the hypothetico-deductive method in action. . .

There is much more in the same vein. However, in spite of the claims proponents of psychology make for their 'discipline', they do admit that 'there is a great variety in the psychology back-grounds of persons presently entering one-year courses, the spectrum ranging from those who have for example done general psychology, experimental psychology, human growth and behav-iour, social psychology, all in various combinations and depths'.

In the case of sociology we are told: 'It also provides a useful preparation for the social worker, facing a variety of problems which require different levels of intervention (or a single problem which could be interpreted as requiring a variety of methods of intervention), since it facilitates an analysis of the problem itself and also provides an analysis of the possible alternative ways of defining one's role as a social worker'.

Social policy and social administration are thought to present difficulties.

A problem identified here was the lack of a single conceptual framework. Different themes and concepts in social administra-tion and social policy were not linked together. Conceptual issues were felt to have diverse sources, and it was difficult to provide an overview.

Several approaches to teaching this subject were identified. The conceptual approach, or focus, centred on values, theories, concepts and themes. The social problem focus looked at a number of different social problems, for example, delinquency, and related material to these. A similar type of approach was where teaching focused on different welfare services. Related to both the previous approaches is the use of various client groups on which teaching is then focused. A more holistic ap-proach is to examine social welfare from the development/ historical perspective.

It is difficult to believe that out of such a meaningless mishmash CCETSW had the effrontery to submit proposals to universities and other institutions offering social work training which, if adopted, would exclude students who had not swallowed large doses of these three subjects in their degree from one-year training courses, and would compel them to undertake two-year courses. Further, an arbitrary requirement of three months' practical work in social work was included in the proposed package. We are happy to report that universities seem likely to resist these impertinent and addle-pated proposals. At a recently convened conference to discuss them (20 April 1979) representatives of the Joint University Council for Public and Social Administration expressed support for the greatest possible variety in undergraduate degrees, objected to outside bodies interfering, and particularly outside bodies like CCETSW whose primary activity was intellectually obscure. John Hudson, Careers Officer at Newcastle University, said that before laying down prerequisites, professional bodies must be able to specify both the content of a subject and the level of attainment necessary for effective practice. He also stressed the importance of providing part-time and short courses to help partially quali-fied individuals to complete their qualifications. He said we should consider whether experience in social work was necessary, or whether any working experience would do as well since it might be maturity we were seeking, or ought to be. He also drew attention to the complete absence of student comment in the CCETSW report. Professor Asher Trop from Surrey commented on the hostility of social work students to the idea of assessment, either of their performance on courses or of the courses themselves. Profes-sor Pinker (whose appointment to a Chair of Social Work at the LSE has been the subject of much social work hostility on account of his lack of social work training) thought it very significant that less than one per cent of social work students failed courses, in con-trast to medicine, where failure rates edge towards 25 per cent.

There was general agreement that one-year courses in social work should remain, though a representative of CCETSW, M. Farrant, declared that it was the firm policy of his organisation to press for two-year mandatory courses for all students. He did not give the grounds for this recommendation, but his sole sup-porter, Miss Z. Butrym of LSE, thought probably three years were needed to ensure professional competence and 'socialisation in professional mores'. June Lait of Swansea asked whether, since one-and two-year courses had coexisted for some years, it would be possible for CCETSW to attempt some measure of effectiveness of the product, always provided they could define effectiveness in social work. M. Farrant said CCETSW was already doing this, but was unable to specify how except 'looking in a general sort of way'.

There appeared to be substantial assent to his and Miss Butrym's contention that social work was impossible to assess, and June Lait was made to feel naive for having asked. She still thinks, however, that discussion of training, employment of armies of advisers, and indeed the whole social work operation could be described as fraudulent if its objectives are indefinable, its skills beyond assessment.

There appears to be nothing in the literature produced by CCETSW, nor in the professional journals, about assessment of personality of students seeking social work training, though we think this may be at least as important as academic qualification. There is some evidence about relation of personality to choice of degree subject, and David Rutherford reports findings about social work trainees subjected to personality inventories. In summarising questionnaires applied to 345 college students on professionally qualifying social work courses, he reports:

> The picture that emerges of this particular group of social work students is an interesting one. While the expected characteristics of human warmth, outgoingness, trustingness and responsiveness to others, are found in abundance, and undoubtedly contribute to good client relationships, the characteristics associated with clear-headed, decisive thought and action are, apart from higher intelligence scores, notably absent. The implications of these findings are clear. Clients can expect kindly, tolerant and enthusiastic sympathy, but very little in the way of coherently planned action. Social work of the future may need two kinds of people, those whose role is mainly emotionally supportive and those whose task is to solve particular problems effectively. (Rutherford 1977)

According to Wasserman (quoted in Rutherford 1977) the qualities demanded of a social worker are almost limitless. 'He must play the roles of wise judge, loving parents, firm advocate, and patient friend' (quite often, one might add, to people twice his, or more likely her age, who only want the gas bill paying). Prins, writing in 1974 (quoted in Timms and Timms 1977), posits that people may be impelled into social work by 'a creative impulse; curiosity about the lives of others; the need to make restitution for early destructive phantasies; the need to express the great mother complex; and the altruistic motive'. He does not disclose whether any of these attributes, singly or in combination, enable their possessors to be effective social workers. He may be correct in some of his guesses. If he is, he inadevertently provides a further gloss on why social work training has taken the heavily psychoanalytic turn it has. Possibly it responds to the needs of the students and their teachers to express the great mother complex or 'make restitution for early destructive phantasies'. What it does for the customers is another matter altogether, of seemingly marginal importance to those who devise training and select students to undergo it.

In our final chapter we suggest an analysis of the jobs social workers are doing now. Such an analysis might provide the framework on which sensible training could be hung. We also suggest outlines of strategies for change. Any one, if adopted, would necessitate further and different training, of a kind we cannot anticipate. We can, however, say with some conviction that we think the present system worse than useless (see Parsloe 1977), very expensive, and overdue for drastic pruning if not outright abolition.

CCETSW's most recent publication, *CCETSW News,* No. 3, Spring 1979, suggests (p. 6) that the Professional Studies Committee, nothing daunted by the hornet's nest it uncovered in the universities, is proposing that from 1983,

Applicants (for one year courses) would be expected to have completed periods of study in social administration, sociology and psychology. A 'period of study' is defined as approximately one-tenth of a three year degree course contributing approximately 50 hours of formal teaching in each of the areas. The study should be at the second or third year level of a three-year degree course, or its equivalent.

From 1986 the requirement would go up from three to a total of five periods with at least one period in each area of study.

Additionally, applicants should have had three months practical placement as an integral part of their pre-professional studies, or one year's employment in the social service field or an equivalent period of experience which the college thinks appropriate.

CCETSW's basic policy is that two years is the normal period for professional social work training and that exemptions should only be granted in specific, special circumstances—degrees, diplomas or certificates which establish eligibility for admission to a one year CQSW course have to be 'relevant' to professional social work training.

There is also a preliminary report on evaluating course work, a study undertaken by Christine Hayward, Research Officer, CCETSW (p. 7). Revealingly, Dr Hayward remarks: 'Social work is not a tidy discipline, and neither is assessment on social work courses particularly reliable. Aims to achieve a precise assessment founder on the richness and variation of discipline content'. More or less admitting defeat, she suggests that 'other criteria' are needed. 'Fairness *or the satisfaction of those affected by the assessment* [our italics] seem at present to be reasonable additional aims, and possibly these are best achieved by broadening the range of opinions involved. A staff/student team approach is suggested'. In other words, if you don't know what you are teaching you cannot really assess it, so why not let the students decide for themselves if they are any good. And give them two years at it while you are about it.

As this book went to press, an important paper by Professor Martin Davies and Joan Brand on was in preparation for the *British Journal of Social Work,* we were generously permitted a preview. 'The Limits of Competence in Social Work: assessment of Marginal Students in Social Work Education' confirms the fears of Professors Pinkes and Trop (p. 43) that many students are hostile to assessment, a hostility shared by many of their teachers, and that the failure rate is unrealistically low. Professor Davies and Joan Brandon suggest that many engaged in the assessment of student's field work fail to distinguish between assessment as a *process* with educational objectives, and as an *event* which licenses the student to practice. Of the sample of 208 students examined, 35 were described as being at risk, but only 4 were not awarded the CQSW. The paper deserves fuller treatment than it can receive here. It concludes: 'In the meantime we are faced with what might look slightly absurd to the outside observer: in a profession which claims to be responsible for undertaking tasks requiring a high standard of performance, all those admitted to training from a wide variety of educational backgrounds are virtually guaranteed success. The fact that not one student in our sample failed solely because of practice incompetence suggests either that assessment standards are too lax, or that an extended period of social work training for all applicants is not so necessary as is generally assumed. The evidence of our study points to the conclusion that it is the former explanation that commands credence, and the position is undoubtedly aggravated by the continuing lack of consensus on what social work practice comprises. Until agreement is forthcoming on this crucial issue it is likely that the limits of competence in social work will remain bewilderingly elastic.' We are grateful to the authors for so conclusive a contribution to our chapter on training.

3

Social work after Seebohm

Confused origin of term 'personal social services'. Imprecise terms of reference and methods of procedure of Seebohm committee. Recommendations stress 'prevention'; what is it? Seebohm's hopes; have they been fulfilled? Two studies of social service departments. The social work strike.

It is one of history's ironies that the issues dividing the Majority and Minority Reports of the 1905-1909 Poor Law Commission should bear a striking resemblance to those that, unacknowledged and possibly unperceived, underlay the deliberations of the Seebohm Committee. The Majority Report recommended that one authority, the Poor Law, should undertake the relief of destitution, whereas the Minority, believing that destitution was the result of bad housing, ill health, poor education and unemployment, recommended the abolition of the Poor Law and the strengthening of what Edwin Chadwick had in 1833 called 'the collateral aids'. These would, they believed, abolish destitution, save in a few exceptionally handicapped citizens. In fact, neither report led to action, though the Boards of Guardians were disbanded in 1929, and their duties transferred to the local authorities. In 1948 the National Assistance Act removed financial responsibilities from the local authorities by setting up the National Assistance Board (which became the Supplementary Benefits Commission in 1966), but left them with the 'welfare' of the elderly, disabled, and homeless. Local authority 'welfare' responsibilities were very sketchily defined—chiefly, we think, because there was no consensus about what they should be, but everyone was feeling generally benevolent in the euphoria of constructing the 'welfare state' (Parker 1965) —and many of these responsibilities were permissive rather than mandatory. It is our contention that these ill-defined, possibly indefinable, 'welfare' functions were the origins of the confusion

underlying the term 'personal social services'. We believe that the
identifiable and treatable needs of the elderly, disabled and homeless were and are for medical care, housing, and money, and that
central and local government agencies already exist to respond to
these needs. The Seebohm Committee, with its terms of reference
'to review the organisation and responsibilities of the local authority personal social services and to consider what changes are desirable to secure an effective family service', was labouring under
many disabilities. Two of the most serious were the terms 'personal
social services' and 'family service', since implicit in them was the
concept that there was some underlying unity which distinguished
the services.

A more intellectually rigorous approach than the one the Committee adopted would have been to attempt to determine what, if
any, the unifying factors were. The present authors do not believe
any exist, and think that the unified social services departments
constructed on a false unity owe much of their ineffectiveness to
the absence of such analysis. The analogy with the 1905-1909 Royal
Commission on the Poor Laws lies in the determination of Seebohm
to construct a unified social services department, as the commis-
sioners were determined to retain the Poor Law. Paradoxically
enough, the only possible unifying factor in the children's welfare
and mental health functions that comprised the personal social
services was that those who received them were all 'disadvantaged'
(to use the current euphemism). To put it more bluntly, the customers were people who had failed or whom others had failed, and
stigmatisation is the nearest we can get to a unified attitude to
them. But Seebohm is at great pains to reject the idea of serving a
stigmatised group. On p. 11, para, 2, he says, 'This new department
will, we believe, enable the greatest number of individuals to act
reciprocally, giving and receiving service for the well being of the
whole community'.

In such ringing, if on closer examination, cracked, tones did
Seebohm herald the New Jerusalem. The sentiment may have
been generous; the effect was, we think, disastrous, resulting in
local government agencies no one understands, and who feel themselves to be bombarded by 'inappropriate' referrals (see pp. 58).
Hall (1976) thinks the term 'personal social services' was coined for
the Seebohm Committee since she finds no reference to it before
1965, when the Committee was appointed. She remarks that the
Committee found 'great difficulty in being precise about their
[personal social services'] nature' and 'preferred to use a func-
tional definition'.

It is at least arguable that the Seebohm Committee was appointed to recommend courses of action several of its members had already decided on (Hall 1976, pp. 59-60). We should not therefore be surprised to find the Committee not delaying overlong contemplating its terms of reference. They do not explicitly grapple with 'personal social services' but say (para. 31, p. 17):

> Although we were anxious to consider the personal social services in the broadest possible way, we took the following present services as our starting point.
> (a) The whole of the work of Children's departments;
> (b) The whole of the work of Welfare departments:
> (c) The *social work elements* [our italics] in health, education and housing departments, *although we recognise that these could not be considered in isolation from the rest of the work of the departments concerned.*

As for defining a family, they say (para. 32, p. 17), 'We decided very early in our discussion that it would be impossible to restrict our work solely to the needs of two or even three generation families. We could only make sense of our task by considering also childless couples and individuals without any close relatives, *in short, everybody'*. They nevertheless continue to use the term 'family service' as if it were capable of some practical application, and was not simply (in this context) a phrase designed to evoke warm sentiments. ('Family' toilet rolls recently caught our eye. The advertisers are unashamedly in the business of selling. Seebohm wasn't, or shouldn't have been.)

The Committee regularly assert that 'resources' for this that or the other service are 'inadequate', but since they fail to declare the objectives for which any of the services are designed, this is a relatively meaningless incantation. Characteristic of the mixture of imprecision and faith in the Committee's thinking is their statement, 'We believe that the services will be more effective if more money, manpower and talent are applied to them' (para. 68). There has certainly been a great increase in money and manpower devoted to the personal social services since Seebohm. In 1972-73, total expenditure on personal social services was £300 million. (Chartered Institute of Public Finance and Accounting and Society of County Treasurers). In 1975-76 it was £800 million, and we expect there has been a more than inflationary increase since. (As we have remarked earlier, it is difficult for governments to resist claims couched in the language if not the substance of benevolence. For an interesting discussion of resistance to reduction of expenditure on anything bearing the label 'welfare' see Chapman

(1979), pp. 47.51). We do not know whether more 'talent' has been applied, since we do not know what 'talent means in this context, and don't think Seebohm did either. Certainly there has been a substantial investment in training. Nor can we say with any more certainty than Seebohm whether the services are now 'more effective'. We can only regret such large investment of public money for such ill-defined objectives, and do not think the word 'irresponsible' inappropriate here.

If the Committee were, as we have suggested, seeking evidence to support conclusions already arrived at, they would have been following a well-established tradition amongst royal commissions and committees of enquiry. Indeed, it would be possible to argue that if a royal commission wants to make effective recommendations this is the only way to proceed. Commissions open to all the winds that blow are likely to make tentative, complicated recommendations, which will be ignored, or even, as in the case of the 1904-1909 Royal Commission on the Poor Law, produce two reports, neither of which led to action. Indeed Seebohm, perhaps recognising that when there is no case for change there is a case for no change, was wise to follow the pattern of the 1833 Committee of Enquiry, which knew what it wanted to find before it began to look, and produced a report instantly followed by legislation along the desired lines.

When one begins to examine the procedures and evidence used by the Seebohm Committee, however, one must conclude that no such sophistication as we have implied in the previous paragraph characterised their activities. There appears to be no fixed purpose in the collection of evidence, and indeed little connection between the evidence produced (such as it was) and the recommendations the Committee made. We do not know what provoked R. H. S. Crossman to describe the Report as contemptible (Hall 1976, p. 82), but amongst the many aspects we think qualify for that description are the Committee's failure to challenge and clarify its terms of reference and its methods of procedure. It is true that in 1965 methods of social enquiry were less well established than they now are (or purport to be), but the presence of one numerate scientist on the Committee or even, one is tempted to say, the use of elementary common sense by the Chairman (who must one hopes possess it, since as Chairman of Funds for Industry he manages huge sums of money; but perhaps when *soi distant* benevolence is at issue he turns it off like most other people, and he is, after all Chairman of the National Institute of Social Work), would have avoided the manifest imperfections that render the Report's conclusions of doubtful value.

The Committee decided that three main lines of enquiry were necessary (Seebohm 1968, p. 42). The first they describe as 'to discover the opinions of all those concerned with the services'. For this read all those concerned with *providing* the services, since the Committee remark (p. 43), 'We were regrettably unable to sound consumer reaction to the services in any systematic fashion. This was also related to the fact that we made no attempt to organise a research programme, as this would have delayed publication perhaps for another year or two'. Such delay would, we believe, have been entirely desirable, since other major reorganisations, notably of local government and the health service, were contemplated and they were of great relevance to the personal social services. In the event, having taken three years to produce the Report, the Committee had to wait another two years to see the Social Services Act passed, pressure group activity by the Seebohm Implementation Action Group being a possible reason why such a foolish, unnecessary, and extravagant measure saw the light of day. (For a full discussion Hall 1976). The five years that elapsed between the Committee's appointment and the legislation would surely have been better spent in undertaking well-managed, precisely focused research which sought to measure and evaluate the demand to which existing services responded, in attempting to assess demand for services not provided, and perhaps most fruitfully of all in insisting as a precondition that those who commissioned the research, i.e. the government of the day, declared objectives more precise than securing 'an effective family service'. The Fabian pamphlet *The Fifth Social Service* (1970) discusses possible strategies the Committee could have adopted, and exposes grave conceptual weaknesses in the actual ones. We are persuaded that the Committee failed to undertake research and formally consulted only *providers* of services because the most influential members were determined to achieve reorganisation speedily and in the form they wanted. It should be remembered that the social work training interest was heavily represented on the Committee (see discussion in Chapter 11). Research and extensive consultation of consumers might well have delayed the Report and led to different and unacceptable conclusions, and there was always the danger that the Maud Committee would recommend patterns of local government which gave greater freedom to local authorities to determine the structure of their personal social services in ways unacceptable to the social work interest. So haste was of the essence. As the Committee revealingly say (para. 40), 'Decisions must be taken very soon which will set patterns for many years to come'.

The second line of enquiry was (para. 42) 'to find out which local authorities had been making or considering material changes in organisation and responsibility, and to benefit from their thoughts and experience'. Local authorities were consulted by questionnaires, reproduced in Appendices A and C of the Report. The questionnaires are conservative, in that they ask for comments on existing services and make no reference to possible unmet need. They are also phrased in such general terms that it is entirely predictable that the answers provoked will be so wide-ranging and unspecific as to be interpretable in almost any way the Committee wishes. For example, having stated that there are 'weaknesses in the present pattern of organisation and responsibility' (Seebohm 1968, App. A. H. 1.), the Committee asks authorities to say whether they could be remedied by 'greater coordination, better training, more resources and other measures not involving radical reorganisation; or radical reorganisation' (Seebohm 1968, App. A. H. 2). We have been unable to discover how the information gleaned from the questionnaires was processed, but we are told with an imprecision characteristic of the Committee that 'nearly all the authorities replied'. Perhaps on closer examination it was something worse than imprecision. Out of forty-five County Councils in England and Wales, eight replied, and out of seventy-nine County Boroughs, fifteen replied. Five London Boroughs out of a possible thirty-two answered. The Committee paid visits to seventeen authorities, chosing them on the declared if unclear criterion of 'what they had said in writing' (para. 47) and of attempting to see authorities 'reasonably varied . . . from the points of view of size of population and the economic structure' (*ibid*). They do not even appear to have stuck by the criteria, since of the seventeen authorities visited, only seven in fact submitted written evidence. We cannot therefore suggest that the Committee visited authorities who had played their tune, nor perhaps should we even wonder whether they chose to visit holiday areas like Cardigan in June and Devon in September because the weather was promising (though this is a suggestive hypothesis since neither authority is listed in Appendix B as having submitted evidence to the Committee). We can perceive no rationale behind their procedure, and suggest there was none.

Once in the authorities, they saw all sorts of people at all sorts of levels. Sometimes 'we took the opportunity to meet people from other services; general practitioners, probation officers, medical social workers in hospitals, officers of the Ministry of Social Security and local representatives of voluntary organisations'. There is no discernible pattern to any of this busy activity, nor perhaps could there be when no precise hypotheses had been formulated for testing. Such random impressions, even those gleaned from officials whose verbal submissions were not 'in accordance with the written submission', nevertheless convinced the Committee that they had acquired 'some idea of the problems facing the services in different parts of the country', and indeed empowered them to recommend solutions.

The third line of enquiry was 'to draw on what information could be made available by central and local government, and by research workers in the universities and elsewhere, on the working of the services'. This line was combined with the first, i.e. to discover the opinions of those concerned with the services, and the Committee 'wrote to 219 other bodies and individuals enclosing a list of points considered relevant to the enquiry, but inviting them to submit evidence in any form they wished. Invitations to submit evidence were also published in the press' (para. 45). Written evidence was received from 160 organisations and 79 individuals. The committee also met representatives from 42 organisations and 54 individuals for discussion. Although unable to meet all who submitted evidence, the Committee remark somewhat smugly that 'we gained a sense of the prevailing opinions on the main issues'. They do not reveal how they estimated the significance of the various contributions, what weight they gave to the opinions of, say, Dame Eileen Younghusband, as against, say, the Women's Gas Federation, both of whom contributed to the Committee's deliberations. Information from central government and research is, presumably, given in Appendices G to S, and a motley collection it is. There is hard data in Appendix O, but it is on salary scales including those of staff nurses and matrons, and Appendix S gives, *inter alia,* firm information about the numbers of amputees, sufferers from TB and diseases of the digestive and genito-urinary system, of the heart, circulatory, or respiratory system, or the skin, in the population (handily divided into age groups) at 31 December 1967. One hopes that these tables are included simply to give a bogus air of authority to the Report, but another and frightening explanation is that the Committee considers anyone who may be unlucky enough to be ill may also be unlucky enough to need the attention of the personal social services.[1] In Appendix Q

[1] Alarming confirmation of this can be found in the fact that those in receipt of a mobility allowance, which is only awarded after a stiff medical by a specially appointed doctor, presumably skilled at spotting fraud, can only get a 'Disabled' emblem for their vehicle from the social services. Almost as if attempting to confirm the worst stereotypes about circumlocutory bureaucracy, the social services need a certificate from the patient's doctor, which the applicant must obtain, before they can contemplate issuing the emblem. One wonders what possible competence they have in the matter.

M. Power and J. Packman attempt to determine numbers of children in 'social' need, along with others suffering from handicaps which have a precise legal or medical definition. They have the grace to put a question mark after their figures for this category, but the Committee quotes them (para. 173) authoritatively in its demands for more resources.

The recommendations of the Report are well known and were largely adopted in the Social Services Act 1970. A new social services department was set up in place of the existing welfare, children's and parts of health departments, and local authorities were compelled to appoint Directors of Social Services responsible to social services committees. Before attempting to assess whether the new departments have lived up to expectations, we should perhaps examine some of the arguments advanced to justify them.

Chapter V of the Report considers that the chief defects of the present services are inadequacies in the amount, range and quality of provision, poor coordination, difficult access, and insufficient adaptability (paras 74-86). They are caused by lack of resources, inadequate knowledge, and divided responsibility (paras 87-100). Chapter VII purports to tell us why a unified social services department will be well placed to remedy these deficiencies. It begins with a series of windy assertions (para. 139). There is the dangerous stress on 'prevention of social problems'— for an interesting discussion on the dangers of 'prevention' see Draper (1979) and Lait (1979b)—and the usual populist flag-waving, 'Much more ought to be done, for example, for the very old and the under fives, for physically and mentally handicapped people in the community, for disturbed adolescents, and *for the neglected flotsam and jetsam of society'* (our italics). In arguing for the 'unified' approach, the Committee tell us that 'the need for a unified provision of personal social services has been made plain by growing knowledge and experience. There is a realisation that it is essential to look beyond the immediate symptoms of social distress at the underlying problems' (para. 141). We are told that people need to be encouraged to use the services, and that unified departments are (for reasons not disclosed) 'an important step in the right direction' (para. 146). Better staff will be attracted to a unified department: 'being large it will have a better career structure' (para. 147). Efficiency, intelligence and planning will be enhanced and the Committee hopes that the new department will engender 'greater clarity than exists at present about the aims of social action' (para. 152). (An odd sequence—create the departments and then encourage them to say what they are about.) Continuous evaluation is essential and 'the new social service department will, we consider, be favourably placed to make a start in this respect' (para. 152). The Committee is at one with the present authors in hoping to avoid 'incorporating our present beliefs and knowledge in an organisational structure that will out-live them', though why they should think the monolithic bureau-cracies they created are flexible structures easy to demolish when outmoded (as we think they now are) we do not know. (See Chapman (1979) for bureaucratic resistance to change, especially when it concerns welfare.)

When talking about services for children, the Committee pins its flag to the joint concepts of prevention and absence of distinc-tion between neglected and delinquent children. They remark that 'public authorities have been given clear responsibility for the medical care and education of children but no such clarity exists over *aspects of their social care*' (para. 187) (our italics). We wonder how it can when the phrase is so vague as to be virtually meaning-less. The Committee also assert that 'the provision of assistance to children and their families on the basis of defined administrative and legal categories inhibits the use of the most appropriate ser-vices, for whether a young child commits an offence, goes out on the loose, or is just unruly and naughty is purely fortuitous'. This kind of unsubstantiated assertion with its ill-defined terms like 'young child' is also characteristic of the sloppy 'philosophy' underlying the Children and Young Person Act 1969, which in the opinion of many, notably and most eloquently Patricia Morgan (1978), disastrously confused welfare and justice.

In the following pages we attempt to assess how far claims made by the Committee for the new departments have been justified in nine years of their operation, concerning ourselves solely with the 'fieldwork' activities. Some of our evidence is necessarily impres-sionistic, but we lean heavily on two studies undertaken by acade-mics. The first, by Goldberg *et al* (1977), monitors referrals to an area office of Southampton Social Services Department over one year. We disagree with many of the deductions made from the material collected, but find the study methodologically sound so far as this is possible. We recognise that one area office cannot be assumed to be representative of all social services departments, and had hoped that evidence using the case review system devised by Goldberg and Fruin (1976) would be forthcoming from other authorities. This has not happened to any extent and is further evidence of the inability or unwillingness of field social workers to evaluate their activities, but we have no reason to suppose that the Southampton experience is not reflected in many other areas. The second study on which we draw is the study by Professors Parsloe and Stevenson (Parsloe 1978) of Area Teams in eight local authorities. Since we believe that the methods of collecting evidence were erratic and inadequate, we are obliged to treat the findings with caution. We have probably selected the findings that best accord with our own preconceptions/prejudices, but in such a formless work that is possibly all one can do. We would remind readers that the joint authors of *Social Work Teams, The Practitioners View* hold university chairs of social work, and so must presumably be considered outstandingly competent members of their profession. The aphorism that springs to mind is, 'In the country of the blind the one-eyed man is king'.

One claim made by Seebohm, that unified departments would attract greater resources, appears to have been borne out. Because of the variety of services comprising the new departments, and the fact that many workers were previously employed in departments which had (understandably enough) no way of separating the cost of 'social work' functions from their other activities, it is impossible accurately to compare the cost of services before the unified departments with the present. Moreover, new duties have been laid on the departments which also render comparison problematic. But there is no doubt whatsoever that more money has been spent, and that the increase cannot be explained merely by inflation. The real value of the money spent has increased substantially. We have cited the overall expenditure in 1972-73, £300,000,000, and in 1975-76, £800,000,000. Table 1 gives details of increases in numbers of fieldworkers and administrative staff, and juxtaposes them with increases in numbers of children and old people in residential care. This table has been compiled somewhat arbitrarily from figures prepared by the Chartered Institute of Public Finance and Accountancy and the Society of County Treasurers, and we are conscious that our interpretation of them is tendentious.

Social work theory, and indeed the Seebohm Committee itself, stresses the importance of people being cared for in families rather than institutions, and much of the focus in 'prevention' is on the prevention of institutionalisation. Many fieldworkers would see this as one of their central tasks. In these circumstances it is odd that the figures show substantial increases in numbers of children in residential care, and constant proportions of old people, while numbers and costs of fieldwork staff have escalated. We suggest that while the numbers of old people needing residential care remain fairly constant because measurable criteria, like degree of infirmity and personal preference operate, numbers of children in care may vary according to the prevailing fashions (and some

Table-1

Expenditure By Social Services Department

	Fieldworkers			Administrators		
	Total	Per 1,000 Population	Expenditure per 1000	Total	Per 1,000 Population	Expenditure per 1,000
1972-73	12,684	0.26	1,008.4	7,365	0.15	987.4
1973-74	11,487	0.28	1,272.2	6,319	0.16	1,199.4
1974-75	17,532	0.37	1,988	15,717	0.33	1,889
1975-76	21,008	0.43	2,625	17,191	0.36	2,502

	Children in residential care		Old people in residential care	
	Total	Per 1,000 Population	Total	Per 1,000 Population
1972-73	39,271	2.88	117,549	17.7
1973-74	31,762	2.02	94,050	16.99
1974-75	94,498	7.1	118,397	17.83
1975-76	96,842	7.3	120,256	17.7

legislation, notably the Children and Young Persons Act 1969 is heavily influenced by fashionable philosophies). This paradoxical situation, so well described by Patricia Morgan (1978), in which attempts to contain children in the community are followed by larger numbers being institutionalised substantiate Karl Popper's belief that the history of social policy is perhaps best understood as the story of the unintended effects of man's intended actions. (The thought is further developed by Andreski, who, in a witty chapter entitled 'The Witch Doctor's Dilemma' (p. 26), attacks psychology on the grounds that, since it advertises itself as an aid to 'adjustment', in those countries where psychologists are thick on the ground, we should expect to find that 'families are more enduring, bonds between spouses, siblings, parents and children stronger and warmer, relations between colleagues more harmonious, the treatment of recipients of aid better, vandals, criminals and drug addicts fewer than in places or groups which do not avail themselves of the psychologist's skills. On this basis we could infer that the blessed country of harmony and peace is of course the United States, and that it ought to have been becoming more and more so during the last quarter of the century in step with the growth in the numbers of sociologists, psychologists and political scientists'.

We have admitted that our use of these figures is tendentious, and we are aware that they could be interpreted in a variety of ways and that to begin to appreciate their significance all manner of other factors and measurements would be required.

Pace Popper, we think that if the personal social services had manageable, definable, short-term objectives of a kind we suggest in our final chapter (and which Popper (1945) would probably call piecemeal social engineering) statistics of the kind produced by the Institute of Public Finance and Accountancy and the Society of County Treasurers would make some measure of success feasible (see Prentice 1978). In the absence of such objectives, the figures merely tell a distressing story of escalating expenditure.

Seebohm's belief that unified departments will enable more people to use their services at first glance receives some support from the Goldberg study. Referrals to the Southampton office increased by one fifth in 1975 compared with 1973, but as Goldberg *et al* (1977) point out, just over half the referrals in 1975 were 're-applications from clients who had previously been in contact, whereas in 1973 only one-third of referrals were old cases' (p. 260). Figures from other social services departments reflected the same trend, which is that the number of new referrals has fallen. Goldberg *et al* also tell us that only 6 per cent of cases were still being dealt with after a year (Table 4, p. 270), and that a staggering 47 per cent were off the books within a week. Goldberg (perhaps wisely) does not attempt to explain these figures, though her discussion of the reasons cases were closed repays study. Our own guess is that many of the people who called at the area office were unaware of its true function (and indeed who could blame them?) and were seeking services the personal social services could not provide. This view is supported by the fact that of clients with 'predominantly material and financial problems'—17 per cent of the whole—half the cases were closed on the day of referral and 85 per cent by the end of one month (p. 276). We are told the main form of help was 'assistance with applications for supplementary benefits and special grants (43%) . . . The area staff have suggested that this time-consuming mediation would be unnecessary if the DHSS staff themselves were better able to communicate with claimants by patient and clear explanation'.

This is not, of course, the only possible view of the matter. We think the existence of an agency with ill-defined functions encourages confusion in claimants, and agree with B. Wootton (1959) that it is irrational to erect institutions to correct others rather than correct the original institutions. It does not surprise us that 'only

30 per cent of cases relating to financial and material difficulties were closed because the social workers considered that their aims had been achieved, and over two-fifths were referred to other agencies, mainly DHSS' (p. 276). Social workers are trained· for other functions than being post boxes, and to find that this is what is principally needed must be frustrating. We have a certain sympathy with social workers trained to sniff out and remedy imperfect 'interpersonal relationships', who, though scenting these difficulties, were nevertheless obliged to withdraw. 'Many closure notes refer to family relationships and environmental problems *which were detected but not pursued*. Among these families were a number who repeatedly found themselves in financial and other crises and the area team's policy was to deal with them on an *ad hoc* short term basis, *rather than get involved in long lasting supportive relationships with very uncertain outcomes'* (our italics). A very significant admission of failure is made on p. 276. We are told, 'When the case review system revealed the frequent reappearance of certain families a small sample of 'repeater' families was selected *with the aim of getting to grips with their more basic problems*. The social workers *found it very difficult to obtain a clear mandate from these clients to explore beyond the obvious trigger events,* and eventually it was decided to continue with the short term crisis help' (our italics). Perhaps if the social workers had read *The Client Speaks* (Timms & Mayer 1970) they would have been saved those basic problems, and have recognised (as the clients apparently did) that many human situations are irredeemably imperfect, concentrating on the limited material help that is the best they could offer.

We do not blame trained social workers for their frustration at not attaining the objectives for which their training had, in its muddled fashion, prepared them. We also wonder whether selection of social workers, either for training or employment, can be done with much skill (see discussion in Chapter 2) when we find that although 99 per cent of a sample of newly trained social workers studied by Parsloe (p. 370 Table 8) had been compelled to deal with financial problems, only 33 per cent liked doing so. Similarly 91 per cent had needed to tackle problems of homelessness and only 25 per cent liked doing so; 80 per cent had had to work with the elderly, 50 per cent wanted to. The mentally ill and handicapped were another unpopular but necessary group, 75 per cent involved and 59 per cent wanting to be (and we think the figures would have shown even more dissatisfaction if the mentally handicapped had been separately listed). The physically handicapped were a client group for 56 per cent of social workers: only 37 per cent liked working with them. These figures seem to describe a lot of square-peg social workers grumbling about the round holes consumers of their services wanted to dig. A strange finding of a profession devoted to helping others.

However, in three areas, job undertaken and willingness to undertake it tally well. Eighty-three per cent undertook 'child care tasks', and 81 per cent enjoyed doing so; 95 per cent undertook 'family relationship problems' while 83 per cent enjoyed them. In these circumstances it is daunting to find (Goldberg *et al* 1977, p. 262, Table 2) that 58 per cent of referrals to the Southampton area office in 1975 were of 'unpopular' categories, while only 14 per cent were of the desired kind. It is also significant and disturbing that although social workers liked working with deep family problems, when they tried to do so in Southampton the families did not seem to appreciate it. The services that *were* appreciated were those social workers least enjoyed providing, i.e. practical help to the elderly and physically handicapped (ibid, p. 275).

Moreover the social workers themselves didn't consider they were very effective. Goldberg tells us (p. 278) that 'in only a third of the family and child care cases did the social workers feel they had achieved the aims they had set themselves' and were compelled to withdraw, 'often aware that many stresses and problems were still present and had remained untouched by their intervention'. Working with mental and emotional disorder (popular so long as not suffered by the elderly or physically handicapped) seemed to have similarly frustrating outcomes, only one quarter of cases being closed because the aims had been achieved (p. 279). Luckily others were at hand who either were not temperamentally inclined to withdraw when the going got rough or whose statutory responsibilities were clearly enough delineated to preclude such quixotic behaviour. Goldberg tells us that in the 137 cases of 'mental and emotional disorder' examined, outside agencies were involved in every single case, GPs in 59 per cent. She allows herself to wonder (p. 279) 'whether lack of specialist training and of familiarity with mental illness or handicap played a part in the social worker withdrawals'. She does not wonder, as we do, whether the introduction of incompetents, albeit expensively maltrained incompetents, deflects resources from the more competent. Far from it; in her conclusions she actually suggests that social workers should be freed from chores (p. 281-2), i.e. dealing with requests for practical help, and should only be brought in to deal with clients 'who appear to need help beyond the specific service requested'. These are clients who 'show early signs of stress, which without intervention may reach crisis point or develop into more chronic and intractable conditions. Time may even become available to engage in some of *the more preventive activities outlined in the Seebohm report'* (our italics). It is difficult to find a clearer example of a profession, confronted with its failures, having the face to demand more of the same. Commenting on the changes in training she considers necessary as a result of the study, Miss Goldberg declares (p. 282) that 'the approaches outlined here demand a broad sociological framework for assessing social factors in the occurrence of problem situations', and talks about a future role for social workers as 'enablers and consultants to others'. (One wonders whether perhaps the time is ripe for CCETSW to suggest that 'enabling' and 'consultancy' should be included as compulsory subjects for undergraduates contemplating social work careers! Or perhaps a postgraduate qualification M.Sc. (Consultancy and Enabling) would be more appropriate. The fact that no one knows what these activities are is unlikely to inhibit a substantial number of people prepared both to teach and to study them. It has not inhibited B.A.S.W. from advertising its study course and A.G.M. 79 as 'Social Work, an Enabling Profession.')

Seebohm believed that large unified departments would be better placed than the existing ones to 'increase the recruitment and training of appropriate staff and to deploy them better' (para. 147), and also to 'provide a better career structure'. Figures already quoted (p. 57) establish beyond doubt that more fieldworkers and administrators have been, and will doubtless continue to be, recruited. Neither can there be any doubt that the better career structure has materialised. As has already been mentioned, comparisons of pre- and post-Seebohm departments present difficulties because of non-comparable increased functions undertaken. In all authorities numbers of fieldwork and administrative staff per 1,000 population have more than doubled between 1972 and 1976, while expenditure upon them has almost trebled (Source Chartered Institute of Public Finance and Accountancy, Society of County Treasurers). We would doubt whether the 'better deployment' Seebohm envisaged is a reality. Since reorganisation large numbers of specialist posts have been created within social services departments. A page advertisement from *Community Care,* 3 May 1979, illustrates the proliferation of 'specialist' posts the one not very large local authority. The London Borough of Waltham Forest Prefaced the advertisement thus.

We have a new approach to managing our Social Services. It will enable policy to be formulated and implemented more effectively and will facilitate the development of specialist and management expertise. We are restructuring our Social Services Department and by extending the management structure laterally, rather than increasing the hierarchial tiers, this creates several new senior posts. They offer challenging opportunities for more flexible ways of working and for developing a better service to the community.

In pursuance of those praiseworthy objectives they declared themselves to need. I, an assistant Director of Social Work (£8817-£9564), two Principal Officers (Social Work) (£7515), a Principal Officer (Home Care), a Principal Officer (Children's Services) and a Principal Personnel Officer (Social Services). All these posts carried salaries of £6798-£7515: additionally the call went up for a Divisional Administrative Officer (Social Work Division), a Planning Adviser (Client Group) in the Planning & Central Management Division on Salaries S.O:2 and P.O.1(a). We don't know what the 1(a) denotes, except probably too much.

We have heard much grumbling about top-heavy bureaucracies in our contacts with social services departments. The complaints have come from field-level social workers, who have expressed doubts about the necessity and usefulness of the various posts created. Professors Stevenson and Parsloe found similar disillusionment in the area teams they studied. We think that of many superfluous appointments in social services departments, specialist advisers are the most useless, since the specialisms they purport to advise upon have no knowledge base. There is of course no direct evidence for our *explanation* of this hypothesis. It would be too much to expect of authors in the business of training, but there is very substantial support for the basic hypothesis (Parsloe 1978, p. 194 para. 7.110).

In general social workers were confused and critical about specialists in the hierarchy. Frequently they could not tell who they were, or what they did, as these quotations, all from different teams, show:

> 'They are just names . . .'
> 'I don't really know what they do.'
> 'Consultants do exist at higher levels of the organisation but who exactly they are and how accessible they are I wouldn't know — what most of them appear to be doing is researching their own positions.'
> 'It's a whole jumble — there's one I'm not sure what his title is at the moment . . I'm not even sure what his job is, all I know

is his name and if you want something you contact him. I know it sounds silly but he's had a couple of changes of title and it's very difficult really.'

'There are two in divisional HQ but I don't know exactly what they are consultants in.'

'I don't know about their usefulness. You know we tended at one point to have a number of visits of people coming round to show us their faces and see ours—and then you say goodbye to them and presumably they are still going round. You get these visions of them going round introducing themselves all the time.'

There were some social workers who said that they thought these specialists in the hierarchy might not be employed to help social workers but rather to assist management and that their advice was meant to go upwards to the director rather than down to the teams. However, if that were the case, the social workers wondered how the advisers gathered their information since they did not seem to look directly to the teams for it.

The social workers offered a sensible explanation for the uselessness of advisers. They said that 'when they needed help they needed it immediately, and from someone they knew and trusted' (p. 195, para. 7.114), and 'the hallmark of a good specialist adviser is that he can be contacted' (p. 195, para. 7.115). Perhaps our explanation for the uselessness of specialist advisers receives some support from remarks like: 'We had virtually no examples of social workers seeking advice about behavioural patterns or pathology typical of a particular client group, nor asking for suggestions about methods of work they might employ' (p. 196, para. 7.117), or, 'Not all social workers were certain that the consultants were actually so knowledgeable about their particular client group or the service for which they had responsibility. Some, it seemed, had been promoted out of areas in which they had expertise and were in urgent need of in-service or post-qualifying training to equip them for their new role' (assuming such a thing to be possible; an assumption we question). The examination of the question of specialist advisers suggests that bureaucracies that tempt directors of social services to acquire staff for prestige reasons are unsuitable vehicles for the delivery of sensitive personal service.

This belief receives some support in Parsloe 78 para. 7.119 (p. 197). While reporting adversely on the general picture of advisers, 'from the team members' perspective, the general picture of the use of these specialists in the hierarchy is a gloomy one.

When used at all by social workers, they are seen as a last resort in impossible situations, and usually seen as failing to produce the necessary magic'. Parsloe and Stevenson report that in one authority they found social workers

> enthusiastic about their access to the hierarchy. This was in a northern English borough where there were no designated posts for consultants. There, social workers felt that senior staff operated an open door policy, and most could identify people in senior positions to whom they turned for knowledge when this was not available in their team. Perhaps the size of the authority, the geographical closeness of teams and headquarters *and the numbers of staff who had grown up in the area* [our italics] are more important factors in explaining this situation than that there were no designated advisory posts.

Earlier, we are told (p. 13, para. 2.12)

> Very many of the social work staff had deep roots in the area, staff with experience in other areas were comparatively few. *Many of the social workers and social work assistants had experience in other occupations, including manual work. The proportion of qualified staff in the authority was well below the national average* (our italics).

It was not, of course, the purpose of the investigation to comment on (or indeed identify) differences between authorities studied, but this reference to the accessibility of advice is one of several clues suggesting that the northern borough, with its compact area and low proportion of trained staff from outside, had fewer miserable social workers than any of the other areas. Neither, unfortunately but not unexpectedly was it the purpose of the enquiry to ascertain which area had the least miserable clients, but it is surely likely that job satisfaction helps social workers to be of at least some use to those they seek to help (Gruneberg 1979). Were it not for the fact that Professor Parsloe herself raises serious doubts about whether training unfits people for work in local authorities (BASW Conference, reported in *Social Work Today,* Vol. 9, No. 4, 20.9.1977) we would be chary of offering this as an hypothesis, but we are encouraged to do so, and we suggest ways of testing it in our conclusions. We also think it likely that untrained staff, at worst compelled by lack of qualification, at best impelled by personal preference to stay in the area in which they are employed, acquire an expertise and a knowledge of local requirements that may be more effective than training. (We are conscious that our use of the word 'effective' presupposes a knowledge of objectives. In this section we use it to mean effective in responding to the requests for help actually made to social services departments rather than effective in responding to hypothetical requests that social workers wish clients would make.)

The Parsloe/Stevenson report gives the first extended account of the use trained social workers make of their expensive training in social services departments, and depressing reading it is. Perhaps even more depressing than Professor Parsloe's honestly reported findings, which, very briefly summarised, are that students make little direct or even indirect use of the social work methods they have spent one or two expensive years acquiring, are the conclusions she draws from these findings. Far from questioning whether the theories on which the methods are based may be invalid, she tends to suggest that the setting in which the theories operate is faulty. Unfortunately that setting is the world as it is, not as it ought to be. An example will perhaps illustrate this tendency. Professor Parsloe reports (Parsloe 78) (p. 342, para. 14.50) that some social workers told her they were using 'the unitary approach' and indeed some courses reported teaching this approach 'based on the work of Pincus and Goldstein and Minahan in the United States, and on that of Specht and Vickery at the National Institute for Social Work in Britain'. It was unfortunate that social workers and teachers tended to be talking about different things when they discussed 'the unitary approach' (p. 343, para. 14.60), but, nothing daunted, Professor Parsloe feels able to tell us that 'while there are possibilities for developing an integrated approach it may be more difficult to implement than the theories allow, and that once again insufficient attention may be paid by those who teach *to the context in which the theory has to be applied'* (our italics). Scientists would bridle at this use of the word 'theory', and so do we. If Professor Parsloe had read Popper (1959) she might conceivably have considered that if the 'theory' only operated in selected contexts it could be considered invalid in other contexts. The implied necessity of manoeuvring the 'theory' to fit the context, instead of abandoning it and constructing another for testing, casts the profoundest doubts on the validity of this particular theory, and by analogy many others used in social work training. (See also CCETSW 1977a for bending theory to necessity.)

Among the many disturbing findings in this work, are that in one of the authorities visited 82 per cent of the reports on boarded out children were overdue, and 53 per cent were more than three months overdue (p. 88, para. 544). (One of us has found considerable dif-

ficulty in getting follow-up reports on adolescents discharged
from an assessment centre, even in the cases where regulations
demand that reports be available.) In only one of the eight authorities was recording of visits up to date. These findings are reported
without comment, and there is no indication that any action is in
hand to remedy the situation. It appears to us shocking that elementary routines designed to safeguard the welfare of vulnerable
people are neglected by workers who have time to tell researchers
(p. 104, para. 5.119), 'you can call it psychotherapy if you will, but
it's psychotherapy that doesn't involve just therapy to the ego,
but involves many other things as well . . . which will heal the total
situation'. We doubt whether it will heal 'the total situation'. It will
not keep the records straight, nor ensure routine visiting to children
boarded out whose only lifeline may be the social worker. The
resistance of social workers to routine record keeping, and their
extreme sensitiveness about attempts to evaluate their work is well
described in Chapter 10. P. Baird (1979), writing in *Community
Care* about a sabbatical term spent working in Birmingham Social
Services Department, says the administration was better than he
expected. 'The difficulty was that social workers themselves were so
unbusinesslike and liable to lose things.' See also Rutherford (1977).
Such difficulties do not appear to have been anticipated by Seebohm when he stresses the ability of the new departments to undertake research based on systematically collected information,
readily available (para. 97).

Another of Seebohm's expectations of the unified departments
was that they would 'enable a natural and helpful division of
responsibility . . . to emerge between the [Supplementary
Benefits] Commission and the new social service department'
(para. 685). With what now seems risibly misplaced certainty about
the nature of social work the Report says (ibid), 'We consider that
the Commission's officers should refer cases to the [social ser-
vices] department and *should not attempt to undertake social
work themselves'* (our italics). There is little evidence in any of the
literature that Supplementary Benefits officials wish to encroach
on this *terra incognita*, and much to suggest that so besieged are
they with routine work that they are all too likely to attempt to
fob some of it off onto social services departments. The success
of their attempts has been facilitated by the provisions of the 1963
Children and Young Persons Act, which enables social services
departments to give material aid to families in circumstances which
may prevent the reception of children into care. There is no doubt
that this provision has enabled some supplementary benefits
officials to refer people with children to social services departments

instead of dealing with the matter themselves. Since local authorities have interpreted their power under this legislation in a highly
idiosyncratic fashion, some never giving cash, others regularly
paying off arrears of rent and fuel bills, the situation for the applicant has become highly confusing. The Goldberg *et al.* (1977)
study shows (p. 276) that of people who came to Southampton social
services departments with financial and material problems, 'over
two-fifths were referred on to other agencies, mainly the DHSS'.
The Parsloe 1978 study (p. 227, para. 96) reports astonishing variations. Uncertainties about the boundary line between the responsibilities of the Supplementary Benefits Commission and the
concerns of social services were made very clear by social workers.
The nature of the work occasioned by ill-drawn demarcations is
startlingly revealed in the remark that in a London authority
'missing social security giros were particularly mentioned as a
regular source of problems for social workers' (p. 227, para. 9.9).
In rural areas of Scotland and Northern Ireland. 'social workers
had accepted arrangements whereby they made emergency payments and subsequently reclaimed the money from DHSS' (p. 227,
para. 9.10). In subsequent paragraphs grants and loans made to
clients to pay off fuel bills are described (p. 229, para. 9.17). 'In
the London borough some large payments had been made towards
fuel bills. Yet even here, in one area, a social worker who was asked
about this said, it was policy to regard fuel bills as a matter for
Supplementary Benefits and the fuel boards. In the other areas
of this authority there was clearly a concern to limit payments
for this purpose'. Interestingly, and to us significantly, the discussion of this obviously confused situation centres on the issue of
whether social workers *like* dealing with money, rather than on
whether their intervention leads to more effective help for their
customers. But the confusion is of alarming proportions. We find
money disbursed to pay for a washing machine, to pay for a 16-
year-old boy to go on a hairdressing course (p. 231, para. 9.25).
We are told that many social workers were vague about the budget-
ary policy of their departments (p. 232, para. 9.30) and more dis-
turbingly still that 'there was no evidence . . . of attempts to co-
ordinate actions taken at team level or to monitor decisions taken
over a period of time. One team, concerned about the extent to
which they felt they were doing the work of the Supplementary
Benefits Commission for them started to try to keep a record
of their decisions, but they soon found they were failing to enter
details in the book provided' (p. 233, para. 9.36)!

The only cheerful outcome from this lax state of affairs is that
in some authorities 'emergency payments may have to be made

out of social workers' own pockets without any absolute certainty of repayment' (p. 231, para. 9.26). Such direct responsibility may deter workers from looking too favourably on these sophisticated clients who 'may know of the money-giving powers and may actually ask for help'. On page 236, paras 9.44 and 9.45, are clearly expressed assertions that customers confuse social services departments and the Supplementary Benefits Commission, though not to our mind any clear exposition of the conceptual differences which distinguish the professional social work giving of money from the bureaucratically monitored (and possibly efficient?) activity of the Supplementary Benefits Commission. (For an interesting discussion of this see Stevenson (1973), especially her discussion of the items proportional & creative justice). In short, we are not surprised the clients are confused or cross when 'they see neighbours get help with electricity or gas bills, and its hard for them to understand whether or not it's right' (p. 236, para. 9.44).

We don't find illumination from the worker who revealingly said (p. 236, para. 9.46), 'Sometimes folk come in with electricity bills and are not the least interested in social work. They don't want help with their other problems anyway, they just want financial help and they won't accept anything else *even though you try to get in under pretext of helping with an electricity bill'* (our italics).

Does one salute the authors' honesty or condemn their stupidity in reporting such a finding? Or are we alone in finding distasteful the confession of a social worker that he manipulated a hard-up client with the promise of money so as to offer a service the client did not want? We consider quite insufferable the assumption that by virtue of training or office, a public servant assumes he knows better than the customer what the customer really wants.

Seebohm hoped that better cooperation between social services and housing would develop from the new arrangements. Goldberg *et al.* (1977) found that of 200 people approaching social services departments with housing problems, two-fifths were referred back to agencies (presumably housing departments) already in touch, and in only 20 per cent of cases did the social workers believe their objectives had been attained. Professors Parsloe and Stevenson also found many difficulties. Since the survey was undertaken, homelessness has been made the responsibility of housing departments, but our information is that many social service departments are still dealing (perhaps tinkering would be a better word) with it, and many housing departments are only too glad to let them. Nevertheless the legislation offers prospects of improvement in the situation described in the following quotations. Parsloe 1978 'The contacts I have had with them [housing departments] have been perfectly OK. Yes, there is tension in the sense that neither side really knows what's going on. I would say that one of the main problems lying with our department is that we seem to get directives saying one thing, and the next day it is countermanded. I'm thinking here particularly of the question of whether you take children into care for homelessness or not' (p. 256, para. 10.38). 'I do not think they [housing departments] appreciate what we are doing, I think they use us as scapegoats, they pass their problems over but they do not want to co-operate' (p. 255, para. 10.36). 'One or two' social workers complained about having a role 'as debt chasers' which was 'subsidising the District Council'. A principal social worker thought his authority had put itself in a false position with regard to housing authorities by being only too willing in the past to develop rent guarantee schemes and take on the responsibility for homelessness (p. 256, para. 10.42). Again, 'It really is a sad state of affairs because the housing department tend to think that once it gets to five o'clock it then becomes a social problem not a housing problem simply because the families are going to be on the street overnight, and so the onus is left to us to find housing, temporary or otherwise, until the following morning. So the following morning when housing come back on the scene it then becomes a housing problem again, you see' (p. 258, para. 10.49).

Both Goldberg and Parsloe and Stevenson find that social service departments spend a great deal of time in 'aid, advice and advocacy'. Goldberg *et al.* (1977) say (p. 280) that the intake team in Southampton was occupied in screening incoming demands, many of them for straightforward practical services; providing practical help of all kinds for the elderly and disabled; acting as a kind of Citizen's Advice Bureau for a great variety of material and inter-personal problems; and taking on the role of a go-between or advocate *vis-à-vis* the DHSS, the Housing Department and other statutory bodies. Similar activities are observed by Parsloe, who also reports social workers' reactions to these duties (p. 260, para. 10.58): 'All you do is telephone them and try and sort out and put the client's problems in a different way. . . . It seems to me a bit silly that it couldn't have been sorted out before you had to intervene . . . this could be sorted out at the initial department without having to come to us *and then go back to them as it always does*.' (our italics). We again refer to Wootton's view that it is foolish to erect new institutions to modify the originals, rather than improve the originals. Advocacy and advice were generally unpopular with social workers. One, seeing a conflict between welfare advice and other aspects of his task Parsloe (1978 p. 261, para. 10.59), said: 'When you start to be seen as the welfare man your credibility in terms of help with relationships, the expertise you bring to situations, can be reduced and diluted'. Are we alone in interpreting this comment as the tiresome real world impinging on the social worker's dream world? Stevenson and Parsloe did not attempt to quantify the amounts of social work time given to 'aid advice and advocacy'; Goldberg reports that 46 per cent of cases received information and advice, and possibly of the 36 per cent on whose behalf 'resources were mobilised' some could be categorised under 'aid or advocacy'. Parsloe suggests that this activity is growing fast.

> Social service departments, and therefore social workers, are faced by difficult dilemmas about being 'tough', about arguing that they are not the agency to deal with these problems. Having helped with some problems of this kind, particularly if they have given money themselves in some circumstances, they are faced by grave difficulties about turning others away. A reputation as a helping agency, once acquired, may lead to a mushrooming growth of demands for assistance (p. 262, para. 10.63).

Or again, 'Just as we know that clients seeking monetary help from social service departments may have differing degrees of success, from authority to authority, area to area, and social worker to social worker, so much the same can probably be said about the extent to which they get other kinds of help with social security or housing problems. Nevertheless, clients' expectations of help of either kind appear to grow and grow' (p. 262, para. 10.64).

Seebohm is somewhat dismissive of the role of health visitors, remarking (para. 370) that 'In recent years some confusion has continued over the respective roles and responsibilities of health visitors and social workers, and this has inhibited collaboration between them . . . there is inevitably some overlap in the duties of health visitors and social workers. . . In our view, however, the main functions of the health visitor and the social worker are distinct, and the two roles may be incompatible in the same person. Moreover, in terms of training it would be uneconomic to combine them'. After stressing the need for close collaboration between health visitors and social service departments, the Report pronounces conclusively (para. 380): 'In our view the notion that health visitors might further become all purpose social workers for general practice is misconceived'. No reasons are given for these assertions, and we suspect that they stem from uncertainty about the competence of social workers, perhaps a fear that their general incompetence might be apparent if juxtaposed with the undoubted skills of trained nurses. Parsloe finds that some hospital social workers see health visitors as their key contacts in the community, believing their services to be more needed than those of social workers (p. 263, para. 10.66): 'One tends to hand on fairly naturally to health visitors because they are part of health and often they need the health visitor more than the social worker. And of course the health visitor is able to visit more quickly and more regularly'. This is remarkable, given the large caseloads health visitors carry. Another hospital social worker remarked, 'I refer more to health visitors than social workers. I feel the need for care is more medical than social work oriented for the elderly. I haven't ever heard a health visitor say she couldn't do it, she was too busy. There are some who say "I will get there when I can". Their case loads are enormous'. We are told that some social workers thought 'health visitors could be more welcome than social workers in some households and were therefore more able to investigate suspected child abuse' (p. 263, para. 10.68). As a social worker said, 'Its a bit more difficult. You are not doing it so directly as the health visitors . . . the health visitor now in cases of the babies that are sort of neglected rather than beaten about, they are sort of neglected, perhaps nappies not changed enough and that sort of thing. Well you can suspect that but really you are not in a position to go and take a nappy off, whereas the health visitor can do that, and if you suspected you can ask her.' We wonder whether this respondent considered she had a general health overnight functions as well as the non-specified social work function? If she did, what were her qualifications for exercising it? The authors remark that 'some of the best relationships between social workers and health visitors occurred when they shared the same premises' (p. 263, para. 10.69). Others attributed poor relationships to the fact that 'health visitors were unsure about the role of the social worker'. This uncertainty is no surprise to us, and in our opinion it is a dangerous uncertainty, for which we propose remedies in our concluding chapters. The nature of the uncertainty was well illustrated at a conference on battered children held at Swansea in 1977. A social worker remarked that the legal responsibility for co-ordinating 'treatment' in families suspected of battering lay with the social services departments, and that when the health visitor suspected battering she should normally hand over the case to the social services department. The same speaker had stressed the need for engaging the confidence and co-operation of parents, so one of the present authors asked how the health visitor should introduce the social worker to the family. What service should she say was being provided different from the one the health visitor was already giving, and indeed how should the health visitor recognise when it was appropriate to consult the social worker? There was a stunned silence. It is our view that the health visitor and the general practitioner are amongst the people most strategically placed to discover child battering, teachers being the others, and that they are probably the people best qualified to judge whether the risk of repetition is substantial enough to justify the removal of the child from its home. We think too that there is more chance of a health visitor undertaking effective 'preventive casework' than anyone else, and we therefore argue in our conclusion for experiment, in which authorities would be permitted to employ larger numbers of these ladies, replacing social workers if that is their preference.

Seebohm stresses the importance of the general practitioner in any effective scheme of family care. 'We regard teamwork between general practitioners and the social services as vital. It is one of our main objectives and the likelihood of promoting it is a test we would like to see applied to our proposals for a social service department' (para. 699). By that test, the relations described in the Parsloe study can only be described as failures near absolute. We reproduce Parsloe's comments unedited.

General Practitioners

75. Social workers indicated that they faced considerable problems in relating to professionals in other fields. Many said that their training did not include any discussion of the roles of other professions:

'Its a big gap really, you spend a long time trying to find out, and in the process make a lot of mistakes and upset people.'

76. Relations with general practitioners seemed particularly difficult, a considerable number of comments were made about the extent to which the doctors distanced themselves. Put at its simplest the complaint about many doctors was as follows:

'GPs I find are extremely difficult to work with, they tend not to see that a social worker has a very valuable role.'

77. Clearly in many cases, GPs had little knowledge about the social work task, and had little intention of doing anything about finding out. Fundamental to this was an attitude which

social workers took to be a lack of respect for social work as a profession. Social workers reported:

'Some GPs are very unconvinced about social work as a profession. They don't think much of us.'

and

'...they don't regard us as being equally professional.'

78. Where there was some understanding of the social worker's role it was often as a local authority functionary with certain legal responsibilities rather than as another 'caring professional' that the social worker was seen:

'They see us as someone who provides home help, does adoption and takes children into care and that's it.'

79. Hence, when social workers volunteered views and advice these tended to be undervalued. One social worker said:

'In most cases I find the GP will generally take the attitude that he knows better or more than social workers ... so you give up.'

Another social worker elaborated this view:

'Some doctors feel a child should come into care immediately whereas a social worker will say "No, it's not as bad as that, we can put in support!" You often find the doctor will say, "Well, you accept responsibility then, I'm telling you what should be done — don't blame me if the client ends up in..."'

80. A related complaint about general practitioners was that they expected social workers to provide domiciliary and residential resources without question:

'They ring up and say "There's an old lady who needs to go into an old people's home. Please arrange it."'

81. Another example of doctors' expecting to 'prescribe' the allocation of social services resources was quoted in the section on home helps. A rural team in Scotland was faced by a situation in which, in the past, the district clerk had been prepared to supply home helps in direct response to doctors' requests. Social work assistants in Northern Ireland experience similar pressure.

82. Social workers were very unsure how to try to overcome these problems with general practitioners. One social worker urged that a 'casework' approach might be appropriate.

'I suppose a lot of the problems are in our own profession because there are some here who will immediately

have words and stand on their professional rights. They
ought to look on GPs as they might look on clients on
occasions and deal with them as such. I'm sure it would
help in the end to see how the GPs are thinking and deal
with it on that sort of level.'

Another social worker, however, objected to such an
approach:

'We've been told to ride them along a bit, but I don't see
why we should. I don't think we're helping ourselves as
professionals. Sometimes I think social workers have got
to stand up and shout for themselves. If we're ever going
to be accepted as professional people we're never going
to do it by being dogsbodies to the GPs or the health
visitors or whatever.'

83. The picture was not, of course, entirely black, Social
workers did report examples of getting on well with doctors.
But the picture certainly seemed to be rather the reverse
of that quoted for health visitors, where rare exceptions of
individuals or groups who were unco-operative were reported. The rarities here were the co-operative and understanding doctors. In this case the findings of the study of
NAI (non-accidental injury) case conferences* and those
of this study do broadly coincide.

84. Some of the best examples of progress with the relationship
between social workers and doctors seemed to arise where
forms of attachment of social workers to doctors' practices
had been arranged. But there were pitfalls with such arrangements. It did not seem to have proved feasible for the attached social workers to be seen as people to whom the doctors
could make direct referrals. Social workers felt that that
played too easily to the 'medical auxiliary' view of social
workers held by some doctors, and in any case came into
conflict with the many other sources of referral to the
team. In one place where it had been tried, the scheme had
collapsed under pressure of work from other sources.

85. The following lengthy quotation illustrates an alternative
model, perhaps of liaison rather than attachment, in which
social workers took on a responsibility for regular visits to
practices:

'Although the GP is receptive, he saw me as just another

* 'Case Conferences: A study of interprofessional communication—cases concerning children at risk'; Desborough C., and Stevenson, O., Social Work Research
Project, University of Keele, 1977. Internal paper, amplified in Parsloe 1978.

para-medic attached for his uses. I was determined that I wasn't going to let it develop on this sort of line, and we had some useful discussions about our roles and functions. I refused to take a list of referrals when I was there and I refused to discuss individual people. I said "I'm here to get to know more about your work and to explain to you more about what we can and can't do, what our roles and functions are, what district we cover, how to make referrals, how we allocate the work", because they had no idea.

I learnt about doctors and I think the basic thing that's got to be understood on both sides is that we work in very different ways. A doctor has to diagnose and act quickly, and make decisions quickly, and he wants to see results very quickly or else he is too late. But he's got to understand that we're on a very different wicket, that we could be doing a lot of damage if we try and jump the gun with the sort of problems we're dealing with. So it's no good him referring and expecting all the problems to be solved by next week because they're not going to, and some you'll never see solved.'

There have been regrettably few well-documented accounts of social work attachments to general practice, though such attachments existed before 1970 and more have grown since. Ratoff *et al* (1973) conducted a survey of social services departments in 1972 which showed only 102 social workers attached full-time to any medical agency, and that nearly 21 per cent of the 225 social services departments had unmet requests for attachments from general practitioners and health centres. The most promising study we know of is that being conducted by the general practitioners' research unit of the Institute of Psychiatry, in which the activities and outcomes of social workers in general practice are being examined with a care and attention to scientific method which makes most of the previous studies look shabby indeed. The opinion of many of the research workers is that a close association between medicine and social work is desirable on the general grounds that it enables a responsive service to clients to be given, but also because the association with medicine makes social workers conscious of the need to evaluate the service they provide. An interesting contrast in styles is provided by two recent papers. 'Mental health care in the community, an evaluative study', by Cooper *et al* published, in *Psychological Medicine,* 1975, attempts to assess the therapeutic value of attaching a social worker to a metropolitan group practice in the management of chronic neurotic illness, and concludes cautiously that the service 'conferred some benefit on the patient population (see p. 62 for a fuller discussion). The research design is impeccable, the reporting accurate, the discussion guarded rather than euphoric. 'Adventure into Health' (Bowen *et al* 1978), on the other hand is an account by social workers of their attachment to a health centre in Croydon. It is hopeful, impressionistic, and, by contrast, more or less useless. A quotation (p. 1514) will give the flavour.

> Our first concern is for our clients but if we are to provide a good service we have to consider our own needs as well. Our satisfaction and confidence stem partly from the fact that through the health centre and group practice we see clients at an early stage in their problems. We have our share of cases where effort seems to lead nowhere but they are easier to cope with because there is a healthy balance of successes. We are not bound by Local Authority priorities as we are researching into all the referrals made to us. The work is varied and interesting and it is possible, despite pressures, to work carefully and well.
>
> We enjoy working as members of the health team, becoming aware of different perspectives and sharing responsibility so there is less chance of something being missed or of our feeling overwhelmed. However, there is a structure of authority already established in the health centre into which we are intruding and at times it has been hard to find our place within it. It has also been difficult to relate to a number of organisations and to reconcile differing interests.
>
> We have been fortunate in having a stable social work team with few changes in the past three years, allowing us to get to know each other well and work together as a team. We also feel we are part of the local community to some extent, although it can be difficult to go shopping quickly when the supermarket seems full of past and present clients. It is a joy to talk to past clients in the health centre and to know that our intervention has had a beneficial effect on their lives.
>
> In conclusion, we find the attachment of social workers to the primary health team has contributed a useful dimension to patient care. We hope our experience will lead to the establishment of similar schemes elsewhere.

These are statements of goodwill and perhaps self-satisfaction, but they are not evidence, and to us they illustrate the need for social workers to be instructed in the habits of scientific thinking and accurate recording.

We cannot help noticing the prevalence in this report of a continued, not to say tiresome, reference to the fact that the workers were *enjoying* their work, with little corresponding concern about whether the patients were also enjoying it. We have observed a tendency in people with a lot of time on their hands and a job without a very clear focus to speculate inordinately about whether the job suits them. Really busy people — most doctors, possibly all dentists — are too busy actually doing the job to indulge in such luxuries. Many of the studies of social work in general practice refer to the different styles of working of the two professions, the doctor having to assess a situation quickly and come to a decision, the social worker more exploratory and indeterminate. In a later chapter we discuss the ineffectiveness of conventional casework, contrasting it with the relative effectiveness of behavioural techniques. We would suggest that working with busy general practitioners might make social workers aware of skills other than the ones they have.

The study of social work in general practice is a minor part of a much larger project at the Institute of Psychiatry which is not near completion. We understand that general practitioners who have received social workers in their practice have reported favourably upon them. The unanswered question, which the researchers are finding difficult to answer (and it may be, for reasons of tact, difficult even to pose to social workers), is whether any spare pair of hands would have been equally welcome. An attempt to examine what the social workers actually do and what special skills they employ has met with substantial difficulty, but the researchers are hopeful of eventual success, and we await their findings with interest. We are very grateful to them for making available to us many of their interim findings.

Seebohm did not say anywhere that the new departments would give rise to happy social workers (though the report did mention better career structures). It seems unlikely that the committee envisaged their recommendations leading to a situation in which the counsellors appeared to be more in need of counselling than those they purport to counsel, yet so to describe some of the social workers and teams interviewed by Parsloe and Stevenson does not seem too wide of the mark. We have already mentioned the declared dislike of many social workers for the activities they are compelled to undertake (pp. 59). This and the impossibility of the tasks they really want to attempt adds up to a situation of very great stress, graphically described in Chapter XIII, Parsloe 78 'Practice, an overview'. We are told that social workers are experiencing pressures of a kind and degree which may inhibit effectiveness (p. 297.13.4). We reproduce two examples of situations producing stress for social workers.

13.15 ...frequently expressed as an area of concern, is the question of vulnerability of certain clients, especially, of course, the young and the old. The following example is quoted at some length because it gives such a vivid picture of the complexities of the situation which the ordinary worker in any locality frequently confronts:

'I suppose the child care ones make me worry. Like yesterday . . . there was a woman. He demanded his conjugal rights over the weekend again. She refused. He battered her. Eldest son tried to come between them and he threatened to assault his son. This is a problem family, eight children, no money. She is going for a divorce and wants to move out but Housing will not accept an application until they get at least a sworn affidavit that she is going to have a divorce. I've been told I'm not to support her application for a house — on the grounds that at some future date it might be said that I encouraged the break-up of the family. Everybody else knows that a split up of some sort is the only answer! What they're doing to the children is. . . Well, I was literally standing between them, not to hold them apart, I happened to be in this terribly cramped room and they were screaming at each other over the top of me. And there were kids all over the place and even when I went from there they hadn't really calmed down. I don't know whether I should have gone when I did, but there was nothing constructive I could do there. They have decided that they are going to split and all I could say was, "Well, if this is really what you've decided" — and I didn't say I endorsed their view — "for God's sake get on with it". But you do tend to think "was there any more I could have done to help?" And even though the answer is usually "no, not really", it doesn't stop you worrying about it, does it, when there are toddlers. . . There's this man and woman *screaming* at the tops of their voices and you look down and the toddlers are just playing — it's an everyday thing to them. So perhaps I'm worrying unnecessarily. If I close my eyes I can see those toddlers playing quite merrily and I think, "Well, maybe I was right just to leave them there".

He added ruefully:

'And when I'm called up before the coroner I shall say the same thing' —

an aspect of the problem to which we shall return later.

16. Again, there is the sadness of cases for which no solution seems feasible or 'right'. A poignant example came from the Welsh study:

'We had one old lady who went into a home (she was not keen to go), and she just gave up and died. So you don't know what is the best, whether to let them blow themselves up through leaving the gas on or . . .'

Parsloe and Stevenson conclude that the solutions to such difficulties 'lie surely, in the main, in staff supervision and general team support' (p. 302, para. 13.20). Given that comments about supervisors and advisers are so uniformly adverse (see pp. 62); given that several of the teams are described as being 'near chaos' (p. 3, para 1.7); remembering that these are the teams permitted to be studied by senior management, others presumably even worse being excluded as not being able to 'cope with the intrusions of the researchers at that juncture'; given that others caused the researchers to wonder after gaining entrance 'whether, if management had been fully aware of particular tensions and stresses, they would have let us in'; given all these daunting conditions, we have not much faith in the solutions proposed. Our own, which we elaborate in our conclusions, involve a contracting and clearer focus in social work activities, and a recognition of the impossibility of preventing all sin and unhappiness. Parsloe and Stevenson describe the reaction of many social workers to the possibility of being involved with battering parents as 'quite simply, fear' (p. 322, para 13.83). One of the social workers said, 'You tend to be frantically searching for clues that perhaps aren't there; and you feel worried they aren't there instead of feeling relieved that this is not an NAI situation'. They attribute much of this fear to 'the concentration of public and media interest about child abuse upon social workers' (p. 322, para. 10.84), and refer to the distortions in 'professional practice' occasioned by fear provoked by the media. Their solution is once again more supervision and better training (pp. 324-5). Ours is that social workers should cease to pretend to a competence they do not possess, since we believe it is the pretence which has raised unreal public expectation.

It is difficult to avoid the conclusion from the evidence we have been able to gather that the social work activities of social services departments have been conspicuously unsuccessful so far (and indeed, we would be prepared to argue, totally dispensable). The latter assertion receives some support from an examination of the effects of the social work strike.

In June 1979 social workers in Tower Hamlets went back to work after ten months on strike. A series of strikes had begun in April 1978 in Southwark and Newcastle upon Tyne and eventually fourteen areas and some 2,600 strikers were involved. We do not propose to discuss in detail the issues (pay and local gradings) about which social workers took action, nor discourse upon the role of their trade union, NALGO. We wish rather to attempt to estimate the effects of the strike, and to consider its implications for the reorganisation of social work that we advocate. It is unfortunate that no rigorous study of the effects of the strike was made while it was in progress. One of us was keen to undertake such an enquiry but, perhaps unsurprisingly, failed to gain entrance to a social services department with the purpose of finding what happened to clients whose social workers were on strike. We understand that a retrospective study of some complexity, involving question-naires to social workers, interviews with voluntary bodies, and interviews with clients is in progress at Liverpool Polytechnic, and short articles about some of the findings appear in *Social Work Today* (Brogden & Wright 1979; Clayton 1979). Another interesting retrospective study was published by Guy's Health District (1979), concentrating on the effect of the strike on health visitors, but in the main we have been obliged to rely on press and radio reports and interviews with interested parties, and our evidence is neces-sarily impressionistic.

The BBC programme, 'File on 4' (Oppenheimer 1978) conduct-ed an enquiry into the strike in Tower Hamlets. The Labour leader of the council said that the direct effects of the strike ap-peared to be negligible, but that the action of supporting unions resulted in unheated buildings, delayed mail and consequent hardship to many. He declared that the absence of direct effect had caused him to advocate a careful look at the usefulness of social work. (We do not know how carefully he looked, but the *Daily Telegraph* of 5 June 1979 reported that sixty vacant posts in Tower Hamlets were not to be filled, and we have heard that another Inner London authority has decided to abolish all com-munity work posts.) A consultant psychiatrist interviewed said he advised social workers against continuing the strike because 'they were in danger of revealing they were not needed'. He said he had missed social workers because 'they were nice people to have around' and they offered a different perspective, but that their work with psychiatric patients was being successfully undertaken by the Community Nurse. (There is evidence for the view that nurses take on many social work tasks in a strike in the Guy's Health District report. They do not appear to enjoy doing so, partly because it is an added chore in an already busy job, but also because many nurses could not see the precise focus of the tasks they were undertaking, and frequently felt 'they were getting nowhere'. Nurses appear to tolerate 'getting nowhere' less readily than social workers, who appear to accept it as an occupational hazard, bearable so long as paid.) Voluntary workers interviewed had not missed the social workers, while citizens of Tower Hamlets expressed views ranging from apathy to blistering contempt. There were unflattering references to the youth and idleness of social workers, and scepticism as to whether the tasks they undertook were 'real work'. Six representatives of the strikers interviewed were naturally all sure they had been missed, and the Director of Social Services gave a tear-jerking account of families without gas and electricity at Christmas because there were no social workers to write off the arrears. (For a fuller account of this enquiry, see Lait 1979c.)

Corinna Adam wrote three articles for the *Guardian* (Adam 1979) in which she interviewed social workers in Cheshire. They too asserted they had been missed, detailing cases which in their judgement would have gone better for all concerned if they had intervened. The cases bear examination, since they can be variously interpreted. One involves the removal of a child from a foster home by the natural parents, who turned up at Christmas and simply removed him. The social worker believed that 'if she had been around as a helpful buffer between opposing parties the drama might not have reached such a potentially dreadful crisis'. One cannot help wondering whether the social worker would anyway have been around at Christmas, and (since we are told the child had been removed from his parents on a place of safety order and placed in the foster home by the social worker), one cannot help wondering whether it was prudent for the social worker to have disclosed the foster parents' address. It could be that she was acting under the fashionable belief that it is always desirable to retain contact with the natural parents, however destructive their previous relationship with the child has been, and it is very likely she was expecting of foster parents a degree of tolerance concerning the shortcomings of defaulting parents few can muster. Such beliefs, based on a utopian view of human nature and on a series of unresearched benevolent hypotheses, have in our view been responsible for avoidable physical suffering and sometimes death in vulnerable children committed to the care of social services departments. We do not discount the possibility that separation from battering parents may result in emotional suffering even in very young children, but we believe that a putative evil should not take precedence over a real one.

The second case is described as follows (Adam 1979):

> Bruce's duties towards one of his families had to be taken over by the police. Four children, father unemployed, mother increasingly depressed.
>
> A month after the strike began (and he stopped visiting) neighbours phoned the police to say that the four-years-old youngest child had been left alone in the house at night. Normally, the police would have contacted Bruce. As it was, a policewoman was sent to the house. After that, the child was removed to a home.
>
> 'If I had been there', says Bruce, 'I could have explained that it was just a temporary inability to cope, on the mother's part. As it was, a residential home was the only alternative. That child is still there after two and a half months.
>
> 'The reason is that there wasn't a social worker available to make an up to date report on the family to the court, when the parents asked for the child back.'

We are alarmed by Bruce's certainty that he was witnessing 'just a temporary inability to cope'. We consider such judgements can only be made on the basis of considerable knowledge and expertise or a very intimate acquaintance, and know that experienced psychiatrists frequently get them wrong. As we have remarked earlier, we have a certain sympathy with the view expressed by social workers that society expects impossible things of them and blames them for mistakes, but consider the remedy lies either in abolishing social workers or in placing many under the guidance of doctors who, while not infallible, have some acknowledged skills. Another, harsher view, is that official 'prevention', a word much used by social workers in the context of baby battering, may be an impossible activity, and that the only way officials can protect children from battering or severely neglectful parents is to establish that an offence has been committed and prevent another by removing the child from the threatening environment (Lait 1979b). Possibly there *cannot* be, certainly there *is* not, a single piece of evidence which establishes that social work intervention, short of removal, has prevented child abuse. There is none at all that the incidence of child abuse was greater (or less) during the social work strike.

Social workers report that the work of the courts has been impeded by their inability to provide social enquiry reports, and Corinna Adam quotes an unnamed magistrate as saying, 'We're fining kids of 14 maybe £50 or £100 for thieving, and I think it's a monstrous imposition on them and their families'. It may well be, but of all the penalties examined, fining comes out in many studies as effective (Home Office 1969). Other courts reported that dispensing with social enquiry reports simply speeded up procedures, and had no other noticeable effect (see also the Leeds truancy study, Chapter 9). Chief Supt. Thomas Farr also saw advantages in the absence of social workers.

'We just dealt with things in a different way. We didn't have to make out referral notices for children in trouble, which saved time. We could take the course of action we thought best without bother.

I expect they do a fine job of work. But compare it with the firemen's strike or the ambulancemen. There's no one queueing up to take over from social workers, is there? Look at it this way. The police have been doing social work for a great deal longer than they have. And we still are.'

Another claim made by social workers is that the strike affected the admission and discharge of old people to Part III accommodation, and there is no doubt that this is the case, as the following extract from an unpublished study (Baxter 1979) reveals.

The second area of priority for social workers is the elderly. The strike has meant that no assessments have been made for admission to Part III accommodation or other types of accommodation. Admissions and discharges to geriatric wards or hospitals have not taken place, elderly people have not been assessed for services such as meals-on-wheels or home helps and perhaps most important of all for a lonely old person, he has not had regular visits from the social workers. The Liverpool Director of Social Services knew of 41 very urgent cases needing admission to a home, he also knew of 85 vacancies in old people's homes which could not be filled at that time. Other old people may have to spend the rest of their lives in a hospital bed where under normal circumstances they could be sent to some type of home or even back to their families for their last days. The geriatric wards are overflowing.

The mentally ill have also suffered, as Miss Baxter points out:

> A third major area of social work activity and responsibility is the mentally ill. Emergency admission of the mentally ill to hospital has carried on as three alternative methods have been found, firstly persuading the patient to enter hospital voluntarily, secondly the police can act if in a public place, thirdly a nearest relative can be found. The police have been very useful in finding nearest relatives, therefore making admissions easier. However, social workers have not been available to protect the interests of their clients, although there is little evidence to suggest that abuse is rife. Also mentally ill patients who may be ready for discharge to some type of rehabilitation unit will have to wait until the end of the strike since a social work report is necessary and also a social worker has to be on standby before the patient may leave.

It is of course obvious that if large numbers of people with statutory obligations withdraw their labour there will be some effect. Where we would challenge the social work interpretation is in their assertion that only they are qualified to undertake these duties, and that free-standing social services departments are the most effective vehicle for administering them. Corinna Adam (1979) reports that voluntary agencies 'almost enjoyed the challenge' and reports a busy lady at the WRVS as saying, 'If the home helps had gone on strike, that would have been something. As it was we really didn't miss the social workers, to be frank'. Corinna Adam also reports that much of the conversation on the picket line was about embellishing the social work image and 'hiving off jobs they reckon any fool could do'. The aforementioned Bruce notes a newly qualified social worker as 'being absolutely fed up with arranging chiropody appointments for old people'. Bruce had the grace to wonder if her resentment was justified: 'If it's a caring profession, doing that kind of thing must be just as important as something which sounds or feels grander'. Do we discern here the phenomenon, already noted, of training 'unfitting' social workers?

In summary, our own interpretation of the strike is that it provided some evidence that the jobs social workers did were either unnecessary or could as well be done by others with less pretentious training and objectives. It may be that it had positive effects on some communities and individuals, causing them to seek for themselves answers to questions they would otherwise have referred to social workers. We recognise that our evidence for these views is slender, but the collection of information we suggest in our final chapter should go some way towards refuting them if they are unfounded.

4

Social work and the mentally ill

More time spent on bureaucratic and administrative tasks than on work directly concerned with clients. Findings of the Worcester Development Project. The fate of the mentally ill. Social workers and community psychiatric nurses.

In spite of the large amount of evidence that most social work activity does not benefit its clients and may actually harm them, relatively few critics of social work have concentrated on the issue of effectiveness, at least until recently and particularly following the strike of social workers in Britain in 1978-79. A more frequent criticism is that social work departments are unwieldy, inefficient bureaucracies in which too much time is spent on conferences and administrative matters and too little time supposedly helping the clients. Criticism of this kind has generally been essentially impressionistic and anecdotal because few time-and-motion studies of social work departments have been carried out. Some indication of the extent of bureaucratic and administrative activity was given by Harris & Palmer (1976) in their useful but limited study of a department in north-east England where they found that case-time—that is time actually spent in contact with clients, or their families, or others directly concerned with the case—came to about 30 per cent of total working time, while desk work and assorted meetings not directly concerned with cases amounted to some 48 per cent of working time. These figures exclude travel time, lost time and educational activity.

A much more detailed study of the work of a social services department has been carried out by Hassall & Stilwell (1976) as part of the Worcester Development Project, which is a long-term evaluation of a new community mental health service. Their study of social work activities during part of 1975—that is, after the two major reorganisations of the social services and the National

Health Service—is valuable not only because of its considerable detail, but because it enables a comparison to be made with an earlier study carried out by Carver & Edwards (1972) which studied social work activity in the same area in 1969, just before the reorganisation which was the outcome of the Seebohm Report.

Although Hassall & Stilwell were particularly concerned with social work activities in relation to the mentally ill in the community, they also looked at the amount of time the social workers spent with all the standard client groups. These were, apart from the mentally ill, children, the elderly, mentally retarded, blind, physically handicapped, and homeless families. A remaining group, 'other and unclassified', amounted to only 4 per cent of total case-time. The results are shown in Table 2.

Table-2

CASE-TIME BY TYPE OF CLIENT— URBAN AND RURAL AREAS

(all grades of social worker)

Type of client	Urban area % Case-time	Hours	Rural area % Case-time	Hours	Both areas % Case-time	Hours
Child care	51	306.25	50	53.75	51	360.00
Elderly	22	131.17	11	12.08	21	143.25
Mentally ill	6	36.25	9	9.92	7	46.17
Mentally retarded	5	28.50	8	7.83	5	36.33
Blind	6	36.42	1	1.42	5	37.84
Physically handicapped	4	21.58	13	13.75	5	35.33
Homeless families	2	12.58	—	—	2	12.58
Other and unclassified	4	22.17	8	9.25	4	31.42
Total	100	594.92	100	108.00	100	702.92

Comparison with the distribution of case-time in 1969 shows many important differences (Table 3). The large amount of time spent in the field of child care in 1975 compared with none in 1969 reflects the fact that, during the earlier survey, child care was not part of the statutory duties of the social workers, as well as the considerable number of statutory duties relating to young persons which have been created since then. This obviously makes comparison difficult, especially as there has been a considerable increase in the number of social workers employed in the area, from seven in 1969 to twenty-seven in 1975. However, the actual number of hours devoted to the mentally ill in 1975 was fractionally *less* than the number of hours devoted to them in a comparable period in 1969. This occurred in spite of the virtual disappearance of the separate social work department attached to the regional psychiatric hospital in the period between the two surveys. As the authors remark, the similarity of the two figures is 'surprising in view of the acceleration of the policy of discharge of long term patients, and maintenance of all patients in the community as far as possible, over the past five years. It underlines the warning in the White Paper that "in a developing social service which is still not equal to all other demands being made on it, there is a real danger that groups such as the mentally ill will be given a low priority compared with other groups whose needs are more overt, as well as being better understood"'. Another disturbing finding was that in spite of the establishment of a case register for psychiatric patients as part of the development project, social workers often seemed unaware that some of their clients were actually on the register. This state of affairs was presumably less likely to occur when social workers had closer contact with the psychiatric services.

Table-3

DISTRIBUTION OF CASE-TIME BY SPECIALITY 1969 AND 1975

	Urban area 1969 %	*Urban area* 1975 %	*All areas* 1969 %	*Both areas* 1975 %
Blind	25	6	20	5
Deaf	—	—	1	—
Elderly	13	22	19	21
Homeless families	—	2	3	2
Mentally ill	28	6	25	7
Mentally subnormal	11	5	8	5
Problem families	1	—	5	—
Physically handicapped	15	4	12	5
Other and unclassified	8	4	6	4
Child care	—	51	—	51

Table 4 shows the proportion of total social work time devoted to particular activities within the department. As will be seen, case-time, as in the Harris & Palmer study, was around 30 per cent, while desk jobs, conferences and meetings not directly connected with clients amounted to some 50 per cent of the total time. Again, this is similar to the findings of Harris & Palmer. It will also be seen that the amount of time spent on these bureaucratic and administrative tasks increased significantly between 1969 and 1975. The largest increase between the two studies was one of 8 per cent in 'conferences, meetings, committees etc.'.

As in the Harris & Palmer study, information about how social workers spent their time was obtained by social workers themselves filling in a time-sheet over a two-week period. The authors say that 'discussions with social workers, both those who took part in the study and those who did not, indicated that they were satisfied that the findings were a good representation of the way their time was spent'.

Table-4

DISTRIBUTION OF TOTAL SOCIAL WORK TIME
BY ACTIVITY 1969 AND 1975

	Urban area 1969 % *	*Urban area* 1975 %	*All areas* 1969 %	*Both areas* 1975 %
Case time	26	30	30	29
Travel and lost time	11	11	16	11
Senior admin. duties	7	2	3	3
Desk jobs	23	27	27	26
Conferences, meetings etc.	15	23	14	25
Other activities	19	7	10	6

*Figures rounded to nearest percentage point.

Subsequently, Hassall & Stilwell carried out a further study (Hassall & Stilwell 1978) in which they examined the work of community psychiatric nurses in relation to the mentally ill, using much the same methods. Some results of this study are shown in Table 5. It will be seen that the community nurses spend approximately 40 per cent of their time as case-time and only 32 per cent on bureaucratic and administrative tasks, including meetings not directly concerned with clients. Their ratio of 'therapeutic' time to 'administrative' time is thus approximately four to three, compared with the ratio in the social services department where it is approximately three to five. The difference would be even more marked if the nurses did not spend more time travelling than the social workers, because they saw more patients in their homes.

Table-5

COMMUNITY PSYCHIATRIC NURSES—
DISTRIBUTION OF TIME BY ACTIVITY

	Hours	*Percentage of total time worked**
Patient contact time		
Interviews with patients in hospital	3.92	1
Interviews with patients in community	111.67	36
Journey with patient	0.67	1
O.P. clinics	8.75	3
Contact with others interested		
Interview with other interested	1.17	1
Ward meetings (medical and nursing staff)	0.75	1
Other activities		
Desk work and discussion	97.42	32
Travel and lost time	68.00	22
Learning (attending lectures etc.)	7.75	3
Leave	7.50	2
Total hours	307.60	100

*(Figures rounded to nearest percentage point)

Hassall & Stilwell's first report, which was intended as an internal document for the DHSS, is somewhat unusual in that the director of the social services department added no fewer than twelve separate comments of his own before the report was submitted. He felt that 'the findings alone could mislead those who are not familiar with either the service or the project'. Among the 'misleading' findings he discusses is the high percentage of time devoted by social workers to conferences, meetings etc. which, he says, 'is to some extent accounted for by a training course which took place during the fortnight of this study'. In view of the similarity of these findings to those reported by Harris & Palmer, this seems a little unconvincing, especially as a further study still in progress reveals little change in the proportion of case-time (Hassall 1979). So, in the light of the available evidence, is his claim that much of the work with children 'could justifiably be described as preventive mental health work'. His argument that 'it is perhaps encouraging that service to the mentally ill in the urban area has held level' (that is, as compared with 1969) seems to take no account of the increase in the number of patients treated in the community since the earlier report.

He seems to have been understandably upset by the implication that the mentally ill might be handled more appropriately by community psychiatric nurses than by social workers. The Director asserts that 'they offer entirely different skills and undergo completely different training'. It is doubtless true that social workers do not acquire the specific and demonstrably useful skills of psychiatric nurses, such as the ability to make clinical assessments and administer medication to the chronic schizophrenic patients who represented some 40 per cent of the mentally ill patients seen by social workers. However, bearing in mind the numerous studies which failed to demonstrate any difference in effectiveness between trained and untrained social workers, it could be argued that while social workers cannot easily acquire nursing skills, nurses could, and in practice often do, add social work activities to their existing repertoire. In their role as potential psychotherapists, there is no evidence that nurses are more ineffective than social workers; and because they are not tied to one particular therapeutic technique, it could be argued that by offering a more eclectic approach than social workers, they provide a better service to the mentally ill. This argument is clearly reinforced if, in addition to the possibility that they can offer a better quality of service, they also offer a more efficient service by spending more of their time in therapeutic activity.

A further argument in favour of a more important role for community psychiatric nurses is that, unlike the social services departments, they enjoy the advantage of close geographical and professional links with the psychiatrists who clearly have a central role in any community mental health service. It is also likely that nurses will have an easier relationship with psychiatrists and other doctors than would social workers, who, as we have seen, not infrequently seem to have difficulty in their relationships with the medical profession. Indeed, there often seems to be a strong anti-psychiatry ethos in social work manifested in fundamental objections to the use of psychotropic drugs, and more particularly to the use of ECT.

We have some sympathy for those who are dissatisfied with many aspects of contemporary psychiatric practice, and as we make clear in Chapter 10 we think that psychiatry suffers from some of the same faults as social work, and for much the same reasons. There is certainly plenty of room for improvement in psychiatry and we are not against unorthodox and experimental approaches, provided they are rigorously evaluated as to effectiveness before they are adopted generally. However, it seems undesirable in principle to encourage what already amounts in some areas to an alternative mental health service, in competition with orthodox psychiatry, but sharing the same umbrella of the Department of Health and Social Security. The Leeds study (page 150) shows how much harm can result when competing ideologies exist within the same system and one group refuses to change its ideology in the light of convincing evidence. There would seem to be a strong case for abolishing the independent function of social work departments in relation to mental illness and bringing them back under the psychiatric services where there might be a better chance of social workers acquiring the sort of experience which is relevant to the care of the mentally ill.

5

Bureaucrat, psychotherapist or child-minder?

Confusion between bureaucratic and therapeutic roles. The similarity between casework and psychotherapy. Influence of psychodynamic ideas. Rejection of behaviourism. Ideology in the curriculum. Ignorance of task-centred methods. Centrality of individual casework. Anti-scientific attitudes in social work. The surrogate function. Difficult cases go to the least qualified. Placement of children; plan or panic?

The preceding chapters reveal a great deal of confusion and uncertainty about the functions of social workers, which evidently affects not only clients and observers but also the social workers themselves. Certain broad generalisations can nevertheless be made. Two of the more obvious features of social work could be described as its bureaucratic face and its therapeutic face. We have already described how the study by Goldberg and Fruin (1976) revealed that many of the things that social workers do come under the general heading of bureaucratic tasks, such as helping clients with 'predominantly material and financial problems' referring clients to housing departments, and arranging mechanical aids or home helps for the disabled. We presume that many of the 47 per cent of their clients who were off the books of the department within a week of their first contact must have been processed in an essentially bureaucratic fashion, since a therapeutic approach which produced even modest results with typical social work clients in so short a time would be enormously superior to anything we have ever encountered.

We have also recorded the fact that despite the prominence of these bureaucratic activities, social workers are generally reluctant to undertake them and evidently prefer what the British Association of Social Workers rather grandiosely describes as 'the purposeful and ethical application of personal skills in interpersonal relationships directed towards enhancing the personal and social functioning of an individual, family, group or neighbourhood, which necessarily involves using evidence obtained from practice to help create a social environment conducive to the well being of all'. What this very often means in practice is the activity known as casework and however it is defined—a task we shall attempt shortly—it seems that it can be regarded as a therapeutic activity in that it seeks to bring about some helpful change in an individual or group of individuals. Furthermore, that change should be at a personal, psychological, or even spiritual level, as well as concerning itself, with certain specific physical needs, which is essentially a bureaucratic activity. We realise, of course, that this may seem a rather artificial distinction, for if the general object of social work is to increase the sum of human happiness, might it not be the case that a man may achieve happiness more readily by having his rent arrears paid than by having his Oedipal conflicts resolved? Nevertheless, we think that most people will accept that there is a distinction, and anyway it is obvious from the preceding chapters that social workers accept it too and wish that it could be made even clearer. We do not propose to devote much space to this bureaucratic aspect of social work, but we may make the point that if social workers are reluctant bureaucrats, then they may well be less effective than those who accept their bureaucratic role more readily.

Another facet of social work which seems fairly obvious to us is the supervisory role. To some extent this too is a bureaucratic function since it involves certain statutory obligations. We have in mind such activities as the supervision of children who are the subject of care or supervision orders, which certainly takes up a significant proportion of social work time (see Chapter 4). The supervisory role often involves a mixture of the bureaucratic and therapeutic functions. On the one hand, the statutory aspects may require the preparation of reports at regular intervals and even a certain measure of inspection. On the other hand, supervision gives scope for casework with individuals or families with a view to 'enhancing personal and social functioning'. Since Professor Parsloe found that 82 per cent of reports on children in care were overdue (53 per cent being more than three months overdue) it seems that many social workers find the bureaucratic aspects of supervision a tiresome distraction from the therapeutic aspects, and we suspect that although a large percentage of social workers said that they liked working with children, what they really like is doing casework with children and their families. According to the CCETSW, 'case work with individuals and families is the method most frequently employed by social workers'. We shall now examine it more closely.

In an introductory booklet for intending social workers (CCETSW, undated), the CCETSW refers to something called 'the social work process' which, it claims, 'equips the social worker with a basic approach to his work'. When it is applied to individuals and families, it is 'usually described as "case work"'' and it involves 'collecting information and observing clients and their situations, whether they are individuals, families, groups or whole communities; assessing their needs and strengths; working out feasible plans of action with them; working with clients to implement the plans by helping them to mobilise both their own resources and those from elsewhere; reviewing their progress and preparing them to cope, if possible, without social work support'. This process seems to us very similar to what is known in other contexts as 'psychotherapy'. After all, the psychotherapist generally collects information and observes his clients/patients and their situations. He also assesses their needs and strengths and thus completes what he would see as the diagnostic aspect of management. He certainly works out feasible plans of action, works with his patients to implement these plans, and will often use any welfare and community resources he can get hold of if he thinks it will be helpful, generally delegating these organisational & bureaucratic tasks to a social worker or his secretary. Finally, he too will review progress and will generally look to the day when the patient can manage without him, although if the therapist is of the psychoanalytic persuasion, progress towards independence may be slow to the point of imperceptibility. The principles of case work and psychotherapy can be applied to small groups as well as to individuals and families with little modification, although the more people who are involved in the process, the more complicated it is likely to get. To some extent they may also apply to community work in which we include such aspects as social action, and the 'radical' approach (see Chapter 6). However, as we explain shortly, neither groupwork nor community work is very widely used. Furthermore, it is our view that once a group gets beyond a certain size, the principles involved are not so much those of psychotherapy or casework as of politics. (We repeat that we are in no way opposed to social workers possessing and acting on their own political viewpoints. Equally, we do not think that social workers have any more rights in this respect than other enfranchised citizens. We find disturbing such confident assertions as that by CCETSW that 'social workers have a special awareness of the effects of social policy'. This sounds a rather elitist idea to us with overtones of the old 'university vote' which once enabled certain graduates to vote twice in parliamentary elections.)

If, then, casework and psychotherapy are similar activities, we must now examine which of the various psychotherapeutic traditions has most influenced the particular type of psychotherapy done by social workers. There are certainly plenty of varieties to choose from. According to Sloane *et al* (1975).

In 1959 Harper described 36 different kinds of psychotherapy. His list was not exhaustive even at that time and since then many new therapies have emerged, each with a different name, underlying theory, and set of therapeutic strategies. Advocates of each believe its novel approach is far superior to others if not in fact the final answer to the problem. Janov modestly describes his new treatment: 'Primal Therapy, the cure for neurosis'. The old army rule — if it works it's obsolete — holds true here; as soon as a new therapy has attracted more than a tiny handful of fanatical supporters, and has reached a point where its effectiveness could be systematically studied, a zealot starts drastically improving upon it. He is usually too busy developing new methods to do any empirical tests. If he does report results, they are repudiated by therapists loyal to the old sect on the ground that he really isn't doing therapy X any more. After mutual recriminations he will come to agree and declare himself to have founded therapy Y at which time the whole mitotic process begins again.

Although not all of these thirty-six varieties of psychotherapy would have had their origin in the great Freudian revolution at the turn of the century, there is no doubt that the psychotherapy industry was very largely created by Freud and his associates and disciples. For convenience, we shall refer to this as the psychodynamic school, and it dominated psychotherapeutic thought with remarkably little opposition until the 1950s. Even then, criticism, such as Eysenck's (1952), was directed mainly at the alleged ineffectiveness of psychotherapy. It was not at that time widely suggested that alternative methods would necessarily be much better. It is not surprising therefore that the psychodynamic approach had an important influence on the development of social work as well. especially when a disproportionate number of social work academics have worked in psychiatric services where psychodynamic concepts have also been influential. (See p. 189 for a discussion of the relative effectiveness, and concern for effectiveness, of psychiatry and social work.)

In the absence of any competition, this takeover of the psychotherapeutic aspects of social work was understandable and it has had some very important consequences. We deal with the therapeutic consequences in some detail in Chapter 10 but here we concentrate on the consequences for the philosophy and knowledge base of casework.

In the 1960s, the supremacy of the psychodynamic approach to psychotherapy was increasingly challenged. It was challenged not merely on the grounds of its ineffectiveness but also on the grounds that more effective approaches to psychotherapy existed. These new approaches were broadly grouped under the heading of behaviourism and their arrival signalled the start of an ideological battle in psychotherapy which is still going on. There had, of course, been ideological differences — perhaps theological would be a better word — between the various psychodynamic schools in the past. This was probably inevitable given that, as one critic put it, 'most schools of psychoanalysis offer not merely the promise of a cure for neurosis but a view of the nature of man. Each strives to interpret human existence in terms of its own, usually rather narrow, conception of the meaning of life' (Sutherland 1976). However, most of these feuds were about specific articles of the faith rather than about the validity of the faith itself. In theological terms, it was as if they were arguing about consubstantiation versus transubstantiation, or about how many angels could dance on the point of a needle.

The effect on the psychodynamicists of behavioural theories was of an altogether different order and can legitimately be compared with the effect of Darwinian theories on the established churches of the day.

But as well as the challenge from behaviourism, the psychodynamic tradition was also increasingly challenged by a number of allegedly new therapies mostly originating in the USA and particularly, though not exclusively, in California. These include, apart from Primal Therapy, Bioenergetics, Encounter Groups, est, Gestalt Therapy, Rolfing, and Transactional Analysis, to mention only a few of the better known ones. Some of these therapies seemed to have at least a tenuous connection with the mainstream psychodynamic approaches, which was sometimes acknowledged. In other cases, therapies seemed anxious to emphasise their difference from the mainstream approach and some group themselves under the general heading of 'humanistic psychology', which may have a nice warm feel about it but is rather vague as to its defining characteristics. The growth of the women's movement led many to question the more obviously male-dominant aspects of much psychodynamic thinking, but while some schools attempted to reconcile Freud and feminism, others felt, perhaps understandably, that a doctrine which was so profoundly mistaken on one point was not to be trusted on any others.

Many of these schools were characterised by the importance of a leader or 'guru' around whom a band of enthusiasts gathered and subsequently tried to spread their particular gospel. Most of them certainly offered 'a view of the nature of man', and almost without exception their claims for effectiveness by any criteria have not been matched by objective attempts to demonstrate whether a particular approach actually does what is claimed for it. In this respect, they have much in common with the mainstream psychodynamic approach, which, as we explain in greater detail in Chapter 10, has also been generally reluctant to submit its theories and practices to objective scrutiny. Although, under pressure, particularly from the behavioural school, the psychodynamicists have fairly recently begun to look more critically at what they do and believe — we also describe, the rather inconvenient results of this scrutiny — objective evidence for the value of the psychodynamic approach was most particularly absent at the very time when it was acquiring such a powerful influence on western thought, particularly on western psychiatric thought.

During the 1950s and 60s, then, at a time when social work was increasingly seeking independent status, it was faced with two approaches to psychotherapy which were not merely different but virtually incompatible: the psychodynamic approach and its successors, which lacked a tradition of self-criticism and the empirical verification of its theories, and the rapidly growing behavioural school, which from its earliest days was almost obsessively concerned with questions of verification and effectiveness, and with making sure by using operational definitions that what behaviourists did was described in such a way that other researchers had a reasonable chance of being able to repeat the experiment themselves. It is our contention that social workers — or at any rate social work teachers — have concentrated largely on the unscientific varieties of psychology (pseudo-psychology would be a better description in many cases) and have largely ignored or actively rejected those therapeutic approaches which possess not merely scientific pretensions but a real scientific tradition.

Without analysing the curriculum of every school of social work, it is difficult to quantify the extent of this bias, but we have little doubt that it exists. Apparently we are not alone in this and we note the comment of Fischer (1978a) in his review of the effectiveness of social work that 'most of the helping professions have concentrated on theories—from Freud to Piaget to Erikson—that help practitioners understand their clients but not change them, emphasizing diagnosis at the expense of intervention. Thus, systematic ways for professionals to implement their theories — the techniques or procedures, what the practitioner is actually supposed to do — either have been given scant attention or ignored altogether'. Baird (1976) and Sheldon (1978) also imply that the scientific behavioural approach has not been treated with the importance which it deserves, given its prominence in academic psychology. Sheldon mentions 'the negative attitudes which many social workers hold towards the concept of science' and makes the point that 'theories containing built-in defences against disbelief, e.g. much of Freud's and Marx's work, although they may have great explanatory range, must occupy a lower position in any hierarchy stressing validity and reliability'. We do not doubt that some of the least scientific and testable approaches to psychotherapy can also seem very attractive, especially to those who are intrinsically suspicious of science. Sheldon remarks that 'social workers often respond to ideas because they are "attractive" in themselves, because they find ready support in our established system of values or because they have flattering implications. Thus, R. D. Laing's proposition that madness is a product of disturbed family functioning (a dimension familiar to social workers) does not have to fight very hard for a place in the curriculum, whereas H. J. Eysenck's rather more "unpopular" but methodologically more sophisticated work does.' Professor Eysenck, of course, is a well-known exponent of the behavioural approach and is unpopular among social workers in Britain. He is disliked for two reasons, for in addition to his behaviourist viewpoint, he also argues that genetic factors are of some importance in human behaviour. Both viewpoints are anathema in many schools of social work, and one group of social science students from a British university actually took their dislike to the point of physically attacking Professor Eysenck at a public meeting, presumably to demonstrate their respect for the traditions of academic enquiry and free speech.

Few schools of social work in Britain seem to give any prominence to the behavioural approach, one notable exception being Leicester (Jehu *et al.* 1972). In many others, if the behavioural approach is taught at all, it is presented in the way described by Sheldon (1978) in which 'theories are often taught alongside each other, the ultimate choice being left to the student . . . .Students are encouraged to believe anything they like from the vast literature available to them'. A further example of antipathy to behaviourism was seen in a review of a recent textbook in a social work journal which the reviewer evidently felt had 'a bias . . . towards a behavioural viewpoint which may not be to everyone's taste'. We ask the reader to imagine a review of a textbook on the treatment of tuberculosis which stated that 'this book has a bias towards the use of antibiotics which may not be to everyone's taste'.

The situation appears to be much the same in the United States. The dean of a major school of social work stated that the behavioural approach had only been introduced into the curriculum in 1977 after a great deal of opposition from many of the teaching staff (Young 1979). Even now, its hold on the curriculum seems rather tenuous. As the dean put it, 'a lot depends on who's teaching it'. Teachers who are opposed to the behavioural approach will tend to teach it reluctantly and thus badly, and it is not difficult for a lecturer or tutor to slant his instruction in such a way that the student feels he need not take the subject matter very seriously. Although there are signs that behaviourism is being taken more seriously at last on both sides of the Atlantic, behaviourally orientated social workers evidently still feel themselves to be a small and rather beleaguered group. In Britain, a Behavioural Social Work Group was formed only as recently as 1978 and its first publication appeared in 1979. In the editorial of the first issue of its journal (which has a faintly *samizdat* air of impermanence and improvisation about it) Sutton (1979) remarks that in the early 1970s she could find few people who were interested in behavioural methods.

This is certainly borne out by the findings of Parsloe and Stevenson who report that 'only a handful of social workers' mentioned that they used techniques of behaviour modification. In task-centred casework, which is very much a behavioural approach ('a task defines what the client is to do to alleviate his problem' (Reid & Epstein 1972)), things are no better. Only 'a very small number' of social workers said they were using this method, and even then Parsloe and Stevenson complain that when these workers described what they actually did with their clients, it usually bore little resemblance to the definitions of task-centred work as formulated by the standard authorities in this field. They add that the infrequent use of task-centred work is 'interesting' (we think 'reprehensible' would be a better word) in view of the conclusion of Goldberg, Walker & Robinson (1977) that task-centred casework was an appropriate technique for a considerable proportion of the average social work caseload.

Apart from providing abundant evidence of ill-planned or unplanned activity without clear goals, Parsloe and Stevenson confirm the essentially psychotherapeutic nature of casework.

We learn that the most common approach was 'working with clients on an individual basis' and that few social workers rated 'assisting clients on a practical level' as more important than 'helping with relationship or emotional problems'. If 'relationship or emotional problems' are not within the province of psychotherapy, we do not know where else they belong. As to the alleged expertise of social workers in group and community methods (see also p. 124) Parsloe and Stevenson found that none of those interviewed said that awareness of community problems 'led naturally to incorporating community work, as such, into their daily work', and that 'none . . . said that group work constituted a substantial part of their method of working'.

No doubt the recent vogue for 'Intermediate Treatment' has altered the picture a little since this survey, but in view of its apparent ineffectiveness (see p. 155) it hardly provides a justification for the wider use of group methods. 'The centrality of casework', they conclude, 'in the sense of work focussed upon individuals and families, was emphasised by our respondents across the studies.' Ironically, although we ourselves are prepared to recognise that many social workers acquire useful knowledge about the workings of the welfare state and can, as any good bureaucrat should, help their clients to navigate the bureaucratic maze, the report states that 'surprisingly few [social workers] referred to the skills required. There seemed to be an assumption that one relied on "common sense"'.

In Chapter 10 we describe some of the differences between the behavioural approach and conventional social work methods. At this stage, we merely ask the reader to accept that there are real and important differences and that these differences may be very relevant to questions of effectiveness. The important point to be made here is that social work education has indeed been guilty of an apparently conscious and deliberate discrimination against a major area of psychotherapeutic thought and practice. We are tempted to discuss what we feel may be the political and philosophical reasons behind this bias, but it might be thought unnecessarily contentious and would inevitably involve a fair amount of speculation. We do wonder, however, whether those teachers of social work who have resisted the introduction of behavioural methods should be considered as fit members of academic communities which are supposed to adhere, and in many other departments actually do adhere, to certain basic standards of scientific debate. We regard this kind of bias as particularly contemptible when it comes, as it quite often does, from social work academics who are highly critical of the methods of certain other professions.

Before concluding this examination of the theoretical basis for the most common kind of casework, it may be as well to give two examples from social work literature of attitudes which seem to reflect both the anti-scientific aspect of social work and the arrogance which social workers sometimes demonstrate towards other professions in the apparent belief that their own training has made them, so to speak, not as other men. Describing some of the problems experienced by social workers attached to a general practice, Bowen *et al.* (1978) wrote that 'some of the doctor's attempts at counselling too easily reflect personal prejudices and advice can be given which is unwanted'. We do not doubt that this is sometimes the case, but are amused — and also rather alarmed — at the implication that social work training somehow prevents social workers from reflecting *their* personal prejudices and from giving their brand of unwanted advice. We think that the studies of Goldberg and of Parsloe & Stevenson provide plenty of evidence of both habits.

The determinedly anti-scientific aspects of social work are illustrated by Hollis (1968) in discussing the argument that the relationship between social worker and client is too sacred to be demonstrated and that research into effectiveness is not really very relevant. Hollis states:

All that has been presented here may seem very theoretical and a far cry from the live process we experience as case workers. Where, one might ask, has provision been made for the *art* of casework? Where are the feelings? Is casework just a coldly intellectual process? Heaven forbid! Casework is in essence an *experience* between two people — a totality which rests upon the feelings of both and upon delicate nuances of interaction that can only be described as art rather than science. (italics in original)

The reaction of one of our colleagues to this illuminating outburst was: 'If she thinks it's an art, perhaps she should be paid by the Arts Council'.

We ought not to end this chapter without some mention of a further function of social workers which is certainly important in terms of the numbers involved although it is not highly regarded within social work itself. Residential social workers have in some respects a much more clear-cut task than field social workers in that they usually have what might be called a 'surrogate' function which is fairly easy to define and understand. They may have other functions as well but these functions are often secondary to the business of providing or being surrogates to those whose homes and families are either non-existent or thought to be inappropriate.

Perhaps the low status of residential work reflects this very ordinary and understandable nature of its functions, which are accordingly thought of as not requiring the kind of specialised skills which are held in some quarters to be imparted by social work training. If there are such things as officers and other ranks within social work, then residential workers come very much into the latter category. It may be that in many cases, ordinary citizens with little or no training or specialised experience are able to do many of the jobs assigned to residential workers as effectively as those who are ostensibly better qualified. After all, not many years ago it was relatively unusual for the elderly to be cared for in institutions, while the rearing of children continues to be, as it always has been, an essentially amateur activity. Empirical evidence that ordinary citizens can do as well as residential social workers even in such allegedly specialised areas as the management of delinquent adolescents comes from a recent study (Yelloly 1979) carried out in Kent. Adolescents who were the subject of care orders and who would normally have been put into community homes went to live instead with ordinary families who acted as foster parents but who were paid in effect as residential social workers. he assessment of this approach has only been partly completed at the time of writing, but the preliminary findings indicate that fostering is no less effective — or as some would prefer, no more ineffective — than residential care.

If social work training is supposed to provide a greater ability to help the more disturbed, deprived, or deviant members of society, it may be thought curious that residential social workers, who often have the closest and most prolonged contact with these groups, generally have much less training than the field social workers, who, in many cases, will have requested residential care when their own psychotherapeutic efforts have been unsuccessful. We both have personal experience of residential establishments and one of us has recently carried out a survey of residential facilities for a large social services department. A significant proportion of these establishments were dealing with people who were sometimes quite seriously disturbed. In one family therapy unit, about a quarter of the families had at least one member who had received psychiatric treatment, not infrequently as in-patients. In practice, the relative lack of qualifications of the staff did not seem to prevent them from using a reasonably systematic approach to treatment which could fairly be described as task-centred. Nevertheless the system presents an interesting contrast to the psychiatric services where 'ordinary' cases will be handled by the general practitioner and only the more difficult or recalcitrant problems will be referred for specialist psychiatric advice. In social work, it is as if the psychiatrists treated all the run-of-the-mill patients and handed over their most intractable cases to general practitioners.

Whether the success rate in residential establishments would be significantly higher if they were staffed by the more highly qualified social workers is another question altogether, and we suspect that the answer to it would probably be 'no'. It is a question which does not seem to be asked very often, possibly because there is no conceivable answer which does not have some rather unpleasant implications for the organisation of social work. If the answer is indeed 'no', it casts grave doubt on the value of training; and if 'yes' it implies that perhaps more of the trained field workers should work in residential establishments, a move which is unlikely to be welcomed by the more highly qualified. When one looks at the figures showing a steady increase in the number of children admitted to residential establishments in recent years, it is hard to escape the conclusion that one reason for the increase is that field workers use these establishments simply because they are there. The increasing number of successful actions brought against social services departments for the return of children to their families provides further evidence for the possibility that some social workers are just as prepared to play pass-the-parcel with their more difficult cases as some doctors undoubtedly are. There is some irony in the fact that during the recent social work strikes in Britain, the residential workers did not join their field-work colleagues. Had they done so, it is conceivable that the effects of the strike would have been somewhat more noticeable than in the event they appeared to be. Even so, we suspect that it is the simple surrogate functions whose disappearance would have been noted rather than the therapeutic ones.

A study carried out at an Assessment Centre in Surrey (Surrey SSD 1979) is more specific as to the confusion which exists over placements for children who take up such a large proportion of social work time (see Chapter 4). Most of the 53 youngsters were within the 13 to 16 age group. 'Nearly half of the children were admitted as an emergency rather than on a planned basis. Although Surrey's policy is to assess all children coming into care, in only seven cases was this policy identified as a reason contributing to admission.' It was found that the Assessment Centre tended to re-examine areas only recently assessed, but in spite of this plethora of assessment, by the end of the follow-up year, 'just over one-half of the children were no longer in the placement to which they had been discharged'.

The report also revealed that there was an almost complete lack of feedback to the Assessment Centre concerning assessed children following their discharge. It states that 'an air of misunderstanding appeared to pervade the formation and follow-through of treatment plans. High residential staff turnover raised further questions concerning the consistency of treatment received following assessment'.

Seldon (1976), in a detailed and comprehensive review of the difficulties of obtaining residential accommodation for children in trouble, documents the way in which community homes can be very selective about their clients and often tend to reject precisely those young persons who seem most in need of help (assuming, as the Seebohm Committee did, that useful help is actually available in the present state of knowledge). He shows that difficulty in finding a place for such cases was not due to an actual shortage of places and that, on the contrary, the places available are generally under-used. Illustrating the conflict between 'care' and 'control', Seldon remarks:

There is still an expectation that community homes will change' individuals. The method now to be used to accomplish such change is to be that of 'treatment' rather than 'training', a term and method borrowed from the medical discipline, but with no clear definition or indication of what it involves. Nevertheless, community homes are still seen as agencies of social control. . . . The superficial view is that of confusion and defence of their operational boundaries without the support of central government departments through an inspectoral system as in the past. Absence of clear objectives together with uncertain operational patterns has had some bearing upon the staff shortages.

Like us, Seldon feels that the imperial ambitions of the Seebohm Committee are an important factor in the apparent disarray at the sharp end of residential care, where therapeutic and/or custodial functions are added to the surrogate role. 'The old children's departments together with others disappeared into monolithic new structures of social services departments, and a wealth of expertise was lost.'

6

Radicalism in social work

Radicals vociferous if not numerous. Proliferation of texts to match university expansion in social sciences. A text examined. Social workers colluding in illegal actions. Low morale in social work. Social work as a 'front' for politics. Social work and homosexuality. Social work and welfare rights. Case Con. How to justify biting the hand that feeds you. The true role of the state.

One of the many causes of friction between doctors and social workers is the tendency of some of the latter, and of many of the more vocal teachers and publicists, to see social work as politics. Doctors doubtless have overt political views as varied as those of any other occupational group, but they do not commonly regard their surgeries as convenient places to propagate them. As we remarked in Chapter 2, people without clearly defined jobs who are not very busy, tend to indulge in all sorts of extramural speculation, as it were intramurally, simply because they have time to do so. We believe this is one of the reasons why social workers attempt to engage in what P. Morgan (1978) succinctly termed 'Revolution on the Rates'. Social workers wield influence without having to submit to a test of public approval: councillors whose policies are unpopular are not re-elected. We should make clear that the 'politicised' social worker who uses his salary to advance his own political cause is a rare bird indeed, but, as we shall try to show, those who claim to speak on his behalf are numerous, vocal, and have access to what passes for the professional press.

One of the more heartening aspects of the extreme radical wing of social work (at least to their opponents) is their almost total inability to deliver their revolutionary message in words comprehensible to anyone save second-rate graduates in second-rate sociology—usually a matter of preaching to the converted. Less heartening is the ability of authors who appear to hover on the edge of literacy to command hard covers. The enormous expansion of universities in the 1960s, and particularly of social studies degree schemes, led to a hunger for textbooks that could scarcely be sated. This coincided with an emphasis on 'publication' as a qualification for promotion in higher education, resulting in any academic, however slender his scholarship, however piffling his research, finding a ready market for his offering if it could be seen in some way as 'relevant' to a voracious yet ill-defined course of study. S. Andreski (1972) writes illuminatingly about this in his chapter 'Censorship through mass production'.

It is difficult to see how *Radical Social Work* edited by Roy Bailey and Mike Brake (1978) saw the light of day except in conditions like this. The book is a collection of essays on the theme of radical social work, tenuously connected by any thread of logic and written in the kind of jargon which has been called 'Desperanto'. (The essay by Stanley Cohen is an honourable exception.) The editors summarise some of the contents as follows.

> Pearson . . . examines the ideologies of social work approaches and suggests that radical social work needs to restructure the roots of the dominant social order. Pearson attempts to rescue the student from psychodynamic reductionism concerning his motivation, and to raise the debate to a valid place in moral and political discourse. Peter Leonard suggests a radical praxis for social work — the use of conscientization, a concept developed by Friere, as a form of liberating education which creates a critical consciousness. Rather than appeal to internal drives located in clinical pathology, Friere suggests a process where people 'not as recipients, but as knowing subjects achieve a deepening awareness both of the socio-cultural reality which shapes their lives and of their capacity to transform that reality'.

Thus are the troops arrayed for the revolution

One of the methods of 'restructuring the roots of the dominant social order' reported by G. Pearson is for social workers to connive with their clients in illegal and sometimes dangerous actions. He reports:

> I heard for example, of an elderly couple who had done a 'moonlight' from a condemned council property thus evading the payment of rent arrears, but who had then moved themselves back into the empty house without the knowledge of the housing department. A senior medical social worker had blundered into

this situation by asking the housing department if there was any chance of the couple being rehoused, only to learn that officially the area in which they were living had already been cleared of tenants. This social worker's account of the matter was rich in its expression of the difficulties of knowing the right thing to do. Her confusion was multiplied when she telephoned the electricity authority who were themselves very concerned about the old couple living in a house without a power supply. On a home visit on the previous day, however, she had talked with the couple before a blazing electric fire: the old man, apparently, was something of a wizard with gadgets and had plugged himself into a main supply some distance away. But although the medical social worker's story was full of confusion about where the limits of her obligations, responsibilities and confidentialities lay, her story was also full of excitement: she had clearly enjoyed her client's deviant ingenuity. In the event her decision was to ask the couple for a full account (which was to be given the status of full confidentiality) of their different dodges so that she could avoid fouling their pitch. And this decision was tinged with a sort of thrill—something which helped balance the more mundane aspects of her working life.

Many stories I heard were told with the same enthusiasm. However, the overall picture is complex and this kind of professional deviance does not fall neatly into Taylor and Walton's 'relief of boredom' category. Stories such as this conveyed a moral: people called clients will not be tied down, and their ingenuity and inventiveness (albeit deviant) was described to me as a fully human response to material hardship. In that sense the excitement which social workers felt about these actions came from the way in which they confirmed the social-work value code that all men (even the downtrodden) have an 'innate dignity and worth' which cannot be squashed. But there is an even more important way in which the social worker's complicity in lawbreaking amounted to more than a sort of deviant kick. In the case I have described, for example, the medical social worker also felt that it was not her job to enforce the regulations of the housing department and the electricity authorities. For even if they were enforced, she argued, the problem would still remain: where were this couple going to live? Similarly, social workers told me that it was not going to help their clients at all if infractions of probation orders were reported to the court: and they added that they (as social workers) were there to help, not hinder. Many people, it was suggested, could not manage effectively on social security incomes and retirement pensions. Ignoring the cohabitation of women claimants, or claimants who had jobs 'on the sly', was thus justified on the ground that it might help to prevent family breakdown, illness or malnutrition because of an impossibly low income. The refusal to pay attention to rules and regulations, therefore, is seen as a way of doing the job more effectively: a complex motivation which might both ease the work process (type 2) and redefine the purpose of the job (type 3). Taylor and Walton (1971, 232-4) argue that for large bureaucracies to function effectively sometimes workers must ignore and break bureaucratic rules. Can we then describe the actions of this medical social worker (and the others) as *good* social work? In order to answer that question, of course, it would be necessary to state unambiguously what the goals of the welfare state are. But the whole point of this type of professional deviance is that it does not just facilitate a more 'effective' accomplishment of the given goals of the job, but also involves a struggle over the control of work and the definition of what the job is.

Pearson comments:

In the case of social work, industrial deviance amounts to a small scale restructuring of the welfare state on a day-by-day extemporised level. It is restructuring (and not just a destructuring) which supports the little man against the big machine, and it is informed by two levels of experience—first the ordinary sense of concepts of equality, freedom, justice, human rights which any citizen might pick up in his daily passage in the world; secondly the *rather specialised* [our italics] sense of those concepts which a social work apprentice obtains in his professional training.

We cannot help wondering what the ordinary citizen who pays his rent and electricity bills, *and* the social workers' salary would make of this 'rather specialised sense' of equality etc. But his small-scale restructuring of the welfare state does not appear to bring the social worker much joy; Mr Pearson tells us (p. 44):

Many social workers talked to me of the problem of personal survival in the hurly-burly of social work departments. One survival strategy was to aim for promotion to senior positions and management posts, to lift clear of the 'firing line'. Another possibility was simply to get out of social work because the job was too demanding, too stressful and too hopeless. There is

even a rumour circulating that social workers are already desert-
ing at an alarming rate. I was told that social workers were only
staying in the job for an average of two years. I do not know
where the figure comes from but I was told the same story on
more than 20 occasions in different parts of the country and
I have also heard it from students on a number of training
courses. I suspect that it is just a rumour, but the fact that there
is a rumour indicates and enhances an inner hopelessness in
the world of social work. If there is an inner hopelessness then
it must find its origins in social work's world and its education.

Mr Pearson's sense of the 'inner hopelessness' of social work is
confirmed by the study by Goldberg *et al.* (1977) (see p. 59).
We agree with his explanation of the origins of hopelessness, especially his reference to education, but we differ in our emphasis.
We have already expounded at some length on unrealistic expectations raised by training in psychoanalytically based 'casework'. We are not surprised if disappointed expectations have led
to disillusion and flight. It is surely downright cruelty to heap upon
inadequate social workers the burden of 'restructuring society' as
well as paying everyone's gas and electricity bill.

Mr Pearson ends his chapter dramatically. 'The test of social
work education is going to be whether it can own up to its own confusion and make a critical contribution to the defence of the weak.
Meanwhile we can only wonder whether it is making or breaking
social workers'. The weak who need defending may well be the poor
old social workers, against such as Mr Pearson (Senior Lecturer
in Social Work. University of Bradford, no less), whose nostrums
cannot (and indeed, to do him justice, are not calculated to),
make the lives of this beleaguered group easier.

An even more prestigous advocate of radical social work, Peter
Leonard, Professor and Chairman of the Department of Applied
Social Science at Warwick University, previously Director of
Social Work Education at the National Institute for Social Work,
and a member of the Seebohm Committee, contributes sage advice
in his chapter, 'A paradigm for radical practice'. He quotes with
approval the Chilean Guru Alfero, who saw social work as 'trying
to raise the level of consciousness of the deprived classes and to
promote in man a critical and reflexive consciousness so that in
fulfilling his ontological vocation, man can overcome the contradictions operating in our society, and assume an effective role in
the structural transformations that it is imperative to achieve'.
He refers to the need to construct 'counter systems' as follows
(p. 58):

Facilitating linkages between people and various informal and formal systems, even if accompanied by conscious reflection on the relationships involved, is frequently not enough. One aim of radical practice will be to help in the building of counter-systems either within or outside the existing systems. Such system-building aims to develop a power-base from which some changes in existing systems can be achieved, or from which in the short or long term such systems can be radically trans-formed or abolished. Within the family, for example, a counter-system may be established consisting of the social worker and an adolescent son or daughter where the aim is to shift the balance of power in the family or to provide a supportive system while the adolescent separates from the family. In residential institutions, it may be necessary to build counter-systems in order to ameliorate the effects of and ultimately to change an authoritarian regime. At organisational and community levels, the building of counter-systems may involve trade-union or pressure-group activity, or the establishment of facilities—counter-information services, or community work-shops designed to encourage neighbourhood opposition to official planning policies, for example—which require conti-nuing maintenance and the input of specific expertise by the social worker.

Both Pearson and Leonard accept implicitly that the reformist activities they advocate, many of which are directed against the agencies that pay and employ social workers, can without moral scruple be conducted within those agencies. Leonard's advocacy is at a level of generality that renders it relatively innocuous, since many aspiring revolutionaries, comfortably settled in their academic boltholes, will read his words with euphoric self-satisfaction, but will not translate them into precise action. Pearson's specific examples are another matter. His discussion of 'professional rule bending' is sophisticated and extensive, and undoubtedly treats of important matters. We would not wish to deny that there may be occasions when a social worker should put the interests of his client (as he interprets it) before a strict observance of law or regulation. The probation service faces this problem frequently with breaches of probation, for example, and the matter is highly complex. What we find contemptible is the use of public position to pursue political objectives under the cover of alleged professional competence. We believe it is partly the absence of any real competence which diverts social workers into political activities as a substitute for work, and we think it high time this subsidised fun-revolution was reconsidered. Social workers and teachers who have the courage of their convictions will pursue their political objectives without the crutch of an official position to provide special and improper advantage.

Another cause radical social workers are counselled to espouse is that of the gay liberation movement. In a chapter characterised by assertion rather than evidence, Don Milligan castigates impartially those who encourage 'integration' of homosexuals in society, and 'most doctors who are hopelessly ignorant about homosexuality'. 'Gay men who "cottage" [that is, solicit or have sex in public lavatories; see Driberg (1978) for an interesting personal account] are victims not villains and deserve our solidarity against police harassment and intimidation'. There is doubtless some justification for this view, but while we certainly believe that the state has no business in the bedrooms of the nation, we are not so sure about its public lavatories.

It is difficult to see what this has to do with bringing about the radical social changes envisaged by most of the authors, given that the proletariat generally has a rather old-fashioned view about sexual unorthodoxy, and the fact that homosexuality is severely discouraged in most of the 'people's democracies'. So far as Mr Milligan connects his diffuse polemic with social work, it is to advocate that 'distressed and isolated gay people who seek help will be counselled by fellow homosexuals. . . . Political struggle and counselling depend on each other'.

In a chapter entitled 'Welfare Rights and Wrongs', Crescy Cannan (who, when he contributed this essay, was studying for an MA in peace studies at Bradford University) talks proudly of the achievements of radical social workers. These include London social workers

> publicly showing their solidarity with homeless families or squatters in their struggle for better housing; some have refused to ask for contributions to the cost of temporary accommodation, or to help clients fill in rent rebate forms under the Housing Finance Act. There has been work with gypsies harassed by local councils, with battered wives, members of the Mental Patients Union and with claimants' unions. In many parts of the country there has been militancy over office conditions, better conditions for residential workers, the struggle over standby payment for emergency duties, and strike action over the London weighting allowance. Many social work students have agitated for the removal of exams (Pinker 1979) and the introduction of course-work that is more relevant to

social problems than casework.

A mixed bag indeed, the unifying theme of which appears to be the sabotaging of any system that gives help to deprived groups unless the helpers accept unquestioningly that 'the system', i.e. capitalism, causes the problem and must be overthrown before we can be rid of wife battering and mental illness. In the whole chapter there is not one shred of evidence for the assertions made; they are seen as self-evident truths. We are told, for example (p. 127), that 'subsistence benefits, low pay and the system of income distribution must be seen as parts of an whole, the function of benefits and supplements being to depress wage levels, while enabling people to carry on consuming as prices and rents, and therefore profits, rise'.

The book fittingly concludes with the *Case Con* manifesto. *Case Con* describes itself as a revolutionary comic for social workers, and has in its time done a useful job debunking professional pretensions. But its political utterances are of a simplicity and circularity that recalls Radio Tirana at its least sophisticated. The last words are: '*Case Con* believes that the problems of our "clients" are rooted in the society in which we live, not in supposed individual inadequacies. Until this society, based on private ownership, profit, and the needs of a minority ruling class, is replaced by a workers' state based on the interests of the vast majority of the population, the fundamental causes of social problems will remain. It is therefore our aim to join the struggle for this workers' state.'

How far does this book represent an important section of social work opinion? One is driven to guessing, and our guess would be that like most other occupations, social work comprises all shades of political opinion, with a slightly heavier weighting to the left than in the population at large. If, however, the teachers of social work and the publishers of books and articles about it are taken into account, the picture takes on a very pink glow. Many of the expanded lecture force of the 1960s were recruited from people who had little or no direct experience of social, or indeed any other non-university work, and who had a penchant for Marxist sociology. The reasons for such a development are complex and outside the scope of this book, but it seems likely that a cadre of slenderly qualified theoreticians have exerted a disproportionate, or at least disproportionately noisy, influence over a profession anxious to establish its academic credentials. When a call goes up for training, and no one quite knows what the task is or should be, there is a natural tendency to accept the services of someone who *says* he can teach it and flourishes a qualification that looks vaguely relevant. Marxist sociologists (we do recognise that there are other kinds) have never been slow to see the advantages of universities as comfortable billets from which to propound their theories, and if departments offering social work courses were the only ones offering opportunities, well *tant pis*.

We do not think Marxist theoreticians disguised as social work teachers pose a threat to any save a lunatic fringe of students, or to society, since even the lunatic fringe tends to abandon theory when confronted with the complex real world. But we do think that having to regurgitate their tedious and irrelevant nostrums to obtain a certificate in applied social studies is a substantial waste of time, and an outrageous waste of money.

A further contribution to the literature of radical social work is *Trapped within Welfare* (Simpkin 1979). Mike Simpkin, a senior social worker from Yorkshire, develops the theme that social work is an attempt to apply a technical solution to problems which are moral and political, and with clarity and more subtlety than is common argues that 'Social work embellishes and preserves forms of relationship (the family) which are neither ideal nor natural but moulded by a particular form of production in which the worker is alienated from his product and in which all members of society are alienated from each other' (Simpkin 1979). He recommends social workers to abandon the pursuit of status and security and join with their clients in attaining the revolution. Asking himself the question we have previously mooted, how one can justify following a profession either useless or serving as a handmaiden of corrupt capitalism, Simpkin writes (p. 159): 'Within the employment opportunities which are open, social work seems as legitimate an occupation as many others, provided that its limitations and contradictions are fully recognised'. While beavering away at capitalism, Simpkin thinks the social worker should be well paid. 'There is no reason why our own ability to serve should be polluted by ensuring that we have a decent wage, at least until we have a society where wages have been superseded' (p. 77).

We recognise that in castigating social workers for a particular political stance we incur the danger of being seen as simply bigots of the other persuasion. Marxists have been the most vocal of the advocates of politicised social work, but Simpkin correctly asserts that other writers have implicit political beliefs which determine the direction of their social work practice. He cites Z. Butrym (p. 87) as being conditioned by her own explicit Catholicism and, more obscurely, B. Jordan (p. 92) as standing for 'the potential good of capitalist society'. It is also possible for social workers to work for beliefs which, while not overtly political, contain within them potential for changing society in a way not envisaged by their employers.

Are we, then, suggesting that only social workers whose views, political and familial, approximate to those of the majority should be employed, and that their task should be to uphold the existing conventions? Indeed we are not, but we are alerting readers to the danger we perceive of those whose job is ill-formulated and well-nigh impossible, diverting their energies to more pleasing tasks which postpone for ever the possibility of admitting defeat.

We cannot too strongly assert that we oppose implacably the prosecution of political ends under the guise of something else, and the attempt to overthrow an established institution while in the pay of its proponents. Quite apart from the issue of why social workers are so well placed to take on almost any activity that appeals to them, we do not consider it the proper function of the state to attempt to influence the intimate arrangements of its subjects' lives. This view is particularly well put by K. Joseph and J. Sumption (1979):

> It is no business of the state to decide in advance what kind of society it ought to be governing and then to manipulate or frustrate known desires in such a way as to bring such a society into being. It must take its subjects as it finds them. It is means not ends which are the proper concern of governments. It is their proper function to provide a framework of laws and institutions within which men can pursue ambitions of their own devising, and thereby create whatever society is the natural outcome of the infinite variety of human tastes and personalities.

In this chapter, we have concentrated on what seem to us the more immediate implications of the radical position and we are aware that behind the 'fun-revolutionary' image lies a more serious philosophical argument which is not so much about the nature of society as about the nature of knowledge. For all our references to the work of Popper, we know that he has his critics and recognise that there are problems in deciding what constitutes knowledge and how we should go about discovering it. (Bernstein 1976; Kuhn 1969.)

While these are important questions to philosophers, the debate about them looks like being a lengthy one. In the meantime, we think it important that less philosophically sophisticated questions be asked about what goes on in the real world of social worker, client and society. We do not seek to devalue the philosophical arguments about how 'real' the real world may actually be, but we doubt the practical value of these arguments to the average Social Worker who knows that in a very important sense there is no doubting the reality of the people and the situations with which he has to deal, and deal quickly. In any case, our experience suggests that while the more overtly political aspects of the radical movement arouse some interest among social workers, the philosophical debate attracts much less attention.

We are also aware that there is much debate about the function of the professions which raises important theoretical questions about professionalisation, and about the structural relationship between certain institutions — doctors, for example — and the nature and functioning of capitalist society (e.g. Bolant 1975; Parry & Parry 1976). At its most abstract, this sort of theorising represents what Wright Mills (1966) dismisses as 'grand theory', and we do not seek to participate in it. Our more modest sociological aim in this book is to clarify the immediate understandings and ambitions which social workers have about their work and their professional status. We are not concerned here with the broader structural consequences of their sociological existence.

7

Private practice in social work

*Saleability as an indicator of need. What private pract-
ice tells us about social workers. Private social work
in the USA and Britain. Arguments for and against.
The hunt for clients. Evidence that private social
workers see themselves as psychotherapists. The
psychodynamic bias continues. Fees and responsibility. Private practice and the poor.*

The notion of private practice in social work is evidently novel and
rather disturbing to many British social workers. We are interested in it for two reasons. First, while we do not regard the saleability
of a particular product or service on the open market as a measure
of its effectiveness, we feel that if such a service can actually be
sold, that suggests that consumers perceive a need for it. Whether
or not this perception is correct is beside the point. After all, there
can be little doubt that the general public perceives a need for the
services of doctors and has done so throughout recorded history,
yet as we explain in Chapter 8 it is highly unlikely that doctors
provided a service of any specific therapeutic value until comparatively recent times.

The second reason is a suspicion that, apart from purely financial considerations, one of the reasons why some people do private
practice is that it enables them to concentrate on a part of their
work which they particularly enjoy, or at which they feel themselves
to be particularly competent. Private practice therefore may tell
us something about how social workers perceive themselves.

In the USA private social work is well established and it may be
helpful to begin with a short description of US practice before
examining the situation in Britain and the implications for social
work in general. In the absence of systematic studies of private
practice we are indebted for our information about the USA to a
number of US social workers whom we have interviewed, at least

one of whom does a significant amount of private practice. Although this social worker indicated that she was prepared to be named, subject to being able to vet the manuscript in advance, we feel that it is more appropriate and no less informative to let her remain anonymous. We ask readers to accept our assurance that she is a senior academic at a large and reputable school of social work in the United States.

It appears that the skill which US social workers manage to sell is psychotherapy, usually of a broadly psychodynamic kind. Some social workers would doubtless prefer to call it casework, but as we have shown in a previous chapter, casework and psychotherapy are very similar endeavours. In the USA private practice has apparently become a significant phenomenon since the beginning of the 1960s, and seems to have grown with the licensing of social workers in various states of the USA. The division of social workers into officers and other ranks which was clearly the ideal of the Younghusband Committee (see Chapter 2) has largely been achieved in the United States. Social workers with a mere bachelor's degree are largely restricted to relatively humdrum bureaucratic tasks — the social work equivalent of hewers of wood and drawers of water. In general, only those with a master's degree are permitted to involve themselves in the more overtly 'therapeutic' aspects of social work, although some social workers with bachelor's degrees have apparently taken legal action against their employers on the basis that a BSW with appropriate experience is the equal of an MSW. In this context, it is interesting that while examinations in social work theory are of major importance in gaining a master's degree, few states apparently require any actual evaluation of the performance of social workers. One or two states have recently introduced video-taped assessment and role-play but in general a master's degree seems to imply a mastery of theory rather than of practice.

Although precise figures about the extent of private practice are naturally hard to come by, if only because not all practitioners wish to advertise that they have an additional source of income, there are certainly several thousand social workers doing some private practice and the numbers appear to be growing. It is thought that very few social workers could make a satisfactory living by doing private practice full-time, and most private practice is done by the holders of full-time agency or academic posts who do private practice in their spare time. Attitudes to private practice in the profession vary widely. The dean of one U.S. social work school made it clear that she regarded private practice as something separate from 'real' social work which — by definition — she regards as something done with or to the wretched of the earth. In her view, any spare time which social workers possess ought to be spent with this group, whom she regards as the main if not the only proper target of social work activity. However, it was said that many social workers see no moral or political objection to private practice and are keen to get involved in it themselves. One view is that private practice raises the status of social work and makes it respectable. We have the impression that, for some social workers, private practice is seen as a way of enabling them to achieve the goal of the British social worker described on page 73 who regretted that GPs did not treat social workers as professional people.

In comparison with the USA, private practice in Britain has barely got off the ground. A report dated mid-1978 prepared for BASW stated that 'it is believed to be not at all widespread'. It then cited two agencies and two individual private practitioners before continuing: 'no doubt there are other instances known to council members, but the current extent of private practice is relatively limited and as a source of employment for social workers, insignificant'. A later report of a BASW working party dated May 1979 indicates the existence of nine private undertakings in England with a few more under development. Feeling about the propriety of private practice evidently mirrors that in the United States. The 1978 BASW report discusses the pros and cons of private practice, and among the points in favour are that 'it is in the interests of social work to be able to produce evidence that there are people who value social work services for themselves highly enough to be prepared to pay for it', and that 'the development of certain aspects of social work, particularly at the psychotherapeutic end of the spectrum, could be helped by the development of private practice'.

Among the points against are that 'social work help is needed most by those least able to pay for it', which is rather questionable considering the well-documented resistance to social work techniques of problem families (Tonge, James, & Hillam 1975). Other possible objections are that 'a strong private sector might lead to the impoverishment of public sector services' and that 'shortcomings in the public sector indicate a need to change and improve the public sector, not a need for a private sector'. This last point is similar to our previously stated view that shortcomings in existing welfare agencies indicate a need to change and improve those agencies, rather than a need to create a new agency in the form of social services departments. It is also stated that 'social work is more appropriately practised in a setting which gives the worker access to a range of resources which would not be available in private practice', and 'there are no adequate arrangements for regulating private practice'. Judging by the findings of Parsloe and Stevenson the arrangements for regulating *public* practice are not adequate either.

BASW has not yet taken any official stance for or against private practice, but the private practice working party recommended, among other things, that 'BASW must make arrangements for recognition and registration of members wishing to establish private practices'. Although the report is not a policy document, its tone seems generally favourable to the acceptance of private practice, and it has already been attacked for this. One council member of BASW was reported in *Social Work Today* (3 July 1979) as saying that 'the association should have no further involvement at all in this field. . . . The charge of elitism has often been levelled at the association. Should BASW now be seen to be supporting private practice, particularly in the context of the most savage impending cutbacks we have ever seen . . . the charge would be substantiated indeed'. Nevertheless, the working party reported that it had placed notices in social work journals about private practice which 'attracted a fairly considerable response and it is evident there are an increasing number of public service social workers who are interested in entering private practice'.

Two social work agencies have been operating for a few years at the time of writing and one of them has reported on its experiences. The Independent Social Work Agency (TISWA), set up in Liverpool in 1975, aimed to 'explore some of the unmet needs that were considered to be properly the concern of social workers' (Farmer *et al.* 1977). TISWA was enthusiastic about the idea of prevention.

> The kinds of needs to which the TISWA workers wanted to direct their attention were well described in the Seebohm Report discussion of preventative strategy. It postulates that an individual family passing through transitional periods in the life cycle demanding substantial role adjustments or realistic changes in attitudes, may well require support or help if crises or damaged relationships are to be averted. Such were the types of referral considered appropriate for TISWA — stressful problems with crisis potential occurring in personal, family or professional relationships; problems, in other words, which whether or not they included practical or 'welfare' elements, might respond to case-work help.

Nowhere in this paper, significantly, is there any mention of the fact that evidence of the effectiveness of preventive casework is even more tenuous than in the case of intervention. Noting the aspiration of the Seebohm Committee that social services should be acceptable to all sorts and conditions of men, Farmer and her colleagues regret that social work should have an image as 'a service available to the lower classes but inappropriate for those more fortunately placed'. They recall a discussion with chief and senior local authority officers in education, health, welfare and child care who 'made it clear that they did not perceive *themselves* as ever being in need of social work help. If problems arose they would turn to friends, doctors or solicitors but not to social workers' (italics in original). Although clearly worried about the notion of payment — a worry evidently shared by some of their colleagues — they argue that for clients to pay for treatment may be seen as an aspect of self-help. 'Furthermore, fees could serve a function in counteracting what, even today, seemed to be stigmatising aspects of social work.'

The first problem in effecting a meeting between TISWA and its potential clients was over the simple matter of advertising. The local papers were puzzled by the notion of a private social work agency and evidently suspected that it was a euphemism for a massage parlour. When this difficulty was overcome, the initial response hardly suggested that the good burghers of Liverpool had been waiting for TISWA with growing excitement in order to gain insight into their personalities at last, much as people were said to have welcomed the prospects of free false teeth and medical treatment at the birth of the NHS a little earlier. Most of the few early inquiries were requests for information or about the prospects of employment at TISWA from social workers themselves. It was some months before the first client arrived, and, happily for the social consciences of the caseworkers, 'the very first self-referred TISWA client proved to be indubitably working class by any standard criteria'.

Unlike some better-known planners of social work services whose activities we have criticised in earlier chapters, the men and women of TISWA were frank enough to acknowledge that this particular social work service was not perhaps as essential as they had thought.

The slowness of the supposedly 'submerged' clientele to surface was, all in all, a surprise, the more so in that when the idea of TISWA was formulated originally and presented to social workers and colleagues in other fields, it was received with a general reassurance that there most certainly existed a need and that such a service would be used. It was even something of an embarrassment, therefore, to find that the demand did not materialise at once, and it became clear that turning need into demand was a more complex process than had been anticipated.

Apart from wondering if it was a case of the social workers' needs that had to be turned into a client's demand, we are reminded of the old adage that 'salesmanship is the art of teaching people to want what you have to sell'.

Indeed, one private practice group has evidently resorted to a rather unusual and ingenious selling technique. According to Fry (1979), at one branch of the Family Welfare Association, the largest group of clients are — social workers themselves! Is this, perhaps, the psychotherapeutic equivalent of Mark Twain's celebrated community whose members 'earned a precarious living by taking in each other's washing'?

The authors do not tell us what type of casework/psychotherapy their clients received, but if the proposed preliminary qualification for Private Counselling Service members of the Family Welfare Association of London, is any guide, it is unlikely to have been either novel or heretical. The FWA requires 'at least two years experience of regular supervision which should have been concerned with the dynamics of client/worker interaction' and adds that 'experience of personal or group analysis or psychotherapy, though not essential, is desirable'. Similarly, all supervisors are required to have seven years' minimum practice experience since qualification, 'of which at least four should have included regular supervision/consultation of a psychodynamic nature'.

The emphasis on psychodynamic techniques is further evidence of the bias which we have noted in Chapter 5 towards outmoded and unscientific methods of treatment with a poor track record of evaluation and effectiveness. The report of the working party also emphasises the probability that psychodynamic approaches will dominate the private field too. While it recognises that the psychodynamic approach is not the only one, it recommends that 'social workers newly established in private practice should, during the first twelve months of their practice, arrange to receive monthly supervision from an experienced and qualified social worker'. It then suggests that 'some established private social workers, for example those operating under the FWA/PCS scheme'—who appear to be, as we have seen, of a generally psychodynamic persuasion—'might be engaged as supervisors for workers new to private practice social work'. We may also add that the apparent belief of the FWA that personal psychotherapy makes for better social workers contrasts with the conclusions of a review of therapist variables in relation to process and outcome (Parloff, Waskow & Wolfe 1979) that 'the contribution of personal psychotherapy to the enhancement of the therapist's usefulness remains undemonstrated'.

If there is any remaining doubt that social workers see themselves to a large extent as psychotherapists, it should be dispelled by the suggested wording of advertisements for private 'social workers provided in an appendix to the report of the working party. It is recommended that social workers should advertise their availability for 'consultation regarding personal and domestic difficulties, family problems, problems relating to children's behaviour, marital problems, children in legal difficulties, adoption counselling, family group counselling, and counselling for members of other professions'. With the exception of adoption counselling, which has certain statutory aspects to it, this list would describe the work of almost any psychotherapist and would cover much of the work of many psychiatrists too. We do not suppose that many social workers will want to take over the management of those who are manifestly mentally ill, but many of Colin Brewer's patients consult him for 'personal and domestic difficulties'.

There is, of course, a much greater market for private psychotherapy in the United States than exists in Britain. Furthermore, in the United States, social workers have to compete not only with psychiatrists and psychoanalysts (medically trained or not) but also with psychologists. This being so, it is interesting that there is a clear financial pecking order in the scale of charges. Psychiatrists generally charge—at 1979 prices—between $40 and $100 per hour. Social workers apparently charge between $20 and $40 per hour. Psychologists charge somewhere between the social work and the psychiatric rate. This financial hierarchy is recognised by the insurance companies, and historically, when psychotherapy has been accepted as a therapeutic activity covered by insurance, the companies have recognised psychiatrists before psychologists, and psychologists before social workers. British fees for private social work are comparatively modest. The FWA recommends £3.50-£6.00 per session. Most British psychiatrists charge upwards of £30 for an hour's consultation and clinical psychologists £15-£20.

When one of our US informants was asked whether she thought that social workers in general provided a different kind of psychotherapy compared with psychologists or psychiatrists, she replied that social workers possess 'community skills' which enable them to organise 'community action'. Although she felt that social work training was important in providing this distinctive therapeutic approach, she agreed that whatever community action is, it probably requires a certain amount of charisma, and that charisma is something which cannot easily be taught, and which may indeed even be possessed by those who are not social workers. An official of the FWA agreed with us that social workers do not provide a unique kind of psychotherapy (Best 1979).

Although, as we have seen from one British study, social workers generally dislike the financial aspect of their work, (page 67) and resent being seen by their clients merely as a source of cash, payments by the client to the social worker evidently present less of a problem. In both Britain and the USA private practitioners may build up a practice either by attracting their clients directly from the community, or by getting them from psychiatrists, GPs and clinics on a sub-contract basis. In some cases the doctor may place the clinical responsibility for his patient entirely with the social worker/psychotherapist, but in other cases the doctor retains overall clinical control and the social worker acts as a psychotherapeutic dogsbody of the kind which so exercised the indignation of Parsloe and Stevenson's informants. Evidently professional dignity has its limits.

Incidentally, we hope that social workers who offer their psychotherapeutic services to clients with personal or domestic problems will turn out to be more perceptive than the non-medical psychotherapists described by Rankine (1978) who in the course of a journalistic investigation consulted each of them with the story that for six months he had been unhappy and less confident in his work, had lost 14 lb in weight in the past month, and suffered from excessive thirst and unusual fatigue. 'These three physical signs, taken together, would suggest to any qualified doctor that his patient might have diabetes. On its own, sudden loss of weight could even be a warning of cancer or tuberculosis.' But five of the six therapists either ignored these symptoms or put them down to emotional problems.

Clearly, few private practice clients will come from the poorer classes, who would generally be unable to pay for a private social worker, even if they felt a need for her therapeutic — as opposed to bureaucratic — services. It might be considered churlish to ask whether private practitioners get more pleasure and satisfaction from doing psychotherapy with fellow members of the middle classes with whom they can fairly readily communicate and identify, than acting as reluctant and itinerant bureaucrats, social policemen, and purveyors of assorted material handouts to unappreciative members of the proletariat who 'just want financial help and won't accept social work, even though you try to get in under pretext of helping with an electricity bill'. We rather suspect that they do.

8

Some facts of therapeutic life

Learning from the history of medicine. Doctors' lack of real effectiveness until recently. Problems in assessing effectiveness of any procedure. The need to believe in effectiveness. Placebo effect. Confusion of spontaneous change with effect of treatment. Concept and history of the controlled study. Application to psychotherapy and social work. Why apparently effective treatments may fail in practice. Importance of effectiveness. Reluctance to accept therapeutic limitations. Doctors more eclectic and pragmatic than social workers. Not necessary to understand causes before one can treat. Principles for selecting a particular treatment.

If therapy in a general sense, and psychotherapy in a more specific sense, is seen as one of the main skills and functions of social workers, then therapeutic effectiveness is clearly a most important issue. We shall deal with it in some detail in the next chapter, but before we do so it seems a good idea to discuss the language, philosophy, principles and concepts that grow out of therapeutic endeavour. Our experience of social workers and of social work literature suggests to us that many social workers simply do not speak or understand the language of therapy. This is hardly surprising, since even doctors — whose therapeutic function is perhaps more overt, and certainly easier to define — are often rather ignorant in this respect. However, there has been a considerable improvement in the standards of therapeutic research since about the 1950s, and some useful lessons have been learned, many of them rather painful.

Social workers, as a group, naturally have relatively little information about the realities of medical practice, but given that both medicine and social work are supposed to be therapeutic activities, social workers have much to learn in principle from the considerable experience of doctors — especially from their mistakes and disappointments, which are numerous.

However we define therapy, it must involve the deliberate production of some kind of change. Clearly this change must be, in some sense, a desirable change, otherwise there would be no point in trying to produce it. Very similar principles apply whether the change occurs in a single organ of the body, in the ability of a patient to move or breathe more easily, in a particular person's attitude of mind or level of contentment, or in that person's relationship with his family or with some larger unit of society. These principles also apply when 'therapy' is directed at the environment, or at society itself.

Those who do not learn from history, it is said, are condemned to relive it. In this respect, the history of medicine is something with which all social workers ought to be broadly familiar. Perhaps the most important fact to grasp is that until about a century ago, it is almost certain that if every doctor in the land had simultaneously dropped dead, the health of the populace would not, on balance, have suffered and would probably have improved. We now know that, contrary to what most doctors and most of their patients believed, hardly anything that doctors did was of any specific value, and many treatments, such as blood-letting, were actually harmful. It is true that even in the seventeenth and eighteenth centuries, the medical profession used certain drugs and other treatments which are known to be genuinely useful, but these remedies were generally used in such a dangerous and haphazard way that, again, they probably did more harm than good. Even towards the end of the nineteenth century an American physician, Oliver Wendell Holmes, felt moved to say that if the entire pharmacopoeia were thrown into the sea, it would be so much the worse for the fish and so much the better for everyone else.

In spite of some improvements, there are still many areas in contemporary medical treatment where it is difficult to demonstrate any real benefit from accepted remedies and there are certainly procedures whose disadvantages seriously outweigh any benefit they bring.

The considerable prestige of medicine was based until fairly recent times on a blind and unsubstantiated belief — particularly among patients — that doctors had real therapeutic skill and also, perhaps, on a shared reluctance to acknowledge — even now — that some varieties of human misfortune cannot be significantly altered in the present state of knowledge. Real progress in medical treatment has, in practice, been a comparatively rare event. Far commoner have been theories and treatments which seemed a very good idea at the time but which did not work in practice.

There are several conclusions to be drawn, and one of the most important is that good ideas and good intentions are not enough. What matters is whether a particular treatment actually works; not whether it *ought* to work.

In assessing the effectiveness of treatment, there are several factors which can make life very difficult for the investigator. Of these, one of the most powerful is what might be called the fundamental therapeutic delusion which is the natural tendency of those involved in therapeutic activity to believe that what they do is useful. People simply do not like to admit to themselves that what they do may have no value or may be actually harmful, and doctors have certainly not been immune from this very human attitude. It means that enthusiasts may perceive benefit where none really exists and turn a blind eye to side effects. This can apply to patients as well as doctors; we may recall the words of another Victorian physician, Osler, that the taking of medicines is what chiefly distinguishes man from the lower animals.

Another factor is the tendency of investigators to confuse the natural history of a particular condition — the spontaneous improvements and deteriorations, whether steady or intermittent, which so often occur in the absence of treatment — with the consequences of therapeutic intervention. Yet another is the placebo effect. A placebo is usually thought of as a pharmacologically inert substance which is taken by the patient in the belief that it has therapeutic value. The patient accordingly believes that he ought to feel better and not infrequently does so. The placebo response applies not merely to the taking of medicines; it may follow any procedure or activity which is defined by the therapist or perceived by the patient as therapeutic.

The placebo effect can be surprisingly powerful, and many modern doctors, forgetting that their fathers and grandfathers often prescribed hardly anything but placebos, find it difficult to appreciate just how powerful it can be. To give only a few examples, a third of soldiers wounded in battle had as much pain relief from an injection of sterile water as from an injection of morphine. Patients who take antibiotics after a common cold recover at much the same rate as those who take placebos. Many insomniac patients sleep almost as many hours on a placebo as they do when they are given a powerful sedative (Shapiro & Morris 1978).

The placebo effect is particularly well seen in psychiatry where, in many disorders, more patients respond to the placebo effect of a tablet than to its specific pharmacological effects. For example, in many antidepressant drug trials, about 40 per cent of patients given a placebo may give an adequate response while the rate may rise to no more than 60 or 70 per cent in those given the active drug (Medical Research Council 1965). Addiction to placebos, including a withdrawal syndrome, has been reported (Vinar 1969), while in one trial, patients responded well to placebos even when they were told that the tablet they were taking contained only inert substances (Park & Covi 1965).

Because the placebo response represents to some extent a response to professional attention, it tends to be increased if the therapeutic procedure is more impressive or elaborate. In one trial involving psychotropic drugs, a placebo response rate of 35 per cent was doubled when patients were subjected to an elaborate series of psychological investigations involving a good deal of electrical equipment, flashing lights, and the insertion of needles (Lowinger & Dobie 1969).

These and other obstacles to objectivity have led to the creation of research methods designed to eliminate them or at least to allow for them. We now have a number of experimental techniques which enable us with considerable confidence to exclude from calculations of therapeutic effectiveness the consequences of both undue optimism and undue pessimism in patients and doctors alike, and which allow for the possibility that any improvement or worsening might have happened even in the absence of treatment. So many seemingly good therapeutic ideas have been shown by these methods to be ineffective or worse, and so few have been shown to be genuinely useful, that the investigator is historically entitled to take an attitude of some scepticism when confronted with a new treatment. This scepticism is institutionalised in the idea of the null hypothesis. This is a philosophical concept as much as a scientific one, and what it means is that in investigating a new treatment, one does not start out from an attitude of neutrality as to its effectiveness or ineffectiveness, but with a *presumption of ineffectiveness* which it is the experimenter's task to refute. In other words one assumes that any new treatment is useless and attempts to prove that that is not the case. Unfortunately, in many cases this assumption will prove to be correct.

As we discuss in the following chapter, many studies of the effectiveness of social work simply do not take account of these pitfalls and are therefore of no scientific value. It is sometimes said by way of apology for the poor quality of these studies that the experimental techniques involved have been developed only recently. This is only partly true, for although the elaborate statistical analysis which is a feature of modern experimental method is indeed of fairly recent origin and application, the principles of objective therapeutic comparison are actually quite old. They are certainly rather older than most social workers.

The principal experimental tool for assessing therapeutic effectiveness is the controlled trial. The fundamental requirement is that at least two groups of patients — or clients, or situations — should be compared. One group must have the treatment under investigation while the other group or groups must be treated differently. They may have no treatment at all, they may have a placebo treatment, or they may have some other form of active treatment — perhaps the established or conventional therapy against which the new idea is being tested. Obviously, the groups of patients must be as similar as possible in respect of the nature of the problem or disease, its severity, and any other characteristics such as age, sex, race or social class which might be expected to influence the outcome. If possible, patients should not know whether they are receiving the new treatment or the old one, or the placebo, and, if possible, the assessor should not know either. As a further refinement, groups taking, for example, active or placebo medication may be switched over after a few weeks so that each group acts as its own control.

If the patient does not know which of two or more treatments he is receiving, the trial is called 'single blind'. If the therapist does not know either, it is called 'double blind'. If the various treatments or placebo treatments are given to all patients at varying times during the trial, it is called a 'cross over' trial. Of course, it is not always possible to compare treatments in this way. This is particularly true where the method of treatment is something other than a medicine, and it obviously applies particularly to the sort of treatments used in social work. However, the principle of the double blind trial can be satisfactorily adapted to most therapeutic situations and where, for example, it is impossible to keep the therapist in ignorance of which treatment the patient is receiving, bias may be reduced by having progress evaluated by independent observers. In evaluating psychotherapy, for example, it is possible to devise 'placebo psychotherapy' in which patients meet the therapist but the encounter is designed in such a way as to contain no specific therapeutic components (see p. 181). In this way, it is possible to see whether psychotherapy confers any advantage over simply meeting somebody designated as a 'therapist' who carefully avoids talking about any of the patient's problems. In one study (see p. 175) — which is perhaps one of the most thorough and rigorous to be carried out in the field of psychotherapy — psychoanalytical psychotherapy and behavioural psychotherapy were each compared with merely putting patients on a waiting list and telephoning them at monthly intervals to reassure them that they had not been forgotten. All patients had the same comprehensive initial assessment interview. The results showed very little difference between psychoanalytic psychotherapy and treatment by waiting list. Behavioural psychotherapy showed modest but significant advantages over the waiting list in some respects, but the differences were less than many people — particularly many psychotherapists — might imagine. About 70 per cent of the patients — who were representative of ordinary psychiatric outpatients — made a satisfactory response to the initial interview, which was designed to be diagnostic rather than therapeutic.

Although clinical therapeutic trials of this complexity were uncommon even twenty years ago, they were by no means unknown. The history of controlled trials goes back at least to the sixteenth century when the French physician Ambroise Paré demonstrated to the King of France that a popular antidote to poisoning was actually useless. He did this by having poison administered to two condemned prisoners. One had the supposed antidote. Both died. Similarly, the use of orange juice for the treatment of scurvy was put on a reasonably scientific basis in the eighteenth century by James Lind, a naval surgeon, who took several pairs of sailors suffering from the disease and gave each pair one of the numerous current treatments. Those given orange juice evidently did much better than the others. This is, of course, a rather unsophisticated method, and it was hardly even single blind, but this approach is often suitable where the changes produced by therapy are reasonably objective and not influenced too much by suggestion.

Perhaps the surprising thing is that although the principle of controlled trials was clearly understood, so few treatments were subjected to them until recently. However, in 1937, hormone replacement therapy for menopausal women was the subject of a very sophisticated double blind controlled trial which would stand comparison with many clinical trials today (Pratt & Thomas 1937). The authors recognised the need for this approach because so many symptoms of the menopause are subjective and thus particularly liable to be influenced by suggestion. It may be significant that one of the best of the early controlled trials took place under the pressures of war. During the preparations for the allied landings in Normandy in 1944, military planners discovered that in landing exercises, many of the troops were seasick by the time they reached the shore, and would have been in no condition

to do much fighting when it came to the real thing. It became urgently necessary to discover a drug which would prevent seasickness
without at the same time being so sedative that the soldier would
be half asleep instead of merely sick. Only a carefully designed
double blind trial could and did provide a reliable answer (Holling
1944). At all events, it cannot truthfully be argued that methods
for the objective comparison of differing treatments are a product
of the last few years. In all probability, the reluctance of social
work to trouble itself with these experimental methods is related
to the pre-eminence of broadly psychoanalytic theories in social
work, psychoanalysts having been notoriously reluctant to subject
their craft to scientific investigation (see Chapter 10).

The inexperienced, the enthusiastic, or the unduly credulous,
may conclude from these examples that choosing a particular
therapy—and leaving aside for the moment all considerations of
personal preference and taste—is simply a question of looking at
comparative trials and choosing the treatment which seems to give
the best results. Unfortunately, the therapeutic life is not quite as
simple as that. It is possible for someone to develop a new treatment, and to show in a well-designed trial that it is effective,
and yet the treatment may not pass into general use. Perhaps the
commonest reason for this state of affairs is that the treatment is
'effective' in the sense that it achieves some or all of the immediate
goals of treatment, but also produces certain side effects which
cancel out the therapeutic advantages, even if they do not make
the treatment altogether unusable. It is a common error among
social workers—as among the lay public—to assume that only
medical and surgical treatments produce side effects. The truth
is that any treatment which can do good is likely to have a potential for doing harm as well. Conversely, those treatments which
really appear to be harmless are often also useless. Although the
Hippocratic oath is now of rather dubious relevance to medicine,
the Hippocratic maxim *primum non nocere*—first do no harm—
is as valid today as it was 2,500 years ago, and as frequently
ignored.

Another reason for the failure in practice of a promising treatment is that it works in some hands but not in others. This may be
because it is so difficult that only a very few highly skilled people
can do it properly. Accordingly, although it may be very effective
when used by these experts, lesser mortals attempting to use it
may actually produce worse results than would be the case if they
used methods which were more familiar or more within their competence. This fact of therapeutic life is seen at its most obvious in
surgery. Objective information about the competence of diff-

erent surgeons is hard to come by for the simple reason that few surgeons are willing to submit to direct comparison with their colleagues and risk being branded as inferior. However, any doctor during his training can hardly avoid making comparisons between the differing skills of surgeons and in extreme cases he will make a mental note to avoid certain operators for certain procedures. Although individual surgeons, as we have said, tend not to publish the results of their own personal surgery, groups of surgeons or clinics not infrequently do so. The wide range of mortality and complication rates reported for seemingly identical procedures may sometimes reflect the unpredictable nature of life in general and surgical life in particular, but they sometimes provide, if unwittingly, strong evidence that some surgeons are a good deal more competent than others.

A subsidiary reason for therapeutic failure, related to the previous example, is that a treatment may be incompetently performed not because of the incompetence of an individual therapist but because the organisation of which that individual is a part is not appropriate to the task. In a medical context, a treatment may fail if the patient is shared between so many doctors that continuity of care is lost and he becomes the victim of conflicting advice. In a social work context, we have seen many cases in which any potential for doing good was lost in a large, impersonal, disorganised department characterised by rapid turnover of staff and a general reluctance to make decisions.

We must not overlook the possibility that a potentially effective treatment may fail if either the therapist or the patient is opposed to that treatment in principle. A therapist who is persuaded by his superiors to use a treatment which he dislikes or distrusts is unlikely to do it well, and this may be particularly true in the case of psychotherapy where the personality of the therapist, his attitudes, and his relationship with the patient are widely regarded as crucial to the outcome. Similarly, a patient who is convinced that his problems will be solved when the doctor prescribes the right tablet for him is unlikely to be greatly helped by a psychotherapeutic approach, even if in theory this would be the most appropriate treatment for the assorted social and domestic problems which are thought to be the cause of his numerous psychosomatic symptoms.

If, as we maintain, the language of therapy is essentially the language of results and of effectiveness, then it follows that the choice of therapeutic approach or technique in any given situation should, if possible, reflect the objective evidence for the overall effectiveness of the various kinds of therapy available.

It should not be influenced too much—or perhaps at all—by the personal tastes and enthusiasms of the practitioner, unless these enthusiasms happen to coincide with the evidence. And, we may add, it is generally desirable that the evidence should not be wholly provided by the enthusiast himself. As Stanley Baldwin—a former British Prime Minister—once remarked, 'considering that enthusiasm moves the world, it is a pity that so few enthusiasts can be trusted to tell the truth'.

Personal taste and enthusiasm can affect the choice of therapy. It is far from uncommon for practitioners to select a comparatively ineffective treatment, or one which is actually harmful on balance, mainly because they like the theory which supposedly underlies it, or because they enjoy doing it. Indeed, at a fundamental level, taste and enthusiasm may dictate whether active treatment is offered in the first place even where the evidence suggests that on balance treatment of any kind merely makes matters worse. It is arguable that protecting people from therapeutic enthusiasm is one of the more important tasks of modern medicine, but it must not be assumed that *furor therapeuticus* is a condition restricted to doctors. It requires a strong will to refrain from overtly therapeutic activity when such activity has been the basis of one's training and philosophy. For example, a bleeding gastric ulcer is one of the more serious medical and surgical emergencies. Even today, it carries a high mortality, particularly as it is not infrequent among the elderly who often suffer from other diseases which may impair their powers of recovery. The choice of treatment lies essentially between medical measures—mainly blood transfusion—and surgical intervention to tie off the bleeding vessels or to remove part of the stomach if bleeding is diffuse. Merely replacing blood and hoping for the best can seem a very passive attitude, especially if the patient's condition is deteriorating, and the temptation to operate is obvious and understandable. Yet the evidence suggests that in hospitals which have a policy of early and enthusiastic surgery, the overall mortality is worse than in hospitals where surgery is resorted to later and more rarely (Bromfield, Atkinson & Longman 1979).

Naturally, enthusiasts for a particular treatment do not like it when that treatment shows up badly in controlled trials. They generally criticise the methodology of the experiment, and since no trial is perfect, they can usually find something to criticise. However, in medicine, when a series of such trials produces consistent results in favour of one kind of treatment and against another, medical practice usually changes to reflect this new knowledge. A number of promising treatments have accordingly been largely abandoned, sometimes within a relatively few years. For example, during the 1950s it was thought that since thrombosis of the coronary arteries seemed to be a major cause of heart attacks, treatment with anticoagulants which reduced the clotting power of the blood would be both logical and effective. The treatment was introduced without adequate evaluation, but became popular and within a few years most hospitals had established a service for monitoring the clotting ability of the blood, and the treatment became virtually routine. Once it was established that anticoagulant drugs were actually of no benefit in most cases, the number of patients receiving anticoagulant treatment diminished very rapidly. The anticoagulant enthusiasts swallowed their pride and went back to their drawing boards.

We may contrast this with the situation in social work where, as Sheldon (1978) has claimed, no treatment ever seems to be abandoned. New approaches emerge, but they are simply added to the existing repertoire. After referring to the 'supermarket' principle of social work education in which 'the in-coming student takes his "basket" to each of the various subject displays, selects the goods which take his fancy and obtains his CQSW at the check-out', he remarks that 'there are many instances of completely and logically opposed views of the same problem co-existing peacefully with each other' and he describes the situation as 'closer to academic licence than academic freedom. It perpetuates a situation where knowledge is merely stored, rather than sifted and refined'. Sheldon continues: 'Whenever I hear students reviewing research evidence as if evaluating a controversial piece of sculpture, I descend into Bateman-type fantasies peopled with chemistry students who still find the Phlogiston theory of combustion "rather attractive" and medical students wondering whether leeches have really had a fair run'.

We agree with Sheldon that social work practitioners seem to be more durably wedded to their therapeutic philosophies than is the case with most doctors, for whom the choice of treatment is generally a matter of pragmatism rather than of fundamental belief. In another chapter, we discuss the possible connection between this state of affairs and the quasi-religious nature of some of the 'psychological' theories which have had such a powerful influence on social work.

However, there is a corollary to the dangers of therapeutic enthusiasm which may be just as important in practice. Personal taste works both ways. It may lead a practitioner to be unjustifiably enthusiastic about a particular kind of treatment, but it may also lead to unwarranted scepticism and pessimism about the effects of those treatments with which he is not personally in sympathy. It is relatively rare in medicine for there to be sustained opposition to a genuinely useful treatment—that is to say a treatment which has established its usefulness by a sufficient number of good controlled trials—but this is not the case with social work.

Quite apart from our personal impressions based on considerable experience of working with social workers, there is abundant evidence from the social work literature that certain types of therapy are indeed rejected by many social workers on principle, and regardless of the evidence for their effectiveness. We have dealt in Chapter 5 with the widespread antipathy to behavioural approaches. Another example is the criticism of the use of drugs and electroconvulsive therapy (ECT, EST) in psychiatry. ECT is often described as a barbaric and damaging treatment, and that is certainly the message of such anti-psychiatric films as *One Flew Over The Cuckoo's Nest.* Yet even if they are true, neither of these criticisms is relevant. First of all, if ECT is 'barbaric' it is difficult to see how it is more barbaric than the numerous other things done to anesthetised patients such as removing, or cutting holes in, various organs. Secondly, unless a form of treatment is so unpleasant as to make it unacceptable to patients, then it is merely one factor to be weighed against the potential benefits. The same goes for such side effects of ECT as amnesia. In a therapeutic context, the main argument over ECT, as over any other treatment, should revolve around whether it has any specific therapeutic effect.

Ironically, as one of us has frequently pointed out (Brewer 1974, 1977), the evidence that 'real' ECT is more effective than placebo ECT (that is, allowing the patient to think that he is having ECT and giving him an anaesthetic, but not actually passing any electricity through the brain) is still rather equivocal and thin on the ground, although some recent and rather belated controlled trials may at last clarify the issue. Yet it is rare for social workers to criticise the use of ECT on the grounds of effectiveness. It is hard to resist the conclusion that such attitudes betray a belief that style is more important than results and that some theories about the origins and management of disturbed behaviour are rejected out of hand if they do not fit in with the prevailing social work ideology.

To say this, incidentally, is not to imply that psychiatrists always use medical treatments in a systematic and discriminating fashion. One of us (CB) has consistently coupled his criticism of social work with a parallel criticism of psychiatry, but at least psychiatry—like the rest of medicine—has taken seriously the matter of effectiveness and controlled assessment. Consequently, psychiatry has rapidly abandoned or curtailed the use of treatments such as insulin coma which have been shown to be without specific therapeutic effect. The response of social workers in Leeds to the demonstration that social work methods of dealing with truancy and associated delinquency were considerably less effective than simple, undisguised threats from the juvenile court, which is discussed in greater detail on Chapter 9, is further and particularly damning evidence of the reluctance of social workers to abandon manifestly ineffective treatments in favour of more fruitful ones.

Perhaps even more depressing than the reaction of the Leeds social workers to the results of this controlled therapeutic trial is our experience that relatively few social workers appear to be familiar with the study. This is unfortunately consistent with the general lack of interest in effectiveness described in Chapter 10.

This tendency to reject certain therapeutic approaches on principle often goes hand in hand with the belief that it is impossible to treat a particular condition or situation without first understanding how it arose. Superficially, this may seem a sensible enough idea and it is certainly one of the more fundamental tenets of the psychoanalytic approach. Yet an examination of medical practice shows that such a belief is entirely mistaken. Of course, there are many conditions whose treatment is greatly assisted by an understanding of their cause, and in some cases it has only been possible to devise effective treatment once the causative factors have been elucidated. Thus, to take only one example, we know that haemophilia is due to the genetically determined absence from the blood of a specific clotting factor, and accordingly it is now possible to treat haemophilia quite satisfactorily by administering concentrated preparations of this missing factor, obtained from the blood of non-haemophiliac donors. However, there are many disorders whose cause is unknown but for which effective treatments exist. For example, we know very little about the cause of most skin diseases yet several of them respond to cortisone-like drugs. Digitalis is often effective in the treatment of heart failure even where the cause of the failure is entirely obscure. Raised blood pressure is a very common complaint and we still do not know the cause of it in most cases, yet effective treatment exists. Accordingly, doctors take a pragmatic or empirical view of treatment and are in principle prepared to use any treatment which appears to work, almost regardless of the theory which underlies it (which may, and often does, turn out to be wrong) and even if no such theory exists in the first place.

Resistance to both behavioural approaches and ECT is often

justified by the claim that such treatments do not 'get to the root of the problem' and 'merely' remove symptoms. It is our contention, and one with which we feel most patients and social work clients would agree, that the removal of symptoms is not to be sneezed at and that getting to the root of the problem—in the sense of understanding how it has arisen—is no substitute for helping the patient or client to feel better. Explaining disease or distress is certainly an interesting activity and one in which patients may be just as interested as practitioners. However, it is our experience that if they have to choose, most people prefer relief without explanation to explanation without relief. As we discuss in Chapter 10, we believe that the psychoanalytic tradition of social work with its heavy emphasis on explanation (or as we would have it, pseudo-explanation) and its sometimes sneering and heartless attitude to symptom removal, must take a heavy share of the responsibility for this illogical and anti-therapeutic aspect of social work.

There are, unfortunately, still many conditions in medicine in which a number of treatments are recommended and none of them has any clear-cut superiority over the others. Indeed, where a multiplicity of treatments exists, doctors have come to realise that this often indicates that none of them is really effective—which is to say, more than a placebo. In medicine as in social work, a number of traditional procedures are in use which have been employed for as long as anyone can remember without adequate evaluation and they continue to be used partly out of habit, partly because nobody has come-up with something better, and partly because of the general tendency of those involved in any kind of healing to prefer doing something to doing nothing.

The first thing to be said about such situations is that where there is no clear evidence of superiority, then there ought to be no dogmatic assertions that one approach is to be preferred on the grounds of effectiveness. This does not mean, however, that all the treatments recommended in such a situation are to be regarded as of equal status. It is true that they may all be equally useless, or be equally but still insufficiently effective for that matter, but it is unlikely that they will be equal in terms of duration, complexity, expense, or the incidence of side effects. If there can be no argument about the benefits of the various treatments, selection must address itself to the question of their costs.

In the field of philosophy, Occam's Razor—an ancient but respected intellectual tool—is still regarded as a valuable method of choosing between competing philosophies. Occam died in 1347 but his axiom *entia non sunt multiplicanda*—is alive and well. The literal translation is 'entities are not to be multiplied' and it means that when two or more hypotheses or explanations are being considered, the one which makes the fewest assumptions is to be preferred. All unnecessary facts or constituents in the subject being analysed are to be eliminated. The principle can be applied to the choice of competing therapies as well, and in the absence of clear superiority, preference is given to the treatment which is simplest, quickest, cheapest, and least likely to produce side effects. If in desperation it is felt necessary to leave none of the available therapeutic stones unturned, unsatisfactory though they may all be, Occam urges us to use the simpler before the more complex, and the quicker before the more lengthy. When there is genuine doubt as to whether any treatment or approach has any specific effect, then there is much to be said for the deliberate employment of placebo treatments or procedures. This is much easier to achieve in social work than it is in medicine, for it is remarkably difficult to prescribe truly inert substances unless the doctor dispenses his own medicines, and many patients are now too sophisticated to be fobbed off with prescriptions for tablets of vitamin C which, though not inert, are for most conditions neither useful nor harmful. In a social work context, placebo effect refers to the improvement which may be obtained from such ordinary non-professional activities as paying attention, making encouraging noises and attending to obvious physical needs. The results of the study by Sloane *et al.* (see Chapter 10) indicate that those who advocate a more specifically therapeutic approach to many problems will be hard pressed to improve on the non-specific effects. Apart from the therapeutic effects of placebo treatments and procedures, they can also have a useful diagnostic function in that any response or lack of it may indicate something about the nature of the condition and its possible cause. The principle is embodied in the Single Case Experimental Design (see p. 211). It is one method of selecting those who may require types of therapy which are more demanding for both client and therapist.

The use of placebo procedures in this way is sometimes a contentious issue, particularly among those healers—medical and otherwise—who have forgotten its long and honourable history. It certainly involves a measure of deliberate deception and there are those who consider any deception, no matter how small, as intolerably damaging both to their own self-esteem and to the client-therapist relationship. There are two answers to this objection. The first is that if we are not prepared to deceive the client for the specific purpose of helping us to ascertain the truth of the situation, then we may well end up by deceiving ourselves, which is surely at least as serious a matter, and arguably even more serious if it means that we thereby inflict our therapeutic delusions not just on one patient but on many.

The other answer is that the placebo effect is so powerful that there ought to be no shame in trying to give our patients the benefit of it. The placebo effect is to be found not just in pills or procedures but also—and perhaps most impressively—in people. All doctors are walking placebos, whatever else they may be as well. So are all social workers, whether paid or voluntary. It is an honourable role, and in view of its proved effectiveness, it is regrettable that so many people seem prepared to minimise its importance or even deny it altogether.

We agree with Shapiro & Morris (1978) that 'a true understanding of the specific components of psychotherapy can only occur when the components of the placebo effect are also understood'; and we would add that they are unlikely to be understood unless therapists are prepared not only to acknowledge them but also to use them.

One of the authors was invited to submit an article to a social work journal questioning some of the common assumptions of social work. He proposed to call it 'The social worker: a walking placebo?' but the editor changed it, as is his privilege, to 'Are Social Workers Necessary?' This had the unfortunate effect of suggesting that the author thought they were not. As ought to be clear, particularly from Chapter 11, this is not the case.

9

Controlled studies of the impact and effectiveness of social work

Mullen & Dumpson's review of US studies; a depressing picture of social work. Fischer updates the evidence; thinks Mullen & Dumpson's conclusions too optimistic. Some more recent studies from Britain and the USA.

Social work emerged from the 50s with confidence concerning its effectiveness. As a profession, it sought expanded opportunities and resources to demonstrate its competence. The 60s witnessed a marked increase in those opportunities, and social work set about to demonstrate its relevance. Out of this confidence social workers boldly exposed their practice to the critical scrutiny of scientific evaluation and assumed that such evaluations would assist them as they refined their technologies and expanded their knowledge. They assumed, too, that these evaluations would clearly demonstrate the effectiveness of their interventive efforts. As the findings from these evaluations became available, it was evident that interventive impact was not so easily demonstrated. . . . The researchers, for many reasons, were rarely able to conclude that a program had even modest success in achieving its major goals.

So begins the sombre Concluding Note of a comprehensive review of the effects of social work by Mullen & Dumpson (1972). Although it may be true that in the USA social workers did indeed boldly expose their activities to critical scrutiny—though we have our doubts that this boldness was really very widespread—social work in Britain has not been noted for an abundance of well-conducted studies of effectiveness. Indeed, there appear to have been no serious attempts—let alone methodologically sound attempts—

to examine the effectiveness of social work before the 1970s. Social workers with a taste for humble pie, as well as those to whom the concept of therapeutic humility is anathema, should refer to Mullen & Dumpson and also to Fischer (1976) for a detailed description of the evidence and for a discussion of its implications for social work. In this chapter we shall merely emphasise some of the more important findings and deal in greater detail with some more recent comparable studies to see whether the situation has changed very much.

We have commented in earlier chapters about the vagueness which characterises the goals of much social work activity. British social workers clearly have no monopoly of vagueness, and one of the reasons why Mullen & Dumpson and their co-authors dealt with only thirteen studies was that in many other research projects the goals of social intervention were either undefined or defined in such a diffuse way as to be meaningless. Jones & Borgatta (1972) are very critical of agencies which carry out

unmeasured and unspecified latent functions such as 'providing employment for qualified personnel and volunteer workers' or which claim that their contribution is 'important in the fabric of government and the network of welfare services'. If this sounds harsh, it might be well to look into the real meaning of statements like: 'it is difficult to say what the objectives of the agency are, as the agency provides so many different types of services to so many different types of client'; or, 'the agency provides vital services, as one can see by the strong demands on the time of our over-worked staff'; or, 'it is difficult to imagine what the community would do without our agency, as we are unable to satisfy the current demands for services'. None of these declarations provides a meaningful indication of what the agency objectives are. Attempting to pin down goals in many cases leads to explanations like 'well, we don't know exactly what we want to do; that's one of the reasons we think it is so important to do the evaluation research'.

Looking at these studies as a whole, Geismar (1972) concludes that they reveal

a range of outcomes the curve of which is skewed at the negative end of the distribution. Four of the projects report almost no significant differences between the experimental and the control group on any of the key measures. The studies report very limited gains. . . . The outcomes of the remaining seven projects either support the main research hypotheses or are in line with the desired objectives, although results reported are frequently described as modest by the report writers and lean towards the non-success end of the continuum.

The studies considered in Mullen & Dumpson's review cover a representative sample of current social work techniques including community work, group work and individual casework. Some combine all three approaches. We shall now summarise their examination of these studies. (Full references to the following studies will be found in Mullen & Dumpson).

Area Development Project (United Community Services, 1968)

This study, carried out in Vancouver, concerned itself with multiproblem families with 'severe and chronic' difficulties who were already known to various agencies. They were randomly assigned to two different social work services, one being a three-year-experimental programme of group work, casework and neighbourhood and community organisation services, while the other was the standard community service. The results indicated a statistically significant increase in certain aspects of family functioning in the experimental group, though it is less clear what this meant in terms of becoming less dependent. Unfortunately, these modestly encouraging results are clouded by the fact that social workers treating the experimental group had lower caseloads than those providing the standard service.

Casework Methods Project (Reid & Shyne, 1969)

120 families, 'first-time applicants to the agency, relatively young, and generally free of gross psychopathology', were randomly assigned to two types of service. The study was designed to test 'the widely held assumption that extended services, based on psychoanalytic theory, are more likely to meet the needs of these clients than is short-term treatment, that rests on no special theories but is basically an abbreviated version of long-term treatment'.

In fact, the results indicated that the psychoanalytically based service was inferior to the short-term service, though since there was no true—i.e. untreated—control group, 'no conclusion could be reached as to the absolute effectiveness of the service'. As will be apparent from Chapter 10, we are not surprised that psychoanalytically based methods showed up rather badly.

Chemung County Study (Brown 1968)

The main aim of this study was to discover whether trained professional caseworkers had greater success than untrained workers in rehabilitating multi-problem families in New York. Families assigned to the experimental group received twice as many social worker contacts as the control families so that they were theoretically at an advantage in both the quality and quantity of their casework. After approximately two years no significant differences in the social functioning of the two groups could be observed.

Community Service Society of New York — New York City Department of Social Services Collaborative Demonstration Project (Mullen, Chazin & Feldstein, 1970).

This study was also designed to test the assumption that an intensive non-standard social work service would produce better results than a conventional and pretty basic social work approach. The control group received essentially routine public assistance while the experimental group were given the benefit of additional casework.

> The underlying assumption was that families needed help to cope with effects of dependency, leading to deterioration in their functioning and a chronic state of dependence. Although it was known that budgets were inadequate to prevent disorganisation, it was assumed that . . . casework would strengthen family functioning, help families take advantage of employment and job training opportunities, and so forth. (Meyer 1972).

The results were not encouraging.

> There was a modest statistical difference noticed in the families' view of help with individual and family difficulties. In regard to internal areas of family functioning — cohesion, relationships and the like — there was no statistical evidence that the experimental group felt that they were helped more than the control group.

A Comprehensive Program for Multi-Problem Families (Marin 1969)

This study tested the hypothesis that family-centred social work treatment would produce better results in Puerto Rican problem families than the conventional welfare services. Seventy-seven assorted objective and subjective variables were measured, but once again 'differences between the experimental and control groups failed to support the hypothesis of greater effectiveness of the demonstration program'.

Experimental Study to Measure the Effectiveness of Casework Service (Behling 1961)

This study again contrasted intensive versus routine casework and those providing the intensive service had only half the normal caseload. In this case, the results did produce statistically significant differences in favour of the experimental group. However, against the expectations of the researchers, greater positive change was also associated with greater relief costs and more cases receiving assistance in the experimental group. This suggests that the 'psychotherapeutic' aspects of casework were only one factor and that the more efficient provision of existing benefits was also important.

Rutgers Family Life Improvement Project (Geismar 1971)

In view of the disappointing performance of conventional casework intervention, this study was designed to test preventative intervention with young families, and again compared the experimental group with a control group receiving routine services. The experimental programme aims to give 'information, advice, advocacy, counselling in inter-personal problems, vocational guidance, assistance in finding jobs and housing, and so forth, with each service pattern adapted to the specific needs and problems of a particular family'. Once again the results were disappointing, with modest differences in favour of the experimental group in one or two areas but no significant changes overall.

Family Center Project (Kühl 1969)

This Danish study was also concerned with multi-problem families and its aim was nothing less than 'the social rehabilitation of multi-problem families by a socio-pedagogical effort'. The workers in the experimental team concentrated on 'giving advice and support, coordinating the family's dealings with social agencies, alleviating pressing problems, and making efforts to modify client attitudes towards children, work and community resources'. Admirable aims, no doubt, but in the event the results showed little significant difference between the experimental and control groups. Such differences as existed were mainly in employment and housing, and it may be thought that similar results could have been obtained by efforts to make the appropriate agencies more efficient and flexible.

Girls at Vocational High (Meyer, Borgatta & Jones 1969)

This well-known study—though when we hear confident claims of the value of counselling, we wonder just how well-known it really is —addressed itself to the proposition that delinquent adolescent girls could be helped to become less delinquent, do better at school, do better out of school, and have fewer unwanted pregnancies, if they received casework and counselling. Once again, there was little significant difference between the experimental and control groups. 'This study resulted in a heated controversy within the social work profession, since the concepts of casework and treatment were seriously threatened by the findings. The controversy was never resolved because the parties to it had no power to change the theoretical articles of faith, professional practices, or blind prejudices of those who disagreed with them' (Walker 1972).

The Midway Project (Schwartz & Sample 1970)

While the studies we have discussed above have generally compared two distinct types of casework or the performance of trained versus untrained social workers, the Midway Project looked at the question whether the state of clients could be improved not by trying to change them directly but by improving the quality of the routine social services already available to them by reorganisation and coordination. Unusually, the Midway Project concentrated on what social workers and their clients actually did, rather than on what they said they did, or on what they felt. This daringly behavioural approach may explain why it is one of the few studies to show statistically significant improvements in favour of the experimental group, though it has to be said that the level of statistical significance chosen was rather more generous than is usually the case. As in the Family Centre Project, the results suggest that much can be done by the improvement of traditional welfare services, and while the study enabled the researchers to compare the effects of reduced caseload with the effects of reorganisation of existing services, the fact that 'the team form of organisation alone produced more than 90 per cent of the benefits obtained through the caseload reduction program' suggests that the specific contribution of casework was fairly modest.

New Haven Neighbourhood Improvement Project
(Geismar & Krisberg 1967)

As with many of these studies, the clients were lower-class multi-problem families living in a low-income housing project. Once again, a control group of families receiving standard services was compared with an experimental group which received a variety of additional social work techniques such as open-door casework for all residents, intensive casework for problem families, a nursery school, a youth neighbourhood centre, social and educational activities for adults, a senior citizens group, neighbourhood-wide cultural events and entertainment, and community organisational activities. A fairly comprehensive package, certainly. The results are among the most favourable of this group of studies with significant differences on various indices of family functioning in favour of the experimental group. However, there were no significant differences in respect of delinquency and economic dependence.

The Pursuit of Promise (McCabe *et al.* 1967)

To test the hypothesis that intellectually superior children from poor environments could be helped to make the most of their abilities, gifted children and their families were assigned either to a control group who had no special attention, or to an experimental group who received a number of interventions designed to 'strengthen their egos, help them to identify with successful adults, and promote educational achievement and aspirations'. The subjects were black and Puerto Rican children, and the results were confusing. Puerto Rican children in the experimental group did better than Puerto Ricans in the control group, but black children in the control group did better than those in the experimental group.

Serving the Ageing (Blenker *et al.* 1964)

332 elderly clients were randomly assigned to three different types of social work of varying intensity and caseload. These groups were also compared with 133 comparable elderly citizens who had not applied for any of the services provided by the city agencies. 'Outcome at follow-up based on physical and mental health, mortality, morale, satisfaction, adjustment, social participation, and so forth, does not support the hypothesis that either experimental program is demonstrably superior to the [standard] service.' Furthermore, at the end of the follow-up period there was little difference between the state of those who had applied for services

and those who had not. Geismar remarks that 'this finding cannot be interpreted to denote failure of the program; but the exact meaning of the results is unclear'.

Fischer (1978b) has reviewed the field of social work effectiveness covering research published up to the end of 1975. Interestingly, he does not confine his critical examination to social work, but has also looked at effectiveness in other fields including counselling, correctional establishments, psychiatric hospitalisation, and education. He concludes that 'lack of effectiveness was the rule rather than the exception' and that accordingly it was difficult to justify any particular approach on the grounds of results. He singles out the results of effectiveness research in the field of social work as 'among the grimmest of all the areas reviewed'. In Fischer's view, the review of casework studies by Mullen & Dumpson (1972), discouraging though it was, may well have erred on the side of optimism. His own review of seventeen studies showed that in three-quarters of them, 'clients receiving services from professional social workers were shown to deteriorate'. He remarks that the data from which this rather shattering conclusion was drawn were often buried in the comparisons of general effects between experimental groups.

We have examined some of the most recent effectiveness research in the field of social work with particular emphasis on British studies. We do this not because we think research in other countries is necessarily inferior to that conducted in Britain (if anything, in the field of social work the opposite is true) but because social workers are evidently not immune to chauvinism and other manifestations of group solidarity. Consequently research done in different countries, even those with similar social systems and patterns of social service, may be held to be irrelevant to practice in one's own country, especially if the results are as discouraging as the ones we have reported. In general, these most recent studies have produced results which are as negative as the earlier ones, though the reader may be pleased to know that the picture we paint is not one of unrelieved gloom.

Suicide Prevention and The Samaritans (Barraclough, Jennings & Moss 1977)

At first sight, it may seem surprising that we have included a study of the effectiveness of the Samaritans since they are an avowedly non-professional organisation and use largely untrained citizens. The Samaritans were founded in Britain in the 1950s but have given rise to similar organisations in other countries. Their main aim is the prevention of suicide and it is claimed that they actually do this by providing sympathy, friendship, and common-sense advice to those who are in despair. Certainly the Rev. Chad Varah, their founder, believes that the Samaritans have saved many thousands of people from suicide.

Yet although the Samaritans are 'amateurs', they do provide a service which is used by many thousands of people and which has grown beyond its original intention of preventing suicide to providing advice and a sympathetic ear for a wide range of people. There is undoubtedly a certain amount of overlap between what the Samaritans do and what social services departments do. Furthermore although some social workers are prepared to accept that they do not have any specific skills and that social work training confers no special expertise on its recipients, they often make the point that social workers still have an important role in performing ordinary neighbourly tasks which today's neighbours, unfortunately, seem less prepared to perform than were their predecessors—possibly because, among other reasons, they feel the existence of 'professional' helpers relieves them of their traditional role and responsibilities. The Samaritans, therefore, may be seen as representing this 'good neighbour' aspect of social work.

Claims that the Samaritans did actually prevent significant numbers of suicides seemed to be given statistical support by Bagley (1968) who analysed the suicide rate in selected towns in England and Wales and found a lower rate in those which had a Samaritan network. However, when Jennings and his colleagues repeated Bagley's study using a more comprehensive range of measures, they were unable to confirm his findings. Suicide has certainly declined considerably in Britain from a peak of about 5,500 in 1963 to about 3,500 in 1978 but the only *method* of suicide to have shown any significant decline is coal gas poisoning, while the suicide rate by other methods has either remained fairly steady or, as in the case of drug overdoses, almost doubled during this period. Most authorities have attributed the fall to the replacement of coal gas by relatively non-toxic natural gas, although there is some dispute as to whether this is the whole story (Sainsbury, Bart & Jenkins in press). At all events, neither formal nor informal social work has been shown to be effective in the prevention of suicide, or attempted suicide. Readers who are social workers may perhaps take some melancholy consolation from the fact that psychiatric treatment seems to have had no measurable impact on the suicide statistics either. The failure of psychiatry in this respect is reviewed by Ettlinger (1975).

The Leeds Truancy Study (Berg *et al.* 1978)

This is, in our view, one of the most important studies of the effectiveness of social work to have been carried out. It is important not simply because its methodology was unusually sound, or because it demonstrates that social work can actually be harmful. It is also important because the social workers taking part in the study were unaware that their activities were being evaluated and therefore it tells us how social workers function in normal circumstances rather than, as is the case with most studies, how they may sometimes function in rather atypical circumstances when they know they are being evaluated and are, so to speak, on their best behaviour.

The results are particularly convincing not merely because of the methodology used but because the study has in effect been done twice with similar findings. In the early 1970s, the Leeds Juvenile Magistrates noticed that an increasing number of truants were being brought before them and were concerned that these truants often committed crimes which they would not have been in a position to commit had they been at school. The usual method of dealing with these cases was a supervision order, in keeping with the therapeutic principles of the Children and Young Persons Act 1969, in which the child was 'supervised'—i.e. seen at intervals— by a social worker or a probation officer. In collaboration with a local child psychiatrist, and without informing the social workers, the magistrates began dealing with a proportion of the truancy cases by repeatedly adjourning the case so that the offending child had to return to court, usually with his parents, at frequent intervals. At these appearances, an educational welfare officer would present a record of the child's school attendance and those who persisted in truancy would either be brought back more often, with increased inconvenience to their families, or threatened with being briefly put 'in care' at an assessment centre if they didn't mend their ways. ('In care' is, of course, the current euphemism for taking children away from their families and even, sometimes, locking them up. The idea of a magistrate saying 'If you don't behave yourself, we'll *care* for you for three weeks' is no more bizarre than some of the philosophy behind the Children and Young Persons Act.)

In effect, then, truants whose cases were adjourned simply had a magisterial finger wagged at them every so often, and this may have had the effect in some cases of engendering pressure from parents to conform to the law's requirements, if only to minimise the number of visits to court. The initial results suggested that this rather unoriginal approach was much more effective than a supervision order in terms of reducing both truancy and other crime. However, although the truants whose cases were adjourned were broadly similar to those who were dealt with by social workers, truants were not randomly allocated to the two treatment conditions as required for a methodologically sound study. The experiment was therefore repeated during 1975-6 with a more rigorous experimental design so that the results would stand up to scientific scrutiny. This time, it could confidently be stated that the two groups of truants were comparable in the incidence of such possibly relevant factors as age, sex, the size of their school class, police record, immigrant status, social class, and the incidence of broken homes. Indeed, since there were slightly more children from broken and immigrant homes in the adjourned group, and since truancy is commoner in children from broken homes, if anything the allocation slightly favoured the group who were managed by social workers. The previous truancy record was identical for both groups, averaging 75 per cent of absences out of 190 possible half-days in the period before their court attendance.

The results again clearly demonstrated the superiority of adjournment over supervision. Sixty nine per cent of the adjourned group improved on their pre-hearing school attendance against only 33 per cent of the supervised group. The average absence in the adjourned group was 67 half-days against 97 half-days in the supervised group. These differences are highly significant statistically. We may add that they also appear to be of some practical significance, which is not always the case with experimental results. The adjourned truants also had a much lower incidence of other crime compared with the supervised group, who had almost five times as many offences during the follow-up period. This result too seems to be of considerable practical importance. Doubtless anticipating criticism that treatment by nasty, unfeeling magistrates might be more psychologically harmful than supervision by caring, sensitive social workers, the research team arranged for the two groups to be tested for psychological disturbance after a three-month period. No significant differences emerged.

Several very important implications emerge from this study. If the magistrates are not seen as providing treatment, and if the adjourned group are therefore seen as a no-treatment control group, then the inescapable conclusion is that the effects of social work intervention in the supervision group were worse than no treatment, which is to say they were harmful. This harm, furthermore, was hardly marginal. Quite apart from the loss of education, the children in the supervised group committed a great deal more crime than those in the adjourned group, which means that they greatly increased their chances of being institutionalised.

Alternatively, if the magistrates are seen not as providing no treatment but as providing an alternative treatment, then it is inescapable that their treatment was very much more effective than that provided by the social workers and that the social workers ought therefore to review both their practice and the theories which supposedly underlie it. In fact, the Leeds social workers appear to have done neither of these things. Instead, they savagely criticised the setting up of the experiment and its results (Reynolds 1978). One can understand a certain amount of embarrassment on their part, but their response is hardly the hallmark of a profession bent on 'enhancing the personal and social functioning of an individual, family group, or neighbourhood', and 'using evidence obtained from practice to help create a social environment conducive to the well being of all'. (BASW 1977)

Quite apart from what this study tells about the harmfulness of social work techniques in some circumstances, it surely has some critically important implications for one of the most fundamental and strongly held principles of social work, which is that many of the problems social workers deal with are best managed by what may be broadly called a 'therapeutic' approach, and that however one defines therapy, it is something which does not involve coercion or directiveness. Yet whether or not the approach of the magistrates is categorised as 'therapeutic', there can be no doubt that it was coercive and there is also no doubt that it was more effective than social work.

Of course, there are very important ethical considerations if coercion is used in any kind of therapeutic context, yet where 'therapy' is a statutory duty, as in the case of supervision orders for truants, then coercion at some level is impossible to avoid. If the 'therapy' provided by social workers turns out to be ineffective or harmful, and if in any case their clients are reluctant to receive 'therapy' (and as we saw in Chapter 3 it is not just truants who may find the therapeutic aspects of social work uncongenial), then the whole therapeutic approach in many areas is surely called into question — unless, that is, social work can produce its own techniques, lacking in coercion, which compare favourably with traditional approaches, or unless society through its elected representatives should decide that for children to attend school is a matter of individual choice.

Another way of looking at what the magistrates did in this study is to view it, as we have suggested earlier, as a therapeutic approach in its own right. In this context, the procedure adopted by the magistrates is an example of one kind of behavioural approach and illustrates some of the salient features of behavioural psychotherapy. First of all, the goals are clearly defined; in this case improved school attendance and reduced involvement in criminal activity. An additional, unstated, but implicit goal was that improvements in truancy and crime should not be achieved at the expense of significant deterioration in other important areas, notably mental health, hence the psychological questionnaires during the follow-up. In this case, of course, the goals will not have been agreed with the patient, as is the case with behavioural psychotherapy in its usual voluntary setting. However, the results suggest that many of the truants did accept the goal of improved school attendance, and if they achieved that goal, a reduction in crime would follow automatically. It can certainly be assumed that all the children at least understood the goals even if they didn't accept them.

After defining the goals, and postulating a set of consequences to which they might be related — in this case, the presence or absence of various kinds of legal inconvenience — the magistrates carefully defined the consequences in advance and also made it clear that if the theoretical existence of these consequences failed to modify behaviour, they would be quite prepared to demonstrate their reality. By often involving the family in treatment, they could increase the number of potential therapists and increase the likelihood of the therapeutic momentum being maintained even away from the overtly therapeutic environment — that is, the court. The magistrates' approach can also be seen as task-centred in that it not only concentrated on specific aspects of treatment, but specifically avoided certain others — such as general but unspecified improvements in well-being, consciousness-raising, greater insight into the nature of society, or the provision of any of the numerous competing brands of existential rebore — which they presumably thought were either irrelevant to or an actual distraction from the specific tasks, difficult to achieve with existing techniques, of dubious value on any reckoning, or beyond their brief as being more appropriately handled by philosophers, theologians, or members of the local or national government.

Although in Chapter 10 we provide evidence for our belief that the behavioural approach is worthy of a wider application in social work and might increase its alleged effectiveness to a point where it can actually be recognised, we have also been at pains to state that we do not regard a behavioural approach as a panacea or anything remotely resembling one. The Leeds study certainly emphasises this qualification, for although truancy was significantly reduced in the adjourned group, it was by no means abolished, and seven children were excluded from the study because they adamantly refused even to consider going back to school when they were asked to do so by the magistrates and presumably told what would happen to them if they didn't. We trust, however, that social workers who dislike the behavioural approach will recognise the professional dangers of criticising a particular technique merely because it does not succeed in all cases.

Whether or not social workers unwittingly involved in the Leeds study approved of the adjournment procedure, its authors, indicate that some social workers at least were not totally opposed to what the magistrates were doing. For some months before the study, there had been pressure on the social services department to give greater priority to truancy, and there was evidence that this pressure had had some effect. Thirteen of the supervised group of children were actually brought back to court during the first six months following their appearance for truancy. Previously, the authors tell us that none of the supervised children had ever been taken back to court. However, our experience suggests that even if social workers are prepared to use essentially 'magisterial' methods, they may not use them in the most effective way. At a case conference concerning an adolescent admitted to an assessment centre for persistent truancy, one of the authors asked the social worker concerned if she would consider taking her client back to court in the event of continued truanting. She replied that she would do so only as a last resort. The results of the Leeds study indicate, as we believe common sense also indicates, that if punishments, 'disincentives' or negative reinforcements are to be used in any kind of psychotherapeutic setting, whether voluntary or under duress, then they should be used strictly according to the programme previously announced or agreed on. If an effective treatment is used only as a last resort, it may lose much of its effectiveness because of the damage done while someone was dithering about whether to use it or not. The old adage, 'a stitch in time saves nine' can apply to surgery and social work as well as to domestic management.

Further evidence of the effectiveness of 'magisterial' methods in dealing with truancy comes from changes in the incidence of certain types of crime following the decision of police forces in certain areas to "arrest' on sight anyone who looked like a truant. According to Tutt (1979), 'Changes in operational services can have an impact beyond that expected. For example, the "truancy sweeps" operated by the juvenile bureaux in various divisions of the Metropolitan Police, in which truants were picked up by patrolling officers and returned to school or home. In one division, this action coincided with a 26% drop in reported auto crimes and a 36% reduction in petty crimes, mainly theft'. We do not say that this is the way to solve the truancy problem. Like any 'treatment' it doubtless entails possible costs as well as possible benefits, and the former may outweigh the latter. We mention it merely as an interesting—and tentative—finding which is relevant to this section. Nevertheless, in view of the apparent ineffectiveness of social work in dealing with truancy, it is perhaps significant that this activity by the police—which at least seems to have had some genuine and useful effects on the problem to offset against any disadvantages—was evidently stopped following an outcry from certain predictable sources.

The Leeds study surely ought to have provoked a good deal of sober debate about the value of social work at least in the important area of juvenile delinquency, and perhaps more generally. In practice, it seems to have provoked remarkably little and much of that has evidently concerned itself more with questions of professional pride and professional ethics than of therapeutic effectiveness (Reynolds 1978). We suspect, though, that any controversy about effectiveness will, as in the case of *Girls at Vocational High* not be resolved 'because the parties to it had no power to change the theoretical articles of faith, professional practices, or blind prejudices of those who disagreed with them' (Walker 1972).

Intermediate Treatment: The Hammersmith Teenage Project (National Association for the Care and Resettlement of Offenders —NACRO—in press).

Intermediate treatment (IT) is the name given to attempts to deal with juvenile delinquency which avoid admitting offenders to expensive and generally ineffective institutions. Indeed, it is seen as preventive in that it concerns itself not just with those who have actually been convicted of offences but also with those whose behaviour is such that there is thought to be a high risk that they will get into serious trouble with the law. Whatever IT actually means in practice—and, as we shall shortly see, there is little consensus about that—social workers are now heavily involved in doing it.

In 1976, the DHSS held two Development Group Seminars to discuss existing IT projects and published an account of twenty-eight of them (DHSS 1977), which reveals a very wide range of concepts and practices. Some, such as the '870 House' in Birmingham, demonstrate an apparently well-thought-out and systematic approach with useful definitions of both methods and therapeutic goals. Indeed, this particular example seems to exemplify some of the behavioural principles which we commend and describe in Chapter 10. Others, such as 'Tyn-y-Pwll' in Wales, seem rather more vague about their goals. Tyn-y-Pwll offers its clients 'an experience of living in a relatively small and well-related group where the questions of communication and relationships are extremely important'. It is 'not . . . a place dealing in miracle cures', but it apparently 'weaves a peculiar magic of its own for all who have lived there'. Just how peculiar this magic is may be deduced from a description of one kind of therapeutic activity practised there.

> We have had a number of examples where by allowing the girls to regress to very early stages of development, we have been able to establish better relationships. Examples such as lying curled in the foetal position in a closed wardrobe, lying on the back kicking the legs in the air having a temper tantrum, thumb-sucking, requests to be cuddled and biting members of staff have all been part of our everyday life.

This and other examples seem to typify the way in which social workers have enthusiastically embraced some of the zanier kinds of psychotherapy which we mentioned in Chapter 6. The use of terms like 'regression' and the fact that IT stands for Intermediate *Treatment* further underline both the psychodynamic bias and the psychotherapeutic pretensions of social work which we have previously noted.

A social worker for whom we have great respect who currently runs an IT project told us that when he visited a number of other IT projects on taking up his post, he was puzzled—the actual word he used was somewhat stronger—at the therapeutic philosophies (or more usually the lack of one) which he found. Many of the projects seemed to be not much more than rather elaborate and expensive playgroups for rather large children, and he suggested that a more appropriate description for them would be 'Intermediate Treats' (De Walt 1979). Apparently, some communities have expressed their anger that recreational facilities which have been requested for years are seemingly denied to tolerably law-abiding adolescents and are available exclusively for those who commit offences (Morgan 1979). However, there are IT projects which require their clients to do generally unpopular work of obvious value to the community—helping with the handicapped and clearing derelict sites, for example—in which there is a distinct element of restitution. (Some IT clients come to enjoy such activities and we understand that this can lead to hostile attitudes from certain magistrates who evidently feel that IT—or anything else done to delinquents—ought not to be enjoyable. It is not a view that we share.)

The Hammersmith Teenage Project seems to be much less ethereal than Tyn-y-Pwll in both its methods and its aims. It is also one of the very few IT projects—if not the only one—to have considered it necessary to compare the performance of IT clients with delinquents or quasi-delinquents submitted to other forms of 'treatment'. It aims 'to provide, through intense community-based support and education, an alternative way of dealing with selected teenage delinquents who have already, or would be likely to get [*sic*] caught up in the criminal justice system'. While the amateur Freudians of Tyn-y-Pwll try to put their charges more closely in touch with their pre-natal memories, Hammersmith merely hopes that 'by working intensively with teenagers in close liaison with their families and schools, the incidence of delinquency can be reduced'. Recognising, presumably, that the only way anyone can hope to find out if IT reduces delinquency is by some sort of controlled study, NACRO — who are monitoring the project — have compared the reconviction rates of IT clients and a group of adolescents given supervision orders. In the first year of the project, 69 per cent of the IT group were re-convicted compared with only 49 per cent of the supervised group. In the second year, the figures were 41 per cent and 47 per cent respectively. However, during this time, the criteria for acceptance into the IT group seem to have been changed, and there is some discrepancy in the follow-up periods of the two groups. Furthermore, the subjects of the study were not randomly allocated to IT or supervision so that the final results of the study—the above figures are an interim report—will be of dubious value whatever they show, though they hardly seem encouraging so far.

We await the completion of the study with an interest which is greatly diminished precisely because of its apparent methodological naivete. Surely it is not too much to expect that if two groups are being compared, then the comparison should be a fair and useful one? Is this really the best that social work research can do in an area of considerable public concern? As academics ourselves, the methodology of this study makes us feel rather like the Duke of Wellington when, reviewing his troops during the Peninsular War, he remarked, 'I don't know what effect these men will have upon the enemy, but, by God, they terrify me'.

The Jackson, Mississippi, Teen Pregnancy Center
(Sherline & Davidson 1978)

Although complications of pregnancy in both mother and baby are much lower in the developed countries than in countries with less sophisticated medical services, there remains a significant gap between the highest and lowest social classes in infant mortality. In Scotland, for example, the perinatal mortality rate per 1,000 infants born to mothers in Social Group 1 is 6.7 while that of infants born in Social Group 5 is 14.5 (Registrar-General of Scotland 1977). There is general agreement that social factors play an important part in this difference and that while the provision of adequate obstetric and antenatal services is necessary, such services are not enough in themselves.

Accordingly, in 1971 the University of Mississippi set up a teenage pregnancy centre to cater particularly for the needs of poor, black and largely unmarried pregnant teenagers. The centre aimed to provide for 'the educational, social and medical needs of the pregnant adolescent' and it was postulated that 'establishment of a comprehensive centre for adolescent pregnancies would (1) stimulate early entry into prenatal care, (2) increase compliance with prenatal clinic appointments and (3) decrease perinatal and maternal mortality and morbidity rates'. The educational aspect of the programme aimed at keeping girls in education if possible, but also emphasised 'preparation for parenthood, family planning, family life education and nutrition counselling'. This was linked with another goal of the project which was 'to assess continued schooling as a means of reducing welfare assistance'. The authors state:

> Effective social service support was considered a necessity all through the project. The social worker used a wide range of techniques: crisis intervention, group work, case work, and family counselling. These often were not adequate and wide use of other community services proved invaluable. Other agency services ranged from service [*sic*] to the development of parenting classes in such areas as (1) adolescent birth planning and sexuality, (2) nutrition, (3) child care and development, (4) legal rights of the single parent, (5) consumer education, (6) financial aid and (7) other supportive services. There was a constant need to help students and their families utilize appropriate community resources and maintain balance within the family.

In reviewing the list of other agencies involved it was apparent that the full gamut of services and information in the area had been involved.

To see if any specific effect on obstetric complications could be ascribed to the setting up of the centre, the obstetric performance of girls passing through the centre was compared with that of other girls aged eighteen or less who were delivered at the teaching hospitals in one year of the project. Although girls were not randomly assigned to the centre it was postulated that the experimental group would do better than comparable girls not passing through the programme. It may be thought that this would make it difficult to draw valid conclusions from the study, and indeed one reason for citing this study is that it demonstrates that questionable methodology has by no means disappeared from this field in spite of the sort of criticism contained in the reviews we have cited. Nevertheless, the authors felt that the population was 'generally the same in all groups' and predicted that the project patients would do better than girls attending the same hospital clinic who had not passed through the programme and girls who had not had much antenatal care.

In the event there was no significant difference between the various groups of patients in the incidence of medical complications, low birth weight, raised blood pressure and anaemia. Neither did the special programme reduce dependence on welfare assistance. (This latter point has more validity because the welfare status of girls passing through the programme was compared in successive years.) It cannot be said that those involved with the project made no attempt to take their ideas into the community.

> Multiple newspaper and television articles and appearances were presented about the project. Project personnel gave lectures and seminars at local colleges. Volunteers worked at the center to help with remedial education and social service projects. Social work and nursing students came to the project and used project facilities for approved individual study projects.

Yet in practical terms, community awareness of the project was relatively low and it proved difficult to excite referring doctors about the project.

The authors themselves appear to concede that in general the aims of the project were not fulfilled and that evidence of any real benefit from the programme was hard to find. Yet in a postscript to this study it is asserted that 'there is no question that programs such as these are beneficial to the clients, their babies, and their parents'.

It seems to us that this study demonstrates a number of characteristics of current social work research. First, as we have already remarked, the research is methodologically deficient not just in relatively unimportant respects but at a fundamental level. Presumably, the research was designed, very commendably, to evaluate the impact of the new centre which had been set up at no little expense. And yet even had the authors reported any positive results, they would have been suspect precisely because certain important variables had not been allowed for. Nevertheless, even without the restraint imposed by proper methodology, no significant results emerged. Insofar as it demonstrates anything at all, this study demonstrates yet again the difficulties of working with people who 'have a high level of alienation' and who show 'distress and estrangement towards others'.

But another point to be made is perhaps even more important. It is that even where, as in this case, the results are unfortunately disappointing, some people will still say in the face of such evidence that the results were very encouraging indeed and merely prove the need for more projects of this kind, and hence for more social workers to run them.

The Evaluation of a Social Work Service for Self-Poisoning Patients (Gibbons, Butler, Urwin & Gibbons 1978)

The taking of overdoses—often, but by no means always, with suicidal intent—has been something of a growth industry in virtually all developed countries in the past twenty years, and social workers are quite often involved with overdose patients both during their stay in hospital and after their discharge. In numerical terms, self-poisoning is a major problem. It is already the commonest reason for admission to acute female medical beds, and it has been calculated (Jones 1977) that if present British trends continue, every acute medical bed will be filled by 1984 with patients who have taken overdoses. (We are a little suspicious of the choice of date, and we are reminded of those predictions in the last century that if London's traffic continued to expand, the whole of Piccadilly Circus would be covered to a depth of six feet in horse-droppings. Nevertheless, the problem is serious enough by any reckoning.) The primary prevention of self-poisoning—that is reducing the number of first-time overdoses—has not proved possible so far (see page 148) but between 15 and 20 per cent of those admitted after an overdose will take at least one further overdose within a year. Since those at risk of further attempts are automatically identified by their first overdose, secondary prevention—that is the prevention of subsequent episodes—becomes theoretically possible. If it proved possible in practice as well as in theory, it could have a significant effect on the incidence of self-poisoning, and since some of those who take overdoses do actually die whether they intended to or not, it might even be possible to save some lives.

Since self-poisoners are typically young and female, and commonly live in the more deprived inner city areas, it seems likely that social factors, in general terms, play a major part in overdoses. Accordingly, it would not be unreasonable to hope that social work techniques might be more useful as a preventative measure than treatment with psychotropic drugs and other types of 'medical model' psychiatric intervention. At the time of this study, there had already been some half-dozen previous attempts to reduce the incidence of repeated self-poisoning, using a variety of approaches and with varying results. However, only one of these studies was regarded as methodologically sound and it suggested that social work was not very effective in this situation. Gibbons and her colleagues evidently hoped that a more intensive and advanced kind of social work might succeed where traditional methods had failed. To test this hypothesis, they randomly assigned 400 patients admitted after deliberate self-poisoning to an experimental or a control group. Following their discharge, the control group received the standard service which involved follow-up by the family doctor, a psychiatrist or an 'ordinary' social worker. Those assigned to the experimental group received intensive, task-centred casework 'based on an explicit contract of limited work which both social worker and client agree to undertake during a defined time period (up to a maximum of three months in this trial)'. Adequate follow-up information was obtained for approximately 80 per cent of both groups of patients, but the incidence of further hospital admissions for self-poisoning was not significantly different between the two groups. Significantly more experimental than control patients reported that they had received 'a lot of help' or that they were 'very satisfied' with the service. However, there was no difference between the groups on a rating scale for depression four months after the initial overdose.

There was a difference in favour of the experimental group in the way patients perceived certain social problems, and the authors remark that the task-centred approach seemed more acceptable to patients than the standard service. As will be apparent from Chapters 3 and 11, we are all for a more precise definition of social work tasks and are thus broadly sympathetic to task-centred social work. However, the fact remains that even this energetic and well-planned intervention failed in its most important task—the prevention or reduction of further overdoses. It is all very well to say that some patients received incidental benefits such as a slight change in the way they viewed some of their social problems, but these patients did not receive social work because of these problems; they received it because, and only because, they took overdoses and were admitted to hospital as a result. We seriously question whether such a service could be justified even if its general psychotherapeutic results had been less marginal. After all, there must have been many other people in the community with similar or worse social problems who for one reason or another did not take overdoses, and as a basis for allocating psychotherapy it seems a rather haphazard and possibly unfair way of using allegedly unique but certainly expensive skills.

Social Workers Versus General Practitioners in the Treatment of Chronic Neurotics (Cooper, Harwin, Depla & Shepherd 1975)

After so many disappointing or equivocal results the reader may be relieved that this chapter ends on a mildly optimistic note, especially as this study revealed that social workers could prove more effective not merely than no treatment, or than other social workers with heavier caseloads and/or unsuitable techniques, but more effective than general practitioners—a group with whom social workers, as we have seen in Chapter 3, have a relationship which is often uneasy and sometimes frankly antagonistic.

Patients who attract the label of 'chronic neurotic' take up a significant amount of consultation time in general practice, and their treatment, which generally consists largely or entirely of prescriptions for psychotropic drugs, is widely regarded as a difficult and disappointing business. Because an increasing number of studies demonstrate an association between neurotic disorders and a variety of social problems, particularly in women from the lower social groups, the authors felt that measures to modify the social difficulties of such patients might lead to clinical benefit. Accordingly, 92 patients in the experimental group were treated in a general practice to which a social worker was attached as part of a general research project into psychiatric illness in general practice. A comparable group of 97 patients, drawn from other practices in the neighbourhood without social work assistance but matched for diagnosis and severity, formed the control group. The study therefore compared a group who had conventional general practice treatment with another group who had conventional general practice treatment plus social work. The results demonstrated an improvement in both groups for neurotic symptoms, the experimental group being modestly but significantly superior to the control group in this respect.

On measures of social adjustment, the experimental group again showed a moderate degree of improvement at follow-up, but this was undeniably a better result than in the control group who demonstrated no improvement at all in social adjustment. The authors say that detailed analysis of the results suggested that the benefits of the experimental service were not confined to the work of any particular member of the team but that it was to some extent a group interaction. They point out that controlled attempts to measure the effectiveness of medico-social intervention in the community are few and that none have previously demonstrated any benefit, however small, to patients so notoriously resistant to treatment as those with chronic neurotic disorders. As usual, a number of interpretations can be put on the results, but even on the most favourable reading it can hardly be maintained that the improvement represented the unique and specific skills which are sometimes claimed for social work. It seems not unlikely that the patients might have responded at least partly to the chance of discussing their problems in greater detail than is usually possible in the average general practice consultation. Similar results might have followed the attachment to the practice of a clinical psychologist, a psychiatrist, or even an untrained volunteer.

The suggestion that the improvement in the experimental group was partly the result of interaction among the therapeutic team might indicate that, as is often implied, social workers may have an improving influence on those institutions to which they are attached. We do not deny that this may occur, though we have given at least one example (p. 17) of how the introduction of social workers may have the effect of splitting rather than uniting the therapeutic team. We think the results of this study support the view we have expressed frequently in this book that social workers may have a better chance of doing good if they attach themselves to existing professions and institutions rather than trying to establish themselves as an independent body. It is significant that some of those involved in this research project have been having considerable difficulty in defining, or getting social workers to define, what it is that they can actually do in a general practice setting. We have already mentioned — but it will bear repeating — that while it appears that general practitioners can indeed coexist with social workers, the GPs tend to see social workers as essentially an extra pair of hands, doing things which the GPs or other mem-

bers of the practice team would often be happy to do themselves
if they had the time. The general practice which treated the experimental group was perhaps fortunate to be assured of the services
of the same social worker over an extended period. The establishment of independent social services departments following the
Seebohm Report has made it more difficult to achieve such continuing team work. This is partly because, as we have seen, staff
turnover tends to be very rapid, and partly because advancement
in social services departments generally means a progressive
withdrawal from actual clinical work and an increasing involvement
in administrative and supervisory activities.

We stated earlier that the results of this study were moderately
encouraging. They are indeed, but it should not be automatically
assumed that similar results can be easily achieved with the present
organisation of social services in Britain.

10

Ineffectiveness and the Psychodynamic Legacy

The intractability of certain social problems. Does training matter in practice? Style and personality. 'Good' and 'bad' therapists. Evidence from educational studies. Effects of the psychodynamic bias. The antipathy to controlled studies. The value of the behavioural approach. Some behavioural principles. Why social workers dislike behaviourism. Psychodynamic and behavioural psychotherapies compared. Defining therapeutic goals. Behavioural attitudes to feelings and the community. Familiarity of behavioural concepts. Putting pressure on clients; a controlled study. Evidence that social workers do not care about effectiveness. Getting rid of ineffective social workers.

If, as it appears, social work intervention in general and casework in particular are usually without any specific effect (that is, over and above the placebo effects of intervention *per se*) and frequently without any measurable effect at all, then a number of possible explanations suggest themselves. The first possibility is that the particular objectives of intervention are unattainable using existing methods. In other words, there are some situations about which nobody can do anything useful. Several studies have commented on the sad fact that in families with multiple problems, there is often a seemingly inexhaustible capacity to absorb social work attention without any corresponding improvement either in the level of function or in the degree of independence (e.g. Tonge *et al.* 1975; Oliver and Buchanan, 1979). This has led some authors to suggest that in view of the disproportionate demands which such problem families can make on social work departments, there is a case for adopting the concept of triage from military medicine and simply accepting therapeutic defeat, devoting the resources thus released to more promising cases. This concept is discussed in Chapter 11.

A second possibility is that the therapeutic goal in question can be achieved by existing methods, at least in some cases, but that those who do social work lack the skills necessary to achieve it, or to produce results better than those within the capability of such existing sources of 'amateur' help as next-door neighbours, the police, and so forth. Such a conclusion would have serious implications for the claim that social work training confers special abilities on its recipients which do not exist, or which hardly ever exist, in the general populace. It is, as we have seen, a conclusion which has certainly been drawn, rightly or wrongly, by a number of people, including some of political importance, when social workers went on strike and there was no apparent increase in the sort of social catastrophes which social workers claim to be able to prevent (see Chapter 3).

A third possibility is that an apparent overall ineffectiveness conceals a state of affairs in which some social workers succeed in producing a specific improvement in respect of defined goals, which is cancelled out by the activities of other social workers who actually succeed in making their clients worse than would have been the case had they not interfered. This hypothesis also allows for the existence of social workers who produce neither improvement nor worsening.

The first possibility need not concern us further because when problems are in practice insoluble by existing methods, social workers need not blame themselves, and should not be blamed by others, for their helplessness. If there is to be any improvement, it will not come about by more and better training but must await the introduction of some new therapeutic approach. (The question of specifically political solutions to certain social problems is discussed in Chapter 5.)

However, if social workers are spending a significant part of their time in energetic attempts to treat problems which are actually untreatable, then it represents a useless and inefficient diversion of their energies away from areas where they might prove more effective. Doctors are rightly criticised for pulling out all the therapeutic stops in manifestly hopeless cases. We sympathise with the natural and understandable feeling in such cases that 'something must be done', but feel that one of the hallmarks of a professional is that his actions are governed by his knowledge and experience rather than by instinctive or emotional reaction. Social workers seem even more reluctant than doctors to admit defeat, and one explanation for this may be that, as we show in this chapter, social workers seem to have remarkably little interest in the evidence for the effectiveness or ineffectiveness of their work. If, as it

seems, they do not seem to care very much whether they succeed.
it is hardly surprising if they are equally oblivious to failure. Like
Queen Victoria during the Boer War it appears that many social
workers are 'not interested in the possibility of defeat.'

We have already presented a considerable amount of evidence
that the effects of social work, even when provided by those with
special training and, supposedly, special skills, frequently cannot
be differentiated from the effects of leaving clients to the atten-
tions of traditional welfare agencies, voluntary bodies and ordinary citizens. In theory, some at least of the problems social
workers deal with might be handled more effectively by those with
appropriate training, and if this is indeed the case, then it may be
that most social workers, although they may have had some training, have simply not acquired the sort of skills which would make
them more effective than those without training. That this can
apply in the field of conventional psychotherapy, too, is apparent from the Vanderbilt Study (Strupp & Hadley 1979).

To test the hypothesis that expert therapists would produce
better results in the treatment of neurotic college students than the
'therapy' provided by non-professional academic staff, two comparable groups of fifteen students were treated either by analyti-
cally or experientially oriented (*sic*) psychotherapists or by a
similar-sized group of college lecturers. The results indicated that
both groups of therapists achieved equal success whether improvement was rated by the patient, the therapist, or an independent clinician. However, the authors noted that, in both groups,
good outcomes seem—to be associated with a certain therapeutic
style — notably an active one — while bad outcome was associated with certain other styles — notably passive ones.

This leads us to consider the evidence for the third explanation
for the overall ineffectiveness of social work — that ineffectiveness
is the consequence of a balance between competent and incompe-
tent social workers. Once again, we must look to psychotherapy
research for our information, partly because psychotherapy and
social work are such similar activities, and partly because of the
relatively small amount of useful effectiveness research in social
work. The current state of knowledge has recently been reviewed
by Bergin & Lambert (1978), who provide powerful evidence for
the view that if treated groups are compared with untreated controls,
the average change in the two groups is often very similar. However, this is because, in the treated group, more patients show
significant improvement but more patients also show significant
deterioration. In other words, as we have already pointed out in
Chapter 8, any treatment can in principle do harm as well as good.

If one were looking at the effects of a single therapist, the conclusion might be that the therapy he provided was good for some sorts of patient but not for others, and research might reasonably be directed at identifying those patients who were most likely to benefit from the approach and those who were likely to be harmed. However, most of these studies have involved the work of several therapists and the evidence suggests that the therapist is an important variable in a range of diagnoses. To put it simply, some therapists do seem to be generally helpful, even if only moderately so, others seem to provide no specific benefit, while others consistently tend to make at least a proportion of their patients worse. Deterioration effects may be particularly relevant where the degree of benefit from a given treatment is relatively marginal, as is often the case in psychotherapy and social work. No doubt there are bad surgeons and bad physicians too, but if they use methods of treatment which produce much better results than no treatment, as is certainly the case for a number of conditions, then the occasional botched job may be forgiven. Furthermore, because the effective elements of treatment are easier to define, it may be easier to correct any mistake which has been made.

Argument about what make a successful psychotherapist has concentrated on two areas: the personality of the therapist and the particular type of psychotherapy employed. Current thinking in this field is well summarised by Parloff *et al.* (1978), and while the picture is still rather confused, some tentative conclusions are beginning to be drawn. Some authorities, notably Fischer (1978a), set considerable store by the qualities alleged by Truax & Carkhuff (1967) to be necessary for therapeutic effectiveness, such as genuineness, accurate empathy, and non-possessive warmth. As we shall see, these qualities may not be as relevant as was once thought, but if they are relevant, or if future studies should point conclusively to the indispensability of certain other qualities, the question naturally arises as to whether social workers and psychotherapists who do not possess these qualities should be allowed to vent their resultant incompetence on clients who presumably already have more than their fair share of misfortune.

Some interesting indirect evidence for the importance of what might be called the therapist's style—that is, some combination of his personality and his philosophy—comes from a recent comparative study of London schools and their differing effects on the children who attend them (Rutter *et al.* 1979). It was found that the schools studied 'differed markedly in the behaviour and attainments shown by their pupils. . . . these differences in outcome between schools were *not* due to such physical factors as the size of the school, the age of the buildings or the space available; nor were they due to broad differences in administrative status or organisation' (italics in original). Perhaps the most important finding of the study was that 'the differences between schools in outcome *were* systematically related to their characteristics as social institutions. . . . The implication is that the individual actions or measures may combine to create a particular *ethos,* or set of values, attitudes and behaviours which will become characteristic of the school as a whole'. The authors add that 'the total pattern of findings indicates the strong probability that the associations between school process and outcome reflect in part a *causal* process. In other words, to an appreciable extent children's behaviour and attitudes are shaped and influenced by their experiences at school and, in particular, by the qualities of the school as a social institution'.

This study utilises a number of behavioural principles, notably a very detailed description of behavioural patterns within a school or classroom. Concern to discover the underlying values, norms, expectations, and standards, and interest in modelling, feedback and consistency are all familiar notions to the behavioural psychotherapist. Characteristically, the authors do not maintain that ethos is the only important variable, and they have gone to considerable trouble to quantify those factors, such as the type of pupil attending the school, which were not determined by the nature of the institution.

Presumably there was little difference in the formal training of those responsible for the running of the various schools, so that if some schools proved to be very much better at their educational task than others, as the investigators found, the vital difference in ethos was due mainly to the personality and philosophy of those staff who set the tone of the establishment. Since casework or psychotherapy, and the closely related activity of counselling, can all be seen as at least partly educational activities, it seems a reasonable hypothesis that similar factors play a part in the differential effectiveness of different psychotherapists. Just as this study has made an important contribution to our knowledge of those aspects of the teaching process which are helpful to children, and those which hinder them, it is likely that studies of psychotherapy involving a minutely detailed description of what the therapist actually does during therapy will point the way towards greater effectiveness.

Although there is a widespread feeling among psychotherapists that personality is an important variable in the outcome of treatment, and some evidence to suggest that enthusiasm can be

useful in achieving stated goals, it seems to us that neither enthusiasm nor genuineness, accurate empathy and non-possessive
warmth will be very useful if they are applied to therapeutic techniques which are ineffective. In medicine, many patients have
died because of misplaced therapeutic enthusiasm and it is not
much consolation to the family of the dead patient to be told that
the doctor who killed or damaged their relation by an unfortunate
choice of treatment was a genuine, empathetic and warm person.
There are several reasons why many social workers may be no
more than walking placebos, and in some cases even less effective
than a placebo, but a prime candidate is surely the heavy emphasis in social work courses and among social workers generally on
what may broadly be called 'psychodynamic' or 'psychoanalytic' approaches to human behaviour. We have already discussed
the evidence for this bias and it is now appropriate to discuss
some of its consequences.

There is no doubt that Freud and his disciples have had a major
and lasting effect on western thought, especially on psychiatry
and related activities, which certainly includes social work. However, although few laymen have any familiarity with the technical
language of psychiatry, many people use — even if incorrectly
— the language of psychoanalysis, which is now to some extent a
part of everyday speech. Such phrases as inferiority complex,
penis envy, castration anxiety, and of course the Oedipus complex, are quite frequently heard, and if they have not yet reached
the lowest social classes, they have certainly reached those people
with the kind of educational level which qualifies them in many
countries for social work. Although relatively few psychiatrists
in Britain actually use a couch, except occasionally to carry out
a physical examination of patients, the standard cartoon figure
of a psychiatrist is almost invariably a bearded, bespectacled
figure talking to a supine patient. In short, the public image of
psychiatry often corresponds closely with the image of the
psychoanalyst.

Again, while theories about the possible biochemical or anatom-
ical origin of certain mental disorders are rarely ventilated in any
detail in the intelligent lay press, and in semi-technical journals
widely read by social workers such as *New Society,* psychoanalytical concepts and language are frequently bandied about, especially in the more literary pages. Sometimes, overtly clinical
psychoanalytic texts are reviewed, even though these publications
would never give any space to a neurophysiological or pharmacological textbook.

If psychoanalysis and its related doctrines were scientific

theories, this selectivity might not matter so much, for even a partial knowledge of the factors which influence human behaviour might be better than nothing. Unfortunately, psychoanalysis, for all its ingenuity, interest, attractiveness, and seductive phraseology, is not merely unscientific, but for much of its history has been rather actively anti-scientific. As Eysenck & Wilson (1973) and others have pointed out, much of psychoanalytic theory is couched in terms which make it inaccessible to proof or disproof and therefore disqualify it from serious scientific consideration. Even worse, where it has been possible to formulate psychoanalytic theories in terms of testable hypotheses, many of these hypotheses have been shown to be unsound and in some cases the very opposite of the truth.

Although psychoanalysis in pure form may not feature very prominently in the average social work curriculum, it has influenced and created many schools of psychotherapy which have as one of their main characteristics a tendency to try to modify the present by paying close attention to the past. The approach of many of these therapies is to study the past, and particularly early life, in great detail with a view to uncovering 'hidden conflicts' which are thought to have an adverse influence on present thinking and behaviour, and in the resolution of which is held to be the main hope of improvement. Although brief forms of psychoanalytic psychotherapy have been devised, psychoanalysis and related treatments are still frequently protracted affairs, and 'classic' psychoanalysis can and not infrequently does continue for years. There is still a strong body of educated public opinion, especially in the USA, which believes that this kind of treatment is the ideal and that anything else is a poor substitute.

This belief may in part be due to the extravagant claims which have been made by psychoanalysts themselves, and yet in spite of these claims, the psychoanalytic literature has been remarkable until very recent times for a distinct shortage of methodologically sound efforts to verify its alleged effectiveness. Readers of psychoanalytic literature will generally look in vain for anything resembling a controlled trial or the formulation of a testable hypothesis. When controlled trials have been done, the results have generally been rather disappointing from the psychoanalytic point of view (see p. 130). The same applies to the works of the better-known of Freud's disciples and spiritual descendants such as Jung, Adler, Melanie Klein and Horney. If the psychoanalytic school had made no therapeutic claims, their lack of scientific rigour would not be very important in this context, but it was Freud himself who insisted that psychoanalysis must stand or fall by its therapeutic effectiveness (Freud 1962). In their dogmatism, reverence for tradition, and the existence of a kind of apostolic succession, psychoanalysis and its offspring have more in common with certain religions than with a scientific activity, and the similarity is strengthened when one observes the fervour and personal insult with which arguments between dissenting sects of the movement are conducted. This latter-day *odium theologicum* has been convincingly documented in many exchanges of letters between the early members of the movement.

As Sheldon (1978) has pointed out, the choice of therapeutic philosophy in most social work courses seems to be a function more of the popularity of a particular idea among students or teachers than of its scientific respectability, and as we have seen, it is the relatively 'soft' and unscientific approaches which seem to be sought and taught in preference to the more precise and testable language of behaviourism. If this state of affairs reflects the unscientific or even anti-scientific attitude of many of those who take up social work, then it is hardly surprising that real and useful progress has been so hard to come by if, as social workers claim (and we agree with them), dealing effectively with the problems social workers encounter might be made easier by the application of specialised knowledge.

An anti-scientific attitude — of which there is plenty of evidence in social work literature — would certainly go some way towards explaining the hostility to behaviourism, since behaviourism is distinguished by a conceptual rigour and concern for testability and evidence of specific effectiveness which would often put medical science to shame. If this attitude is general, as Sheldon maintains (see also p. 184), it surely demolishes any claim of social work to receive serious consideration either as a science or as a useful specific therapeutic endeavour. If, on the other hand, the emphasis on psychodynamic concepts is defended as a scientific choice based on a consideration of the available evidence, then the antipathy to behaviourism is rather surprising for exactly the same reasons and suggests an ideological bias.

Whatever the reason, it is certainly very regrettable, because the behavioural approach has proved to be of real and almost undisputed value in certain conditions including some, such as obsessive compulsive disorders (Marks, *et al.* 1975), which have in the past proved notoriously resistant to conventional psychotherapeutic approaches and very often to medical treatment as well. There are now a number of studies comparing behavioural psychotherapy with more traditional kinds of psychotherapy, and while they often reveal that almost any kind of psychotherapeutic intervention can be beneficial if it is perceived by the recipient as helpful, and that non-specific factors in treatment which are common to all types of psychotherapy are often more important that the specific features of a particular therapeutic approach, there is still a tendency for behavioural approaches to produce better results than other kinds of psychotherapy, even if the superiority is sometimes fairly modest. At any rate, the rejection of behavioural approaches on the grounds that they are ineffective simply cannot be justified by reference to the growing body of literature. The reader is referred to Bergin & Lambert (1978) for an up-to-date assessment of the state of knowledge.

Apart from certain characteristic therapeutic techniques, one of the most distinctive features of behaviourism is its concentration on defining the aims and objects of treatment in any particular case. It is probable that some of the success of behavioural methods in certain areas is attributable not only to the evolution of specific techniques but to the fact that the clear and unambiguous definition of the aims of treatment enabled behaviourists to be correspondingly clear about whether they were achieving their goals or not. This in turn enabled them to modify their techniques by identifying the successful elements and eliminating the redundant or harmful ones. Whatever technique they use, behaviour therapists are generally clear that they are indeed trying to produce some change in their client (which does not exclude changing the environment in which their client lives). They accept that the object of treatment is that the client should be different in some respect, be it in behaviour or apparent attitude, compared with the beginning of treatment. In contrast, many social workers seem to be very vague about what they are actually trying to do. Of course, they will doubtless hope, as all behaviour therapists hope, that their clients will feel generally better or happier, but 'feeling better' is far too vague and diffuse a therapeutic goal to be of any value. We have already seen in Chapter 3 just how vague social workers often are about their goals, and there is often an inference that setting specific goals represents an altogether too hard-headed approach. Yet it is surely the case that almost any aspect of social work presupposes the existence of certain goals even if these are implicit and unspoken. Insofar as a social worker is disappointed at the outcome of certain cases, at the failure of a client or his circumstances to change in the hoped-for direction, then there must have been some kind of standard against which the actual outcome was to be judged. In the behavioural approach, these implicit goals and expectations tend to be made explicit and there is evidence to suggest that this makes life easier for both therapist and patient (see p. 180).

Indeed, behavioural psychotherapists tend to regard as axiomatic something which other types of psychotherapists often seem to find difficulty in accepting, namely that behavioural change is the goal of *every* kind of psychotherapeutic endeavour. The only way of making a diagnosis or assessment before beginning psychotherapy is by observation of the patient's behaviour, including his verbal behaviour, and therefore the only way in which progress — or lack of it — can be assessed is by observing changes in behaviour. Even the kind of labyrinthine speculation which is the defining characteristic of so much psychodynamic psychotherapy must in the end be based on what the patient says and does. That is not to say that behaviourists never speculate, but behaviourists draw a much clearer line between untestable speculation and testable hypothesis. It may be thought that a therapist who knows that his goal is the modification of behaviour is likely to have more success than the therapist who is actually working towards the same goal but tries to convince himself and others that he is really working towards a very different object. Even environmental change is only 'desirable' to the extent that the affected individual, or his family, or 'society', sees the change as desirable and says so.

Yet among social workers these fundamental characteristics of the behavioural approach are often obscured behind a barrage of comments about the nastiness of behaviourists in general and of aversion therapy in particular, as if this were the main or only technique of behaviourism. As Sheldon — a teacher of social work — wrote recently (1979), 'it is difficult to teach social workers how to make proper use of behaviour modification techniques. . . . they keep raising spurious ethical issues about things like the Alabama State Penitentiary scheme (when really the shocks only lasted a second or two, and anyway we all have to earn our bed and breakfast, don't we)'. In reality, electrical aversion therapy is now rarely used by behaviourists, partly because it has been shown to be not particularly effective, partly because in the case of sexual deviation — the field in which the use of aversive techniques has perhaps been the most controversial — the relevance and validity of the theory on which treatment was based is now very seriously questioned, and partly because most behaviour therapists actually dislike causing their patients pain and are acutely aware of the complex ethical issues involved in this area of treatment. Aversion therapy is very much a product of the early days of behaviourism when its use probably reflected an understandable tendency—common to the early stages of most new therapeutic developments—to concentrate on relatively concrete and obvious aspects before concerning itself with more subtle ones.

Since those days—and we must remember that behaviour therapy did not really get going as a distinct professional and academic activity until about the middle of the 60s—there have been numerous developments in both technique and theory, and current methods concern themselves not only with the more obvious aspects of behaviour but also with feelings. Yet to read much of the social work literature, one would hardly think that behaviour therapy had advanced beyond the stage of giving powerful electric shocks to reluctant homosexual patients. Even in 1976, the distinguished social work academics and others on the working party which produced the publication *Values in Social Work* for the CCETSW described the behavioural approach as dealing 'only with overt behaviour since this. . . was all that could be seen and measured. It would not deal with sensation, perception, image, purpose and thinking or emotion as these were subjectively defined'. Subsequently, they stated that 'behaviour conditioning therapies [*sic*] treat the patient as a reactive being, moulded by stimulus contingencies to which he is subjected. The aim is behaviour change according to a standard established more by the therapist' (CCETSW 1976). In the same fashion, Baird, although suggesting that social workers should take behavioural methods more seriously, talks about their 'sinister aspects' (Baird 1976). Behaviour therapists are consistently presented as cold, calculating, unfeeling manipulators with about as much sensitivity as a bulldozer. They are often contrasted unfavourably with practitioners of other approaches, especially those of the analytic school, who, whatever their shortcomings, are often depicted as kindly, caring individuals who tease out infantile traumas with all the skill of someone entrusted with the repair of the Bayeux tapestry.

In their comprehensive study *Psychotherapy versus Behaviour Therapy*, Sloane *et al.* (1975) remark on 'the fact that behaviour therapy has been at times characterised as a rather impersonal process with little regard for the patient as a human being in contrast to the close empathic relationship of psychotherapy'. As they found in their study—apparently somewhat to their surprise—this view is not merely untrue, but may well be the very reverse of the truth. The Sloane study is one of the most thorough of its kind and is characterised not merely by its attempt to compare the relative effectiveness of behaviour therapy, psychoanalytic psychotherapy, and a control group who had the same initial assessment procedure but no treatment; it also studied what the two kinds of therapists actually did in the course of therapy, in the hope that any differences in style might prove to be related to differences in outcome. In fact, the differences in outcome, though generally favourable to the behavioural approach, were not very marked, especially by the time of the long-term follow-up, so that the relevance of any differences in style is not clear-cut.

However, the study has provided very valuable information which enables these differences in style to be quantified, and they are not at all what conventional psychotherapists have tended to claim. Among various measures of therapist variables, they used the well-known Truax triad of accurate empathy, depth of inter-personal contact, and unconditional positive regard, devised to test the assumptions of Rogerian counselling. Although, as Parloff *et al.* (1978) have pointed out, 'evidence for the hypothesis that judged these qualities to be the necessary and sufficient conditions of effective treatment has become increasingly clouded', they are still widely regarded as being of value, and were doubtless thought even more relevant when Sloane *et al.* carried out their study some years ago. They found that 'behaviour therapists showed a significantly higher level of interpersonal contact than did psychotherapists. In addition, behaviour therapists showed a significantly higher level of Accurate Empathy and of Therapist Self-congruence than did psychotherapists. Both showed an equal degree of warmth or unconditional positive regard towards the patient'. On an inter-personal contact scale, 'behaviour therapists were functioning at about stage four in intensity and intimacy which indicates that they were "concernedly attentive" to the patient while the psychotherapists were between stages three and four'. (Stage three is 'attentive but not engrossed'.) They also remark: 'It might have been expected that patients in psychotherapy would have discussed their problems on a deeper level than would patients of behaviour therapists, but again this was not so'.

Lest it be thought that these ratings, made by observers from tape-recorded extracts of several interviews, were affected by observer bias in favour of behaviourism, it should be pointed out that the perceptions of the patients themselves were in the same direction. Unlike the trained observers, patients saw no statistically significant difference between behaviour therapists and psychotherapists on accurate empathy, non-possessive warmth, or concreteness (although the trend in each case was in favour of the behaviourists), but they rated the behaviour therapists significantly higher than the psychotherapists on genuineness and the overall assessment. For all that the working party on 'values in social work' claimed that behaviourists aimed for 'change according to a standard established more by the therapist', behavioural psychotherapists have shown themselves to be sharply aware of the rights and powers of their patients in this respect. The draft ethical guidelines issued by the British Association for Behavioural Psychotherapy states: 'The aims and goals of treatment are discussed and agreed with the client at the onset of treatment and may be renegotiated, or treatment terminated, or a referral made to another therapist, at the request of either party if the goals are not being met after a reasonable period of time, or if they later appear to be inappropriate'. Far from rigidly and unimaginatively applying standard techniques to, patients who are human and therefore variable, behavioural approaches are, to a much greater extent than most other types of psychotherapy, tailor-made to fit the individual case. To take a simple example, although there is a superficial similarity between all spider-phobic patients, in that they are all frightened of spiders, they will not all be frightened about the same feature of spiders. Some may tolerate small spiders but panic at big ones. Others may panic only at the sight of hairy spiders. Others, still, can cope with stationary spiders but become anxious when they scuttle about. In all cases, the behavioural approach is to find out those details which seem to be particularly relevant to the problem—whether these be aspects of behaviour, attitude, or the environment—and concentrate upon them. And contrary to the view of the working party cited above, it is perfectly possible to measure changes in subjective matters such as fear, anxiety, confidence, and mood, by using such techniques as the visual analogue scale, inventories, and the semantic differential. Even in these areas, the emphasis is still on measurability, and we may make a point which we have made in other places in this book that where there are no reliable measures of improvement or deterioration, there can be no convincing claims of effectiveness.

Nor can it be claimed that the behavioural approach ignores that aspect of therapy with which social workers claim to be particularly concerned—the environment. Since they accept that their task is essentially to modify, behavioural psychotherapists have never seen any reason why they should not try to modify the environment as well, where appropriate. Although therapy is often directed at the client rather than the environment because it may be easier and is often quite effective, behaviour therapists are quite prepared to carry the therapeutic battle into the patient's home or into the wider community. For example, in the treatment of obsessive-compulsive states, it may be relatively easy to modify compulsive, repetitive behaviour in a hospital setting, but if the compulsion is long-established, as is usually the case, it may relapse quickly on returning home unless the family is involved in treatment and, indeed, trained to take over the role of therapist. Similarly, in treating a patient with a phobia involving shops, the therapist may seek the cooperation of a particular store so that the patient may be able to practise shopping by, for example, going past the check-out a number of times in one afternoon. There is surely no great difference between these techniques and the use of group and community methods in which social workers are prone to claim that they have something approaching a monopoly of wisdom. Of course, this is community work on a fairly small scale, and with the consent of all those involved. Behavioural methods can certainly be applied to community work on a larger scale, but that inevitably involves certain political considerations which are often overlooked (see Chapter 5).

In its habit of paying close attention to the present while looking at the past in fairly general terms, behavioural psychotherapy contrasts markedly with the psychodynamic approach where the opposite tends to be the case. Behaviourism uses techniques which are familiar to most parents, and the fact that the principles underlying it are readily understood by almost everybody is a great advantage when compared with the complex and often jargon-infested hypotheses which underlie many other approaches. The principles are also familiar to anyone who has trained a dog or to any instructor of military recruits. Perhaps it is these authoritarian and military overtones which have helped to make behaviourism so unpopular in social work.

The fact that some—though by no means all—behavioural techniques involve encouraging patients to expose themselves to distressing situations is another objection frequently raised by social workers. This applies not only in such obvious cases as aversion therapy, which as we have remarked is rather rarely used, but also in many desensitisation procedures. For a woman who has been housebound because of agoraphobia for many years, to make even a short excursion from her home may indeed cause a lot of anxiety and distress even with the use of drugs or relaxation techniques designed to reduce that distress. If it were possible to produce similar therapeutic results in the same time or less using gentler techniques, then behavioural therapists would doubtless use them. However, where the evidence suggests, as it does in this case, that other approaches do not produce such good results, and that a certain amount of metaphorical arm-twisting may assist the therapeutic process, then the behaviourist takes much the same view of the situation as does a surgeon who knows that operation is necessary. Since the vast majority of patients receiving psychotherapy of any kind receive it voluntarily, they are free to refuse a behavioural approach just as surgical patients are free to refuse surgery. Neither can it be said that patients seeking psychotherapy have little choice in the matter of style. At present, although behavioural psychotherapists are becoming increasingly numerous, psychodynamic psychotherapy is probably still the norm, and the patients of behaviour therapists are quite often referred after more conventional approaches have failed. We submit that a surgeon who declined to operate on the grounds that surgery was painful would be a pretty useless surgeon. We submit that a social worker or psychotherapist who refuses to use behavioural methods of proved effectiveness in certain conditions is an equally useless therapist. If there is some truth in the old joke that a psychiatrist is a doctor who cannot stand the sight of blood, then perhaps we can say that anti-behavioural social workers are psychotherapists who cannot stand the sight of psychological and therapeutic reality. Although the unpleasantness of a therapeutic procedure is certainly an important factor in deciding whether to use it, we regard effectiveness as of at least equal importance. In any case, it is in the end for the patient to decide whether he thinks he can tolerate the degree of unpleasantness involved. From the large number of people who submit to surgery more or less cheerfully, we surmise that the unpleasantness of treatment is not a major objection for most people if it produces the desired results.

We have already referred to the fact that the behavioural approach uses a number of principles which are widely understood—and, perhaps even more important, widely accepted—by the majority of ordinary citizens. That is not to say that behaviourists never use jargon and always express themselves in simple language. Indeed some behavioural texts are written in a way which must seem at least as confusing to the layman as the average psychodynamic text, if not more so. After all, whatever his faults as a scientist, Freud was once considered as a candidate for the Nobel Prize in literature, and we cannot think of many behavioural writers who would be likely to qualify for it.

Nevertheless, because the principles of the behavioural approach are so readily understood, it is at least possible to translate the requirements of a behavioural approach in any particular case into language which is very likely to be understood by the client, and because these principles seem to be common to most societies, the behavioural approach is valid even among clients who may not share the 'western' values to which most social workers subscribe. It is not necessary to be unduly sceptical about the value of the psychodynamic approach to question the utility of trying to explain the concept of unresolved Oedipal conflicts to the barely literate breadwinner of a poor immigrant family.

Another advantage of the understandability of the behavioural approach is that there is more likelihood that treatment goals can be devised which will be shared by both therapist and client. It may seem obvious, even to laymen, that unless clients both understand and share the treatment goal, they may have some difficulty in achieving it, but it does not seem to have been obvious to all social workers. As Baird (1976) remarks, 'it says something rather depressing about social work that we need research evidence to show that it is important to share goals with clients'. Yet there is plenty of evidence that the social work profession as a whole continues to plug away at the psychodynamic approach even in the most unpromising circumstances. Richan & Mendelsohn (1973) describe

> a social work agency located in a sprawling horror in Brooklyn, New York, which offers psychoanalytic services to a population reeling under the impact of crime, slums, rats and despair. Precious few of the residents of this ghetto are 'motivated' to seek this kind of service. Of these, only a small proportion actually receive psychotherapeutic support from the social worker. These select few are seen individually for the traditional psychoanalytic hour; obviously, very few people can be seen. There are psychiatrists on staff who also offer psychoanalytic hours—not to the population but to the social workers! This agency and its services are as remote from their community as if they were located in the Himalayas.
>
> If this particular agency were an exception in the practice of social work in the United States today, its practice might be experimentally justified. Since this agency is closer to the *norm* of professional practice, however, and since this example may be multiplied a hundredfold, then legitimate questions concerning the nature and function of social work practice today should be raised.

Perhaps the one thing even more depressing than the picture of American social work described by Richan & Mendelsohn is their belief that any kind of psychoanalytic approach might still be 'experimentally justified' in the light of so much evidence against it.

Although the behavioural approach is sometimes criticised as elitist and manipulative, what could be more elitist than this attempt to persuade the inhabitants of a New York slum to look at the world through the bourgeois-tinted spectacles of *fin de siécle* Vienna?

What could be more manipulative than persuading clients that their material needs are less important than the need to restructure their psychic apparatus? And as we have seen, this attitude is by no means restricted to a few Freud-besotted frustrated psychotherapists on the American side of the Atlantic. The social worker described on page 68, who regretted the preference of his clients for material aid when what he wanted to give them was psychotherapy, displays exactly the same attitudes. No. If any approach is to be categorised as 'the people's therapy' it is surely the behavioural one rather than the psychodynamic tradition.

We return to the charge that behavioural approaches may involve putting pressure on clients even if it is pressure to achieve goals with which the client agrees.

We realise, of course, that as well as social workers, many other people who are involved in a general sense in therapy have both philosophical and practical reservations about putting pressure on their clients. It is sometimes suggested that any change made under pressure will not last and that with the removal of pressure the *status quo* will be restored, if not something worse. If this were true, it would certainly be a valid objection, but we have already presented some evidence which indicates that it is not true. Even if it were, an apparent reluctance among social workers to apply pressure on individual clients contrasts strangely with the enthusiasm which some social workers demonstrate for persuading whole communities to involve themselves in certain group activities even against a background of apathy and mistrust. We do not necessarily disagree with these activities, though as we have remarked elsewhere we think their political implications have been insufficiently thought out. We merely remark on the contrast, and do not know whether it represents a preference for the collective ethic over that of the individual, a Marcuse-ian mixture of politically aggressive Marxism with psychotherapeutically passive Freudianism, or some other explanation.

Further evidence of the value of even modest amounts of arm-twisting is to be found in a carefully controlled study conducted by Crowe (1978). Although the study was done by psychiatrists, it is of considerable relevance to social workers because it concerned itself with marital problems, a field in which social workers are not infrequently involved.

Crowe randomly allocated couples with marital problems to one of three groups. The 'directive' group were treated using 'a simple model of marital disturbance. The couples are seen as not producing enough rewarding interpersonal behaviour, and an attempt is made to negotiate behavioural change to increase such behaviour. The therapist thus gave advice on "give to get" principles...' This was combined with Masters & Johnson techniques for dealing with sexual problems, which employ similar principles. In this group, dynamic interpretations were expressly excluded.

The second group used an interpretative psychodynamic approach based on the work of Skynner (not to be confused with the behaviourist Skinner). The therapist 'made interpretations to the couple centering on conflict, defences, manipulation... Ventilation of feelings was encouraged. Advice of any sort was expressly excluded from this approach'.

The third group acted almost as a placebo control. They received 'support' which avoided both advice and interpretation, 'the main objective being for the therapist to remain passive and impartial, to encourage talk...'

Three different therapists were used, though some of them provided more than one type of therapy, modifying their styles accordingly. That the three therapeutic approaches really *were* different is apparent from the fact that independent observers, using recorded extracts from the therapeutic sessions, were able to identify correctly, in most cases, the group from which the recorded extract came. It is interesting that in the case of the directive group, the independent observers correctly assigned the recorded extract in 91 per cent of cases, but they managed to assign interpretative and supportive extracts correctly in 74 per cent and 72 per cent of cases respectively.

While both the directive and the interpretative group were to some extent 'client centred' in that both attempted to deal with the way in which the couples themselves saw the problem, it was very much a trial of a directive versus a non-directive approach, which is particularly significant since the non-directive Rogerian philosophy seems to be so popular among social workers.

The results demonstrated the superiority of the directive approach over the interpretative (which itself was superior to the support group in some respects), and it is interesting that there was also a higher rate of defaulting in the interpretative group than in the other two. Apart from the superior improvement of the directive group on the various scales and assessments used, it also had the lowest incidence of separations. This superior performance held true even after eighteen months follow-up.

We have already discussed the evidence that it is the psychotherapeutic-casework aspects of their job which many social workers particularly enjoy. That is one reason why we have devoted so much space to the topic. We do not find this preference for psychotherapy surprising because we know that many of those who do psychotherapy seem to find it enjoyable and stimulating. (That is certainly true of Colin Brewer who does quite a lot of it.)

Yet, as we have stated in Chapter 8, choosing a particular treatment merely because one enjoys doing it is surely a rather strange approach to securing maximum effectiveness, and we would even suggest that it is an inherently unprofessional approach. If the concept of professional integrity means anything at all, it surely means that the interests of the client should generally take precedence over the interests of the practitioner. This holds true not just for the choice of a psychotherapeutic approach as opposed to any other, but for the choice of a particular type of psychotherapy over other types. It certainly seems that social workers not only favour psychotherapy as opposed to other and possibly more mundane and unexciting aspects of their work, but also favour methods of psychotherapy which do not give the best chance of success. Even worse, it seems that they often specifically and sometimes vituperatively reject approaches and philosophies which on the available evidence are likely to be more beneficial or less time-consuming.

We have also devoted a lot of space to the question of effectiveness — not just in respect of psychotherapy/casework, but of social work techniques in general. This is partly because one of our themes is that social workers cannot expect much in the way of public and political respect or financial support if the evidence for their superior effectiveness as compared with existing or traditional agencies is so noticeably lacking. As Baird (1976) has said, 'we cannot . . . escape from the centrality of the issue of effectiveness'.

The other reason for placing so much emphasis on effectiveness is, in some respects, a more serious one. It is that, very often, social workers are simply not particularly interested in the question of effectiveness.

Apart from the manifest importance of effectiveness for the future of social work itself, it seems obvious enough that unless practitioners of social work are interested in effectiveness, it is unlikely that there will be much progress towards the discovery of better methods of intervention.

The charge of relative indifference to effectiveness is a serious one to make and we do not claim to make it on the basis of a series of methodologically sound inquiries conducted among a large number of social workers. It is certainly supported by our own personal experience of social workers, but having previously criticised those who rely on their 'personal experience' to tell them that social work is highly effective when objective evidence suggests that it is nothing of the sort, we could hardly complain if the reader were to reject the charge on the grounds that we are hostile witnesses, though we would argue that our hostility is not to social work but merely to unjustifiable therapeutic claims.

However, we are not alone in making this charge and it may be considered particularly convincing when it comes from those who are involved in the training of social workers.

Sheldon (1979) describes a lecture he attended at which H. T. Meyer (joint author of the *Girls at Vocational High* Study; see p. 146) addressed an audience of social workers. It is clear that Sheldon was greatly disturbed by the ineffectiveness of social work which the study revealed, but he goes on to say: 'I was much more worried (and still am) by the complacent smiles of colleagues all around me'. He categorises the typical response among social workers to demonstrations of their ineffectiveness as: 'let's pretend nothing of importance has happened'.

In their survey of British social work departments, Parsloe and Stevenson complained that 'results and outcome were discussed in very general terms. . . . Nowhere in our studies did we find departments or social workers who were subjecting any part of their direct work with clients to empirical testing'.

Similarly, Fischer (1978a) states that 'the human services professions never developed a tradition of basing even part of their practice on the results of research. In fact, many professionals appear to be so resistant to research findings — especially when they are negative but often even when they are positive — that major structural or institutional changes appear necessary in order to alter that pattern.' Fischer echoes a point which we have made frequently, which is that unless there is a major change in the attitudes of social workers to the question of effectiveness, financial support for social work is likely to decline and that 'the public and government may not, indeed probably would be unwise to, wait much longer'.

Ironically, Fischer's warnings seem likely to go largely unheeded, at least in Britain. The reason is not so much that they fall on unreceptive ears as that they fall on hardly any ears at all, receptive or otherwise. During the preparation of this book, we found some difficulty in getting hold of a copy of Fischer's *The Effectiveness of Social Case Work* (Fischer 1976) and his more recent *Effective Case Work Practice; An Eclectic Approach* (Fischer 1978a). We would have been distinctly encouraged had this difficulty been due to unexpected demand for both books by social workers anxious to improve their effectiveness, but the real reason was that they were not stocked by the main bookshop serving the largest university in Britain because there is no demand for them. Similarly, the library of that university stocks only Fischer's earlier (1976) book and then only a single copy which, when we inquired, had been taken out some months earlier and had not been returned because nobody else had requested it.

This is doubly unfortunate because Fischer not merely reaches very similar conclusions to ours about the urgent need to rescue social work from its pretentious incompetence, and agrees that the best of way of doing this — indeed, in the present state of knowledge, the *only* way of doing this — is the adoption of the behavioural approach which we have advocated, but in his second book goes on to describe this approach in considerable practical detail, certainly in much more detail than we propose to provide here. Like us, Fischer has a fairly broad conception of the behavioural approach which goes beyond the mere application of a few isolated behavioural techniques such as implosion therapy or massed practice. He, too, advocates not merely a concentration of effort on those approaches which appear on present evidence to be genuinely effective (with the corresponding implication that ineffective practices must be frankly discouraged if not actually forbidden) but also the application of these techniques in a systematic way in order to achieve specified and attainable goals.

Fischer evidently believes, as we do, that changing the habits of social workers, though urgently necessary, will not be easy. He remarks that

> for case workers, this means a turn from preoccupation with methods of practice developed solely by case workers to a careful examination of all available sources — whether from within or outside the profession — for knowledge that may lead to greater effectiveness in practice. This must be done whether or not that knowledge easily fits into our traditional theoretical molds. Case workers cannot afford paying continuing allegiance to theories developed by case workers . . . *because* they are developed by case workers. Again, this does not mean that traditional approaches should be eliminated merely because they are traditional. But it does mean that when there is recourse to new and better methods, no matter who develops them or what their professional point of origin is, case workers should use them. (Fischer, 1978a)

To some extent, this is beginning to happen. We stated in Chapter 5 that there are signs of greater interest in behavioural methods in social work, and the idea of brief, task-centred, and contractual varieties of casework clearly owes much to behavioural principles.

Yet the indiscriminate application of a particular therapeutic technique can be just as undesirable as its indiscriminate rejection. There are disturbing signs that some social workers are using potentially useful methods in an unthinking, unselective, and sometimes slapdash way. For example, the use of contracts between social worker and client is becoming quite fashionable in some areas, but we have seen a number of cases in which the social worker involved evidently thought that a contract simply involved drawing up a list of goals and presenting it to the client. In other cases, the contract seems to have been entirely unilateral with no suggestion that failure to achieve client goals will result in any change of behaviour on the part of the social worker.

Parsloe and Stevenson remark on the vagueness which characterised the use of contracts in their survey of social workers and indicate that it was common for allegedly contractual treatment plans not to be shared with the client. No wonder they state that 'it was not clear why some social workers accorded the status of contract to the plans they had formulated and sometimes shared with clients. The significant feature of so-called "contract work" in this context was the absence of any shared discussion about time limits or the roles of the social worker and client'.

In casework, as in law, a contractual agreement implies not only a measure of negotiation between the two parties but also the existence of sanctions if the contract is breached. There is an element of coercion in any contract and, as we have seen in the aftermath of the Leeds study (p. 150), coercion often seems to be alien to the prevailing ethos of social work.

A further reason for doubting whether many social workers are actually capable of making effective use of the behavioural approach is that it needs to be applied in a rigorous and systematic fashion. It involves an attention to detail, and to the *recording* of that detail, and we have seen that neither of these is characteristic of current casework. The principles involved are often simple enough to grasp, just as the principle of asepsis in surgery is simple enough to grasp, but in both cases, unless the principles are rigorously and consistently applied in practice, they will lose much of their theoretical effect. We have previously mentioned the finding of Rutherford (1977) that social work students show a notable lack of the characteristics associated with clear-headed, decisive thought and action. 'Clients can expect kindly, tolerant and enthusiastic sympathy, but very little in the way of coherently planned action.' Coherently planned action is exactly what is required for the successful application of the behavioural approach (and probably of most other therapeutic approaches too for that matter), and if, as it seems, it is a rather scarce commodity in schools of social work, then it is unlikely that things will improve very much. It seems more likely that social workers will prove to be as Pavlovian and unimaginative in their choice of therapy as many doctors still are. They will use desensitisation for anxiety and cognitive restructuring for depression because they have read somewhere that these approaches may be 'good for' these conditions. They will use these approaches and will think that they have done their job. They will not fit them into any overall plan and they will be surprised when they do not work. They will be behaving in the same way as the doctor whose treatment for depression consists *only* of antidepressant drugs and whose treatment of obesity consists *only* of slimming tablets. Unfortunately, this describes the practice of a large number of doctors in Britain and in the USA, and we have seen nothing to suggest that social workers will use the techniques available to them any more wisely. Given the anti-scientific attitude which we have described, they will probably be even worse.

In this respect, we disagree with Fischer that social workers have the potential to be uniquely beneficial by adding their own particular perspective to psychotherapy/casework. Fischer claims that 'the knowledge base for case work, and for social work as a whole, is broader than the base used by other professions concerned mainly with clinical practice. . . . and perhaps most importantly, social case workers operate in the context of social work philosophy and values and a particular orientation to people . . . characteristics unique to social work and to social case workers in clinical practice'. (Fischer, 1978a) This suggests that Fischer believes social workers have the interests of the poor at heart in a way that nobody else does and that only social workers engage in such activities as advocacy and brokerage. We think that this is manifestly untrue and that the growing interest in private practice social work in both the USA and Britain (see Chapter 7) suggests that many social workers feel no exclusive commitment to treating the wretched of the earth. Indeed, the suggestion that all social workers subscribe to a particular philosophy or view of life would be rather disturbing if it were true, which it surely is not. We live in a pluralist society and we have observed that while many social workers subscribe to what might loosely be called a 'progressive' viewpoint, many of their clients have decidedly unprogressive views about life. We think that it would be an unhealthy state of affairs if clients found themselves under pressure to view the world through some sort of standard social work spectacles. Perhaps the most charitable explanation of Fischer's assertion is that having, through his researches, sawn off the branches on which many of his students had planned to sit for the rest of their professional lives, he feels under some moral obligation to keep the remains of the tree alive.

If social work is to respond effectively to attacks on its lack of effect, it is not enough for it to become more selective in the therapeutic techniques which it uses and encourages. It may also have to be a good deal more selective in its choice of people to carry out these techniques. Since the behavioural approach lends itself to definitions of therapist activity as well as of client/patient activity. it is much easier to identify effective therapists and to separate them from ineffective ones. We have tried to make it clear throughout this book that some social workers can be genuinely effective as psychotherapists. But unless social work training improves to the point where it can demonstrate that training does actually confer significant increases in effectiveness on its recipients, which is far from being the case at the moment, it will be necessary to dispense with the implication that social workers with equal qualifications are equally effective. Something fairly drastic will have to be done about ineffective social workers and ineffective techniques. We know that incompetence is not the prerogative of social workers and that there are plenty of bad lawyers and bad doctors. Nevertheless, social work does not enjoy anything like the esteem of these two groups and, unlike them, its function is not rooted in any established traditional base.

Social work seems to lack a reservoir of good will and is accordingly very vulnerable, especially at times of financial restraint. In Chapter 11 we argue that social workers might more usefully be employed within existing organisations rather than trying to compete as an independent profession on ground which is already quite strongly occupied by experienced troops from a variety of opposing armies. Even in a subordinate role, they would still have to compete against those such as clinical psychologists, who might well find it easier to absorb the bureaucratic and administrative aspects of social work than would social workers to master the disciplines of psychology.

Without major and painful changes, social work may well have to struggle not merely for funds but for its very survival. Indeed, as Fischer himself says (1978a), 'unless such changes are made, it is not clear that as a field we deserve to survive'.

In Chapter 8 we urged that social workers might benefit from adopting some of the habits of thought which have helped bring about improvements in medical practice. It is only fair to add that it may be unfortunate that the branch of medicine which is likely to have had most influence both on the philosophy of social work and on the practical experience of many social workers is psychiatry. Like social work, psychiatry has also suffered from a therapeutically unproductive flirtation with psychodynamic concepts, and it suffers more than most branches of medicine from arguments which are essentially about ideology rather than effectiveness.

A feature of British psychiatry which may be of some relevance is that it is not a popular speciality, and while some centres enjoy a consistently high standard of practice and research, many others may be less fortunate. Some psychiatrists can be as unselective and unthinking in their approach to treatment as some of the social workers whom we have described. They too may be relatively ignorant of the language of therapy and, given the considerable overlap between psychiatry and social work, it is probable that social workers may encounter rather less concern for effectiveness than they might meet in other specialities.

Yet it cannot be said that psychiatry has ignored the question of effectiveness in the way that social work—especially British social work—seems to have done until recently. The first controlled trials of drug treatment in schizophrenia took place in the early 1950s, and the positive results reported then have been repeated in numerous subsequent trials. Although the results of drug treatment in psychiatry still generally leave a lot of room for improvement, virtually all of the standard treatments have been adopted on the basis of several carefully controlled trials. Psychiatry does therefore have a few areas of genuine effectiveness which help to offset a record which in other respects is often rather undistinguished. Furthermore, psychiatry has shown itself much more responsive to behavioural methods than has social work, even though it could be argued that they represent as much of a 'threat' to the prevailing medical model of psychiatry as they do to the prevailing psychodynamic casework model in social work.

We said earlier that we have a fairly broad concept of the behavioural approach. To some, behaviourism means only those treatments based on learning theory, but as we stated in Chapter 5, our position is that what matters in any type of intervention—'therapeutic' or otherwise—is not the underlying theory (which may be unsound) but the level of effectiveness. Effectiveness has to be measured if intervention is to be on a more than random basis, and measurement of effectiveness must involve defining the goals of intervention. This in turn requires a concentration on what people do and say, including what they say about their own attitudes (which can be observed) rather than on what it is believed they may be thinking at a conscious or unconscious level (about which few confident statements can be made).

It is this concentration on behaviour and objectivity which characterises the behavioural approach for us, though we welcome any other approach which can be shown to be effective. However, we insist that there are certain rules governing the establishment of effectiveness which cannot be side-stepped. The behavioural approach seems to be the only psychotherapeutic one which has consistently recognised this fact, which is why we suggest that the unpopularity of behaviourism in social work is causally related to the ineffectiveness of social workers.

In our experience, too many social workers seem to think that when science comes in at the door, compassion flies out of the window. We are all for compassion, but we also believe that compassion which is applied without regard for its consequences is both misplaced and dangerous.

11

What is to be done?

BASW calls for an enquiry. We agree; but what sort of enquiry? Shortcomings of previous enquiries. A royal commission or a committee of enquiry? Composition. Terms of reference. Procedure. A few comments on recommendations. Our own views on how social work might develop.

Social services departments have now existed for ten years, and there seems to be some agreement that an enquiry into their functioning is called for. There is little agreement about the form the enquiry should take, and some evidence that social workers are attempting to ensure that an enquiry is conducted by the profession itself. Chris Andrews, the secretary of the British Association of Social Workers, wrote to Social Services Secretary Patrick Jenkin in August 1979. A report in *Social Work Today* (Vol. 10, No. 48, 14 August 1979) summarises his submission as follows.

> BASW is continuing to urge the government for an inquiry into social work, despite indications that the DHSS hopes to establish an inquiry into the personal social services as a whole.
>
> In a letter to Social Services Secretary Patrick Jenkin, the association's general secretary Chris Andrews says: 'If a House of Commons departmental committee inquires into the personal social services we shall, of course, cooperate fully with it. I hope you understand our concern, however, that such an inquiry may not answer the case we have made for an inquiry into social work *per se*. and we continue to urge such an inquiry'.
>
> Mr Andrews believes that the time is right to look at the 'regulation of the social work profession, the establishment of minimum standards of competence, and the identification of tasks which should only be entrusted to qualified practitioners'.
>
> He says: 'Given a statutory framework social work is now

well able to undertake these functions for itself. A self-regulating profession would surely relieve your department of many responsibilities which are more appropriately carried out by the profession itself (with adequate lay influence) than by government'.

BASW wants an inquiry into the function, training and organisation of the social work profession. As an agency's structure and policies can improve or impair a social worker's performance, the association also calls for an inquiry into agency function, statutory responsibilities and relationships between one service and another as well as the quality of work undertaken by professional social work staff.

'The strikes of last winter', says Mr Andrews, 'are indicative of the confusion and frustration which many social workers feel. It is extremely stressful to be in daily contact with distressed and demanding people and to know that more could and should be done to help, but because of lack of resources, training or support, or because of over-load, little help is actually being provided'.

The letter says that cuts 'will prove costly, not only in human terms and even lives, but also financially. Cutbacks in domiciliary services will increase the necessity to provide residential facilities in hospitals or elsewhere for persons unable to care for themselves or whose families cannot cope without support'.

With the closure of children's homes and old people's homes in the personal social services cutbacks, and with home-help, day care and social work services being similarly cut back Mr Andrews asks: 'Who will be in the dock when children are found to be unprotected from parental abuse, or old people are found dead in their homes? It is not likely to be the politicians'.

Social Work Today is the official organ of the BASW, and we can therefore assume that the report is accurate and that the views expressed are those of an influential, or at least vocal, group of social workers.

We too consider that an enquiry into the social work function of social services departments is necessary, but are certain that to place it in the hands of those who make their living from it (either directly or indirectly) would be disastrous. (We use this word advisedly, and were the subject of greater import would use the term catastrophic.) We hope we have provided enough evidence of the unfortunate influence of the over-representation of the social work interest on the Seebohm Committee. Lord Seebohm, a banker and industrialist, was and is chairman of the National Institute for

Social Work; R. Huws Jones was its Director. P. Leonard and R. Parker were both involved in social work training, and Baroness Serota had strong interests in professional child care, so that the chairman and four of the nine members could be presumed to share a certain direction, to put it no more strongly. We note too that when the DHSS conducted an enquiry into the death of Maria Colwell (DHSS, 1974) Professor O. Stevenson produced a minority report which suggested that the social work viewpoint had been neglected, but did not clarify what that viewpoint was. When an enquiry into the death of Paul Brown, aged four, in 1976, conducted by a barrister, a consultant paediatrician, an area nurse and a deputy director of social services, made specific criticisms of social workers, BASW (1979a) set up its own enquiry which, Turner (1979) in *New Society* wrote, 'firmly lifts the blame off the shoulders of the social workers involved' and 'criticises [the report] for saying little about the omissions of health service staff'. It has been the experience of both authors that the social work establishment, as exemplified by BASW, *New Society* and the Social Service Correspondents of most quality newspapers, is reluctant to publish material that poses difficult questions. For example, one of us wrote asking whether *New Society* thought social workers should conduct their own enquiries, and, if so, whether the police should do the same? The letter was not published. Another letter was slightly augmented without the author's permission to give an emphasis the original did not carry. The journal also failed to publish a reply to a letter personally attacking one of the authors, though a representative had provisionally agreed on the telephone to do so. We are conscious that personal pique and vanity may colour our views of these incidents, not in themselves significant, but they add to our conviction that it would be a mistake if any enquiry were dominated by representatives of the profession. We also think the reiterated emphasis (see p. 77) on whether social workers *enjoy* the jobs they do rather than whether their jobs are useful, and their apparent reluctance or inability to assess usefulness (see Chapter 10) makes their inclusion on an enquiry problematic. (See Gruneberg 1979 for a discussion of effectiveness and job satisfaction.)

It is one thing to recommend an enquiry into the social work functions of social services departments, quite another to say how such an enquiry would best be conducted. If academics in faculties of social sciences had justifiable reputations for impartiality, or alternatively if, as in the natural sciences, the material being studied imposed a degree of accuracy upon the investigators, one could recommend a research project funded by the DHSS. Precedents for this are, however, most inauspicious, with *Social Work Teams. The Practitioners' View,* (Parsloe 1978) a particularly expensive (£120,000 worth expensive) recent example of social workers gazing at their own navel. The problem seems to be that in subjects without an established knowledge base and frail techniques of investigation the presuppositions and prejudices of university researchers are accorded the respect that has been properly earned by others in more rigorous disciplines. There is perhaps a special reluctance to question the credentials of those recommending solutions concerned with 'welfare' which, like the 'family', has connotations of virtuous benevolence, and when combined with assumed expertise is powerful indeed. We have no confidence that researchers would not be wearing one or other set of professional blinkers, however much they protested, and in many cases (including our own) believed they were not.

For these reasons we think that a royal commission or a committee of enquiry would be more suitable than an internal enquiry by the profession or an academic enquiry by social scientists.

There is a diffuse literature on royal commissions, little reliable information on how members are appointed. It is obvious that in technical matters members with technical qualifications must be included. This often means members of involved professions, and there is always a danger they will smockravel the lay members. We do not believe that social work is in exclusive possession of a body of knowledge demanding professional expertise to elucidate it, and think that one possibility for membership of the committee is to choose ordinary citizens, possibly in the same way that jurors are chosen, excluding those professionally involved in social work or related fields. One serious problem would be to persuade such people to serve, another to find a chairman of sufficient intellectual stature to interpret for the committee the doubtless partial submissions professional pressure groups would make to it. Our experience tells us that a numerate scientist is most likely to have the necessary regard for evidence, and capacity to distinguish fact from professionally inspired fiction (though the career of Sir Derman Christopherson as chairman of CCETSW gives pause for reflection, and few numerate scientists are available for tasks of this kind). We recognise that our suggestion of a lay committee may sound extremely naive to the politically sophisticated. We hope it is not dismissed out of hand on this account, since we think most of the functions social workers undertake are well understood by ordinary citizens, who perform many of them spontaneously without benefit of training, and are after all compelled to finance them.

The more usual approach to appointing members of a royal commission or committee of enquiry—which title the investigation is given is of little moment, as Chapman (1973) makes clear, and we shall refer to it henceforth as the committee—is to attempt to secure balanced representation of the various interest groups. If this approach were adopted, we would argue for the exclusion of the social work interest, on grounds we have already outlined, and suggest that the profession's role be confined to compiling secure evidence to support whatever case they wish to put to the committee. If this seems to skew the committee towards becoming an enquiry into malfunctioning, the authors' opinion is that such an approach would not be wholly unjustified.

If it were decided that interest groups should be represented, at the very least medicine (probably subdivided into hospital, general practitioner, and community physician and with a health visitor representative), education (with possibly an education welfare officer representative), supplementary benefits, housing, probation and police should have a place. We are conscious that many would question our inclusion of the police. Their relations with social workers and probation officers are of the first importance, and our impression is that the 1969 Children and Young Persons Act has not made them easier, an impression confirmed by a call for its repeal by the Police Conference 1979. We believe that the police are almost as strategically placed as are doctors in discovering people who need help, and that, provided they do not become obsessed with the mania for training and the acquiring of paper qualifications, they have in some police constables effective and sympathetic social workers who enjoy the confidence and trust of those they seek to protect. We can hear the cynical laughter of those who believe the police are racist pigs. Undoubtedly a few are (as a minority of social workers are ineffectual Marxist twits), but unlike social workers the police have functions understood and accepted by most citizens. An unpublished study undertaken in the University College of Swansea in 1970 reveals that in a series of situations thought to be especially appropriate for social workers to deal with, doctors were the first choice of consultant, closely followed by the police. A survey undertaken by the Independent Broadcasting Association in 1979 in connection with their series *The Do Gooders*, confirms this order. Racial tension in areas of high social need may have diminished the confidence of some groups in the impartiality and sympathetic attitudes of the police, but we are convinced that the majority of citizens still regard them both as guardians of liberty and as ports of call in all manner of situations involving disturbed relationships. One remembers that it is the police who take on the delicate task of advising relatives of sudden deaths or serious injury, that it is they who comfort victims of motor accidents, that it is they who intervene in dangerous or potentially dangerous matrimonial disputes.

In these delicate matters the police, though 'untrained', act with great skill, and we have rarely heard complaints of their conduct in such situations. Some police authorities are experimenting with greater police involvement in the community, and an interesting account of one such venture is given in the Chief Constable of Devon and Cornwall's book *Communal Policing* (Alderson, 1977). Some, especially campaigners for women's rights, believe the police are too inactive in domestic violence, too unwilling to intervene between husband and wife, parent and child. We tend to prefer the judgement of experienced empiricists to that of fanatical campaigners for the latest in group fashion, though of course experienced empiricists will sometimes make mistakes. Not claiming infallibility endowed by training in human relationships, the police are ready to admit this, and do not generally seek utopian solutions. In sum, then, we think the police have achieved much in helping people with problems, and have great potential. We hope that if an enquiry were undertaken the police would submit views and experience to the committee as well as serve on it.

Since it is the social work section of social services departments that we consider most urgently requires investigation, we would not think it inappropriate if other sections of social services departments, for example residential workers and/or home helps, were asked to serve, and can see substantial advantage in ascertaining their views, whether as members of the committee or as respondents to research enquiries or both.

A difficulty in structuring a committee to reflect interest groups is to include voluntary bodies with related interests. They are so many and varied, some being akin to large social services bureaucracies, others near to tiny consumer pressure groups. These difficulties appear so great that it seems to us fairer to exclude voluntary bodies, urging them, like professional social workers, to submit cogent evidence to press their particular case. It must not be assumed that because we do not suggest their inclusion on the committee we do not consider voluntary bodies and their relation to social services departments important; indeed, we know they are vital. But their very idiosyncrasy, a great source of their strength, precludes the same sort of treatment as is possible for standardised agencies of the state. If it is difficult to include voluntary bodies, it is well-nigh impossible to include 'typical' consumers of services, unless the committee is to comprise several hundred people, an obvious nonsense. (For a lighthearted but useful discussion on size of committees see Parkinson, 1968).

Having set up the committee, either of laymen with a professional chairman or of interested professionals (and as one looks at the complexity of professional groups, one leans more and more to the lay solution), to enquire into the functioning of social workers within social services departments, how should those terms of reference be interpreted, refined and made more specific?

The first task would undoubtedly be to find out, as exactly as possible, what social workers do at present. We have already referred to the case review system used by the National Institute of Social Work in Southampton (Goldberg and Fruin, 1976), and had hoped that its undoubted usefulness to social workers 'to discover what they are doing' (to use Goldberg's memorable phrase) would have led to its adoption in other local authorities so that there would be other evidence available. So far as we can ascertain, the system has been used and reported upon only in Strathclyde (Latiry, J. 1978) and Cambridge (Warburton,1978), and in a modified form in connection with research by Bangor University College (Turner, 1979) (a most promising project on social service in rural areas, only at the pilot stage but worth watching), though there are proposals to use it in a few other authorities. Statisticians would deny the need for every social services department to use the case review system, and of course if compilation of information were the sole objective so time-consuming an exercise would be unjustified. We nevertheless recommend that the committee *require* all local authority social workers to operate the case review system (CRS) or a modified version of it for a minimum of three months, and that a representative selection of authorities do so for a year. The authorities selected for extended use of the CRS should agree to spot checks by outsiders on the accuracy of the information provided, and we would hope that members of the recently formed Social Service Research Group would undertake this duty with payment only of expenses. We agree with the designers of the system that it has value in encouraging social workers to attempt analysis of their own work. As Goldberg (1978) says in the Eileen Younghusband lecture, 'it helps social workers to establish who their clients are, what problems they are trying to tackle, by what means, and with what objectives in mind. It enables them to compare aims with actual achievements. In aggregated form the Case Review System can present information to social work teams, to management and the general public on client populations by case type, problem, service provided, by whom and with what results'. Bravo Goldberg! (Yet how sad, that having staked so clear a claim for the use of the CRS, she needs to dot her i's and cross her t's in the jargon-laden sentence: 'This system showed for the first time that it was possible to provide in an ongoing way an integrated and wide range of activity data for all clients in a social service agency'.)

We find it odd that the statistics required of social services departments do not furnish material on which to base analysis of functions undertaken. (For a learned and suggestive discussion of this problem see Fitzgerald 1978.) One would hope that the material thrown up by the operation of the case review system would encourage the requirement of fuller and more standardised statistical returns by all social services departments. But our chief objective in suggesting that all social workers should experience the case review system is our desire to engage them actively in analysing what they are doing so that the evidence they submit to the committee will be as well informed as it can be. We would not anticipate that all the material collected would be processed and used by the committee, but would hope that each department would analyse, report and debate its own findings. The social work journals might well find themselves embarrassed by the profusion of quality material submitted to them and the level of debate be raised from its present somewhat impressionistic defensive condition.

Our approach to the examination and possible restructuring of social work is essentially a consumerist one. We see consumerism as a thoroughly democratic process originally emerging in response to some of the characteristics of a competitive capitalist society. However, the principles of consumerism are applicable to almost any type of society and certainly to any institution within a society which claims to provide goods or services. One of the cardinal principles of consumerism is that you do not rely on the manufacturer's word alone in an attempt to discover the true nature of the product. When consumer organisations want to know about a particular model of dishwasher, say, they not only take it to pieces and test it themselves, they also ensure that the specimen they examine is a truly representative sample. They do not ask the manufacturer to supply one for testing, for that would obviously alert him to the impending investigation and he would naturally arrange that the specimen he provided was of the finest possible quality. We think that the same principles should apply to an investigation of social work, and suggest that the idea of using a spy in the camp may be particularly informative. This has already been done for psychiatry by Rosenhahn (1973) who sent bogus psychiatric patients round to various psychiatric hospitals, with some rather alarming results.

We should like to see, concurrently with the case review system, evidence collected on a systematic basis detailing contact (co-operative or otherwise) between social services departments and what in the jargon are called 'significant others'. These would be principally doctors, nurses, health visitors, officers of the Supplementary Benefits Commission, housing officers, teachers and education welfare officers, probation officers and policemen. This enquiry would try to find out what sort of cases they referred to social workers, with what purpose or expectation, and with what outcome. We do not on the whole consider the people we have called 'significant others' to be in quite the same need of encouragement to analyse their own activities as are social workers, and we do not suggest that large numbers should be involved. The selection of respondents would need to be undertaken rigorously, volunteers being avoided because of the probability that they would hold strong and therefore untypical views.

Consumer surveys present enormous difficulties (Shaw, 1976) but they are difficulties with which the committee should and must grapple, otherwise any enquiry will share the defect of all its predecessors, the absence of the view of those for whom the service is, after all, provided. The National Institute for Social Work has undertaken two studies involving assessment of consumer opinion. The first (Goldberg 1970), is seriously flawed, and is in itself an interesting study of social workers wearing social work blinkers. It seems preposterous that in purporting to compare services provided for the elderly by two groups of workers, trained and untrained, the trained workers should, unlike the untrained, have been told the purpose of the experiment and should have carried lighter caseloads. The second study (Glampson & Goldberg 1976), 'a first systematic attempt in England to obtain views from a random sample of clients of the newly integrated social services departments', was reported briefly in *Social Work Today,* and so far as the authors can judge was well designed and replicable. We are grateful to the Institute for making material available to us relating to this study, and think that something similar to their questionnaire (see p. 212), applied and interpreted by uninvolved researchers, might be used to test the views of users of social work services.

Until it is clear what material is produced by these enquiries it is difficult to suggest what form the second stage of the enquiry should take; whether, for example, in seeking evidence from professionals, volunteers and the public, the committee should suggest headings under which it would like to receive evidence, or whether it should seek in general terms views on how the service provided could be improved.

When all this systematised information has been processed, we would expect a cogent and speedy summary to be circulated to all social services departments and others who had contributed, and for the findings to be widely reported in the media. The committee would then declare its readiness to receive evidence, setting a time limit of not more than six months, and preferably three months. We have given much thought to whether a survey of public opinion as opposed to consumer opinion should be undertaken. We believe it is so difficult to devise unloaded questions (i.e. not to put words in people's mouths) (Shaw 1976) for people whose knowledge of the matter at issue is limited, that a general survey is unwise. It is, however, possible that the material collected in the case review system, the consumer survey and the survey of significant others, would suggest questions of sufficient specificity and relative simplicity to make a survey of this kind possible. It may indeed be that a lay committee would have its own ideas about the sort of research it wished to commission. Lack of sophistication in research methods can be an advantage in that the unsophisticated are not inhibited from asking important questions by knowledge that the answers are almost impossible to obtain, and may sometimes see ways of obtaining them unavailable to those shackled by methodology.

The assessment, or at least summary of evidence received would be the next task for the committee. Its most vital task would be its last, to outline possible strategies for change. Assuming that a nationwide situation similar to that in Southampton was revealed, i.e. that social workers were predominantly engaged in providing practical services and information and advocacy, and that the 'casework' aspects of the service were little used and largely unsuccessful, we would expect the committee might consider recommending experiment, carefully evaluated, with different areas operating different administrative schemes. Our present preference is for one in which social workers are attached to agencies like DHSS, general practices, supplementary benefits offices, housing departments and schools, since it is in these agencies that many of the problems with which social workers attempt to deal, arise. We expand our ideas about attachment to general practice later in this chapter. We have been struck when examining the work of previous enquiries by the absence of two components in their analysis which some would see as making nonsense of the whole operation. The first is the absence of precisely defined objectives that the various proposals are intended to attain—we have already referred to this weakness in discussing Seebohm's desire to achieve 'an effective family service'. The second defect is the absence of any attempt to take into account resources likely to be available for the implementation of proposals, and to cost proposals made. Seebohm (paras 24-29) makes a nodding gesture to the fact that fieldwork services may save heavier residential costs, but otherwise indulges in the universal but meaningless professional strategy of calling for 'more resources' as the panacea for all ills. We are grateful to Professor P. C. Thonemann, Department of Physics, University College of Swansea, both for his constant emphasis on the importance of defining objectives and for alerting us to the importance of costing proposals at the time they are made. We had simply assumed the latter was done, and were astonished to find it was not, except in the Birch Report, which as we have shown was attempting an impossible task. We recognise that costing proposals requires skills laymen and many professionals do not have, and we recognise that governments may not be able to predict exactly what sums will be available for particular services. We nevertheless believe that proposals made without attention to cost and likelihood of meeting it are so much wind and might as well not be made. As L. Chapman (1979, p. 187) remarks, 'In a large number of cases merely to state the cost will be to state the answer'. Interesting experiments in allocating fixed sums to area social services teams in Kent and Gwynedd and allowing workers to establish priorities within these sums are proceeding. If reports were available they should be useful to the proposed enquiry.

When considering objectives, we think it would be useful if the committee 'though small' rather than 'thought big'. Objectives of the kind favoured by Townsend (Fabian Society 1970), like 'achieving greater equality' are high-sounding but difficult to evaluate. K. Joseph & J. Sumption (1979) believe them to be impossible and misguided. We prefer for the social services objectives like 'Provision of X numbers of home helps per 1,000 population over 65', or 'Reduction by X per cent within two months of casework trained social workers', (As a matter of fact we like the last one very much, but do not wish to pre-empt the committee's options.) We do not believe that it should be the function of social workers to attempt large tasks like putting the world to rights, though we recognise that this is a matter of opinion. More certainly we believe that the pursuit of nebulous global objectives leads to constant defeat and disarray amongst social workers, and dissatisfaction amongst those they try to help. Manageable, small-scale objectives appear to lead to greater satisfaction all round (Prentice, 1979). Social workers who still want to put the world to rights when they have seen that Gran has her meals-on-wheels and her home help and can get to the club if she wants to, should perhaps recall that they are citizens as well as social workers, and

should go in for politics. There is another book to be written about
the presumptuousness of expecting pay for social work and really
going in for politics (see Chapter 6), and we are grateful to
Miller & Scott (1979) of the National Institute of Social Work for
suggesting this theme by saying 'the reality is that social work is
a political activity . . .'. If it is, perhaps the workers should stand
for election and lose their pay if defeated? But it appears to us
that there are likely to be enough modest and essential taks to be
performed for pay without social workers needing to indulge in
such dishonest activities as seeking political ends while purporting
to do something else. We hope the case review system will reveal
what they are, and that a rational attempt will be made to devise
training for them if training seems to be necessary. We hope that
if an enquiry of the kind we suggest outlines proposals, the decision
about which are best will not be taken by involved professionals
but by the electorate which surely has some right to determine the
direction of its social services on the basis of sound information.

Given that information about what people seek from social service
agencies now is lacking, and given that their very existence may
have raised expectations of which the present authors, like everyone else, are ignorant; given that we consider the objectives of
social provision to be political and that we have not declared our
political beliefs; given these substantial caveats, what changes in
provision would we suggest, working from the knowledge we already
have?

   We have already said that we think attachment of social workers
to agencies with clearly defined functions is likely to be worth
trying. Medical social work and mental welfare before 1970 provide examples with both strengths and weaknesses (see Chapter 2).
We do not know whether it would be more economical and/or efficient for existing social services departments to second social
workers or for the DHSS, housing, etc. to employ them direct,
though a competent organisation and methods team could determine this. But since we are sceptical of the value of 'professional'
training for the bureaucratic tasks we see as likely to form the bulk
of social workers' activities, and since social services departments
would be likely to insist on such training if for no other reason
than to justify their separatism, we would incline to an arrangement
in which workers from the basic agencies, with an interest in, and
preferably temperamental and intellectual suitability for, working
with 'difficult' people, undertook an apprenticeship. This might; as
with most apprenticeships, involve working with someone experienced, plus day release in which the apprentice had the opportunity

to discuss his experiences with others from related fields. It would have the advantage that the recruit had experience of exacting work before thinking he could undertake more of it.

It appears unlikely that many of the people presently engaged in training social workers would willingly participate in secondment and apprenticeship schemes, or be capable of undertaking training in methods which have been shown to have some prospects of success. We think no more people 'unfitted for training' (Parsloe, 1977) should be recruited, and that many, if not all, existing training courses should be shut down. We think that social work trainers and social workers who, in spite of evidence to the contrary, believe their methods are effective, should consider private practice. When we have suggested this in the past, it has been greeted with howls of execration from social workers, who have argued that social work clients who seek help cannot afford to pay for the service. This is of course true of many who seek practical services such as meals-on-wheels and home helps. We do not think the provision of these services requires lengthy training in 'interpersonal relationships', neither do we suggest that the state should cease to fund them. They are acceptable, popular, and useful. Whether they are most effectively provided by social services departments and whether they go to those most in need are questions we do not wish to raise at present. But the expensive 'casework services' have not generally been shown to be acceptable, popular or useful, and we see little reason for retaining them under public funding; absolutely none for expanding them. It may be that casework-trained social workers have skills which are marketable to middle-class neurotics who are deterred from approaching social services departments because of their stigmatic image, but we believe the only real test of this hypothesis must be a market test.

In Chapter 7 we have documented the limited appeal of casework in the private sector. We have also described the apparent similarity of casework to psychotherapy provided by a variety of other therapists and we find no evidence that social workers provide a distinctive type of psychotherapy which cannot be provided by anyone else. In keeping with our belief that it is better to improve existing services rather than to create a separate all-purpose service, we think the therapeutic aspects of social work should be much more closely integrated with the medical profession which is the main provider of 'therapeutic' services and has a well-established therapeutic image which social work does not have.

If we were empowered to make only one mandatory change in present provision, we would opt for the attachment of social workers to general practice. We recognise that this statement begs all manner of questions about how such social workers should be trained, and ignores the likely reluctance of many doctors to give them house room. We realise that it would often mean that social workers would have to take a more subordinate role than most of them would probably wish, and we know that the relationship between doctors and social workers is often a difficult one, especially perhaps in recent years. However, we have described an example of successful and apparently effective cooperation between general practitioners and social workers (p. 162), and we think that cooperation and respect will come more readily from doctors when social workers show more evidence of the concern for the effectiveness of what they do, which, we have argued, is such a vital aspect of therapy. For the moment, we think it not unreasonable of doctors to have some reservations about using the services of people who, as we have shown, are often very confused about what it is that they can actually offer.

We accept that some social workers may be reluctant to acknowledge the rule of medicine, and we note the apparent desire in some quarters to see doctors taken down a peg or three. However, we think it unlikely that medicine will be dislodged from its present commanding position in the foreseeable future and feel that those social workers who groan under the yoke of medical imperialism have to make a strategic decision about whether they fight, or surrender more or less gracefully. If they cannot beat medicine but are reluctant to join it, then they should no more expect peace of mind than any other unsuccessful insurgent. Equally, they can hardly expect to be liked by doctors if they treat them as an enemy.

We have cited evidence that adopting a behavioural psychotherapeutic model rather than traditional approaches may lead to greater effectiveness and to considerably greater clarity about what social workers actually do. We think that these changes could prove attractive to social workers as well as doctors, except those Balint-trained psychodynamically oriented GPs who might well welcome social workers similarly trained in psychodynamic casework. However, we have some reservations about the ability of many social work leopards to change—or even to diversify—their psychodynamic spots and accordingly we think that change is unlikely to be rapid. Even if it comes about, we think that social work will still have a hard job to convince doctors—or indeed the rest of society—that it offers a service significantly different from that provided by other paramedicals, either individually or in various combinations, though we do not rule out the possibility that it may some day develop a style which is both distinctive and distinctly useful. GP attachment offers one way to test this possibility. To achieve this desirable objective reluctant GPs could be encouraged to accept social workers into their practices by building in a financial advantage, not to say a bribe. The arrangement could be treated as a trial (possibly in more senses than one) during which the social workers would have the opportunity to demonstrate the special nature of their contribution. At the end of the trial (perhaps experiment is a more judicious term) the practice would have the option of retaining the social worker on the same financial terms as apply to health visitor attachments.

We see rich possibilities for comedy in this situation, as in other areas of social work, but we are entirely serious in our suggestion. We know that many social problems surface in GPs' surgeries, and that emotional problems may manifest themselves in physical illness. GPs seldom have time, and some neither inclination nor capacity, to grapple with these problems. Few deny their existence or suggest they should be ignored. We think attachment would be an unrivalled opportunity for social workers to demonstrate their skills to professionals with industrial muscle, who could prove most powerful allies in a struggle for recognition, if not survival. In Chapters 2 and 3 there is much evidence that social workers believe doctors undervalue and fail to understand them. One reported by Parsloe (1978) goes so far as to suggest that doctors might best be regarded as fractious clients (p. 74). We think this approach to some of the more trenchant GPs of our acquaintance would be injudicious, but concede that to gain acceptance from a group sceptical if not downright hostile would indeed demonstrate some of the skills in 'relationship' that caseworkers hold central to practice, and would cause the present authors to revise their opinions.

A further change in social work practice which might improve its image, and which would probably stem from greater concern for the question of effectiveness, is a more selective approach to its clients and a greater readiness to recognise a hopeless case when it sees one. That is not to say that problem families which have been a problem for years should be denied assistance, but it does mean that there should be a greater readiness to admit the futility of energetic intervention and that the therapeutic role in such situations will often be inappropriate. We note that the concept of triage is making an appearance in the literature of social work and psychiatry (Seagrave 1978; Gritter 1978). The concept has its origins in military medicine, and according to Gritter, is applicable to any situation in which there are many casualties and insufficient resources so that it is impossible to provide optimum treatment for everyone who needs it. Under those circumstances practical necessity requires a procedure to bring about the greatest good for the greatest number. This is done by a system of prompt and dispassionate sorting of casualties into three groups: (1) those whose condition is so poor or injuries so severe that survival or benefit is improbable. They must be relieved of suffering then set aside. (2) Those whose illness or injury is relatively minor so that they will do fairly well without immediate treatment. They must be sent away. (3) Those for whom prompt and thorough attention will probably make a great difference in outcome. All available resources must be applied to them.

Applying the concept of triage to social work does not mean that intractable problems or minor problems are simply ignored. But it does mean that a deliberate decision may have to be made to offer only nominal support or purely bureaucratic/administrative services in some cases, reserving planned and specific therapeutic intervention for those cases selected on some reasonably objective basis as being at least moderately likely to respond. *The Single Case Experimental Design* (Sheldon 1978) can provide a useful framework for sorting out the treatable wheat from the unresponsive chaff, as well as being a useful therapeutic and research instrument in its own right. (See Appendix)

One of the criticisms levelled at this book when it was in draft form was that we imply social workers have nothing to do. In fact, we believe that social workers are overburdened with mandatory legislation and hampered by elastic permissive laws. Both of us know large numbers of social workers who work excessive hours and slump physically and emotionally spent after a 48-hour day. We have dealt in some detail in Chapter 5 with the way in which social workers spend their time. Here we would like to reiterate that unformulated jobs with imprecise objectives are indeed especially exhausting because one can never say when one has finished, nor even when one has made a good attempt. We think our idea of attachment to general practice could help social workers to recognise the necessity of good organisation and precise objectives, and might even prevent some of them complaining about pressure of work when they see the bombardment that is the lot of the average GP. We do genuinely sympathise with the excessive strain which many social workers suffer, and our suggestions are an attempt to help them restructure (or should it be structure?)

their work and reformulate (or formulate?) their objectives in ways which may be more helpful to clients, less painful to social workers, and less costly to taxpayers.

We have indicated that we would welcome opportunities for local authorities to conduct their own area-based experiments, preferably absolved from the mandatory provisions of social service legislation. We recognise the problem of the negligent, slothful, ill-endowed local authority, and concede that central government would need to employ a fail/safe inspectorate of the kind that used to be employed to monitor standards. We nevertheless prefer local approaches to local problems, especially those concerned with intensely personal services. If some local authorities chose to abandon social work provision, or even social services departments *tout court,* we would hazard that no substantial hardship would result. The social work strike provides evidence that some necessary functions would be undertaken by official agencies, some by volunteers. The latter would, we think, be wholly desirable, as would the resumption by parents of responsibility for their children, and by children for their aged parents. It would be utopian to suppose that the withdrawal of official care for deprived children and old people would at a stroke restore a sense of duty to defaulting citizens. Humanity would not permit such a withdrawal, since incapacity as well as irresponsibility causes neglect. There are, nevertheless, grounds for suspecting that the existence of 'professional' care persuades people to seek it who might otherwise do their own caring. This is not always a culpable evasion of responsibility; some have been led to believe that old people are genuinely better off in hygienic old people's homes than muddling along in their own. June Lait remembers with awe from her 'professional' child care days a well-heeled middle-class mother of a two-year-old, living amicably next door to her own mother, who requested the child's admission to a council nursery when she was confined. She had read in the *Guardian* newspaper that the Children Act 1948 incorporated nursery provision, and thought 'it would be nicer for her little boy to have others to play with' than to be with his grandmother. The latter was anxious to have him, and deeply wounded by her daughter's attitude, but accepting and respectful of what she thought was official policy.

We do not (though we think we could) argue against collective provision on ideological grounds. We simply record our observation that officially provided substitutes for families are uncomfortable, expensive and usually unhappy billets. It may be that officially provided advice on personal matters suffers from the same defects, especially if unsolicited; and we hope that withdrawal of state funding for particularly ineffectual forms might throw some capable people firmly back on their own resources.

We have talked at length about the unwieldy, bureaucratic nature of social services departments. If they are to remain in any form, we should like to see each one providing services for not more than 50,000 people and preferably fewer. Such an arrangement which would inevitably lessen the size of the administrative unit, might have the incidental benefit of removing any pretence that hierarchical structures with all the paraphernalia of specialist advisers, useless as they have been shown to be except to themselves (see pp. 62, 63), are needed. We would hope that if work at present being undertaken by Professor R. Hedley and associates at Lancaster University confirms his and our suspicions that social work undertaken on a small scale by a locally based worker, which he terms the patch system, is more effective than centrally administered provision, irrespective of the qualifications and funding of the worker, notice will be taken of his findings. An early exponent of this view is Robert Lait, whose submission to the Seebohm Committee was, it seems, unheeded. Bob Holman, former professor of social work at Bristol and now a community social worker for the Church of England Children's Society, is courageously testing similar views, and will record his experiences in a series of articles in *New Society*. His experience will undoubtedly be valuable, though we think it very likely that the success or failure of experiments of this kind turn on the personality of the worker. We fear that the hand of officialdom, with its necessary reaching for regularities and accountability, might well destroy the spontaneity that is the mainspring of such ventures, and indeed we suspect that the whole concept of professional social work may be flawed for the same reasons.

We are also concerned that when compassion goes public, the involvement of ordinary citizens diminishes, either because they are intimidated by the 'professionals' who corner the market, or because they feel that taxpaying absolves them from caring or entitles them to get their money's worth. To paraphrase Octavia Hill, when the public purse is open not only is the private purse shut, but the private heart begins to grow calluses.

We do not dispute that many therapeutic activities (open heart surgery, for example) are best carried out by competent professionals unhampered by enthusiastic lay participants. Social work is not, in our view, one of them, and we find irritating complaints by social workers that councillors 'interfere' in 'professional' decisions. While local authorities retain control of social services, we would like to see more, not less involvement of elected members in social work activities. We have made only passing reference to 'community work' in our chapter on radical social work, and it is not an area that either of us pretends to understand. But we are unconvinced that the current vogue for 'community workers' employed by local authorities does more than absolve councillors from doing the job for which they were elected. We think it highly probable that local councillors will comprehend the social, personal and community problems of their constituents better than imported strangers, however trained. We therefore urge those who wish to enter 'community work' to seek the approval of the electorate rather than embark on training of untested merit, or to work in a voluntary capacity when they see an opportunity to do so.

From the dual considerations of the desirability of lay participation and the unsatisfactory nature of 'professional friendship', then, we hope some local authorities will disband their Departments of Applied Love (as the *Daily Telegraph*, quoting the British Association of Social Workers' pamphlet *The Social Work Task*, once styled them). Being optimists about the capacity of individuals and communities to behave humanely to each other when left alone to do so, we anticipate that volunteers would step into any genuine breaches, but that the genuine breaches would be narrower than anticipated. If the history of social policy is any guide (and Popper might deny it) official support would be given to the volunteer activity when it had demonstrated a need, but we would hope that official takeover bids would be resisted. We think as good a way as any of demonstrating social need is the readiness of ordinary citizens to respond to it; and there is no surer way of drying up the springs of human kindness than mandating them through official channels. Edward Baines writing in 1846 remarked:

> The tendency of all things committed to government is to become stagnant, frozen, bound in chains which it requires a Hercules to break. At first infinite diligence, excellent arrangements and the most charming annual reports. By and by stiffness, formality, indifference. Ere long a positive hostility to all reform, complaint or disturbance.

Local committees, like the ones that for so long and so effectively have provided and overseen those admirable institutions, Citizen's Advice Bureaux, would seem to be more flexible instruments for mediating sensitive personal services. Complaints by social workers that such bodies are staffed by ignorant do-gooding nosey parkers accords ill with their reiterated calls for 'community involvement'. Can it be that community involvement is all right so long as a 'professional' is in charge?

We are well aware that we shall be accused of heartlessness when we suggest the possibility of abolishing social work, and told we do not care about battered babies and neglected old people. Against such charges we can only say that neither of us is careless of the needs of vulnerable groups, and though we do not think it appropriate to flaunt our liberal qualifications both of us have campaigned actively for causes that benefit the vulnerable. It is simply that we can find no convincing evidence that the intervention of social workers has prevented a single case of baby battering except where they have physically removed the child from the threatening environment (a course they are frequently unwilling to undertake on account of their beliefs about the importance of the biological tie). As for old people, visits from social workers may be better than no visits at all, but the evidence is that the services needed are practical and can be provided by competent untrained officials, who are just as likely to be kindly, sympathetic people as are social workers, and if Rutherford is to be believed (see p.44), marginally more likely to be reliable. They may also be less resentful of practical tasks than the young lady (p. 84) who found chiropody such a bore.

Finally, provision of social services is not a once-for-all activity, but will obviously be affected by changes in society. We are not so naive as to suggest that, having found what social workers are doing and what 'significant others' think about it in 1980, a definitive position will have been reached. There are important questions to be debated about the effect of state provision of personal social services on the quality of family life, about the role of charging for social services, about the place of volunteers and a host of others which have only been hinted at in this book. All we have sought to do is to examine one small area of an immensely complex series of provisions, and to suggest how information about it might be obtained with a view to improving its effectiveness, leaving it as it is, or abolishing it. The decision as to which it should be must not be left to those with a professional interest in maintaining the *status quo*. If this book has contributed to the debate it will have been worth writing. If it has caused involved professionals to reflect on their roles and to question their usefulness it may have contributed, however modestly, to providing more effective services. We hope that is what it has been about.

Appendix

The Single Case Experimental Design (after Sheldon)

Step 1 Problems are loosely defined in conjunction with the clients and other interested parties on the basis of a collective understanding of current supporting factors as well as their historical origins. Hypotheses about the origins of problems and their potential solutions are erected. These may be modified to suit later developments, but should be as 'risky' as possible at each stage. E.g. (i) 'Mr. Brown's coolness towards his stepson is born of a fear of rejection'. This hypothesis may be tested in conversation with Mr. Brown — does it 'feel right' to him, does he conceive of the problem in these terms, etc. It may be more rigorously tested by the addition of the following clause: (ii) 'A counselling experience which provides Mr. Brown with opportunities to discuss the problem, and to prepare in advance his reactions to potentially hurtful comments, will result in Mr. Brown spending more time in joint activities with his stepson'. 'Amount of time, etc.' thus becomes an indicator of positive or negative outcome, and is given equal status alongside reports of the emotional experience of spending time with stepson.

Step 2 Negotiations take place to 'anchor' qualitative definitions in observable behaviour. Thus, information will be required about what client X visibly does, or does not do, which leads others to describe him as having, for example, 'an inferiority complex' or 'an aggressive personality'.

Step 3 From these new behavioural definitions a hierarchy of problems is constructed and an attempt is made to establish 'contractual' obligations for the parties involved.

Step 4 Selected problems are then baselined. That is, a record of instances is kept, either by the client himself, or by others concerned, prior to the main attempt to influence the problem.

Step 5 The main social work effort begins. Records continue and recorded variations in behaviour are placed alongside verbal progress reports.

Step 6 If the social worker and/or the client wish to know whether or not it is a specific pattern of intervention causing any changes, it is possible in *some* cases to return to baseline at this point; i.e. to temporarily halt, then restart the social work programme and observe what happens. This has the advantage that the factors controlling the problem are clearly demonstrated to the participants.

Step 7 If this kind of suspension is not possible, then evaluation in terms of amounts of behavioural change, and the client's impressions of the process of change, takes place. Just as 'increased levels of social contact' as an outcome, is of little use if this has not lead in the long term to greater enjoyment, then, if 'greater social confidence' as an outcome, does not result in the client doing anything different, it is also of doubtful validity. The qualitative aspect acts as a check on the quantitative aspect at each stage and vice versa.

(We had hoped to reproduce the case review system devised by the National Institute for Social Work, but technical difficulties prevented this. The document can be obtained on application to the Institute, Mary Ward House, 5 Tavistock Place, London WC1.)

References

Adam, C. (1979) 'Social Work Strike', *Guardian,* 12-14 March.

Ainsworth, F., (with Hunter, J.) (1975) *A Unitary Approach to Social Work Practice,* University of Dundee.

Alderson, J. (1977) *Communal Policing,* Devon and Cornwall Constabulary.

Andreski, S. (1972) *Social Sciences as Sorcery,* Deutsch.

Bagley, C. (1968) 'The Evaluation of a Suicide Prevention Scheme by an Ecological Method', *Social Science and Medicine,* Vol. 2, pp. 1-14.

Bailey, R. and Brake, M. (eds), (1975) *Radical Social Work,* Arnold.

Baird, P. (1976) 'Process or Outcome?', *Social Work Today,* Vol. 7, No. 1, pp. 10-11.

Baird, P. (1979) 'The Sharp End', *Community Care,* No. 266.

Barraclough, B. M., Jennings, C., and Moss, J. R. (1977) 'Suicide Prevention by the Samaritans: a Controlled Study of Effectiveness', *Lancet,* Vol. 2, pp. 237-238.

BASW (1977) 'The Social Work Task' *Working Party Report.*

BASW (1978) 'Private Practice in Social Work', *Report of Professional Development and Practice Committee,* June 1978.

BASW (1979a) 'Inquiry into an Inquiry', *Working Party Report.*

BASW (1979b) 'Private Practice in Social Work', *Working Party Report.*

Baxter, K. (1979) 'Social Work Strike', unpublished essay, University College Swansea.

Behling, J. H. (1961) 'An Experimental Study to Measure the Effectiveness of Casework Service', Franklin County Welfare Department, Columbus, cited by Mullen and Dumpson (*op. cit.*).

Bell, E. Moberly (1961) *The Story of Hospital Almoners,* Faber.

Berg, I., Consterdine, M., Hullin, R., McGuire, R. & Tyrer, S. (1978) 'The Effect of Two Randomly Allocated Court Procedures on Truancy', *British Journal of Criminology,* Vol. 18, No. 3, pp. 232-44.

Bergin, A. E., & Lambert, M. J. (1978) in Garfield, S. & Bergin, A. E. (eds), *Handbook of Psychotherapy and Behaviour Change*, 2nd edition, Wiley.

Bernstein, R. J. (1976) *The Restructuring of Social and Political Thought*, Methuen.

Best, D. (1979) Personal communication.

Birch, R. A. (1976) *Manpower and Training in the Social Services*, HMSO.

Blenker, M., Jahn, J. & Wesser, E. (1964) *Serving the Ageing*, Community Service Society of New York, cited by Mullen & Dumpson (*op. cit.*).

Bolant, J. L. (1975) *Profession and Monopoly: A Study of Medicine in the United States and Britain*, University of California Press.

Bowen, B. *et. al.* (1978) 'Adventure into Health', *Update*.

Brewer, C. (1974) 'ECT: White Man's Magic?' *New Psychiatry*, 14 November 1974.

Brewer, C. (1977) 'In The Country of The Blind, The Double-Blind is King', *World Medicine*, Vol. 12, 30 November 1977, pp. 53-8.

British Association of Social Workers: *see* BASW.

Brogden, M. & Wright, T. (1979) 'What About the Workers?', *Social Work Today*, Vol. 10, No. 37.

Brown, G. E. (1968) *The Multi-problem Dilemma*, Metuchen, N. J.: Scarecrow Press, cited by Mullen & Dumpson (*op. cit.*).

Carver, V. & Edwards, J. L. (1972) *Social Workers and their Caseloads*, National Institute for Social Work Training.

Central Council for Education and Training in Social Work: *see* CCETSW.

CCETSW (1972) Teaching Sociology in Social Work Courses.

CCETSW (1975a) Report no. 2, pp. 73-4.

CCETSW (1975b) Paper no. 9.1.

CCETSW (1976) 'Values in Social Work', Discussion Paper.

CCETSW (1977a) Consultative Document no. 3.

CCETSW (1977b) Paper no. 9.3.

CCETSW (1978a) Report no. 3, pp. 74-7.

CCETSW (1978b) Workshop with Nottingham University, undated Paper no. 10.

CCETSW (undated) *Introducing Social Work*.

Chapman, L. (1979) *Your Disobedient Servant*, Penguin.

Chapman, R. A. (1973) *Role of Commissions in Policy Making*, Unwin University Books.

Clarkson, E. M. R. (1974) *Medical Social Work*, University of Rajshahi.

Clayton, P. (1979) 'Looking back on the Strikes', *Social Work Today,* 22 May 1979.

Cooper, B. *et al* (1975) 'Mental Health Care in the Community. An Evaluative Study', *Psychological Medicine,* Vol. 5, No. 4.

Corney, R. & Briscoe, M. (1977) 'Social Workers and their Clients', *Journal of the Royal College of General Practitioners,* May 1977.

Crowe, M. J. (1978) 'Conjoint Marital Therapy: a Controlled Outcome Study', *Psychological Medicine,* Vol. 8, pp. 623-36.

Curtis, M. (1946) *Report of the Care of the Children Committee,* HMSO, Command 6922. Department of Health and Social Services: *see* DHSS.

De Walt, B. (1979) Personal communication.

DHSS (1974) 'The Report of the Committee of Inquiry into the Care and Supervision Provided in Relation to Maria Colwell'.

DHSS (1977) *Intermediate Treatment: 28 Choices,* Social Work Service Development Group, London.

Donnison, D. (1975) *Social Policy and Administration Revisited,* Allen & Unwin.

Driberg, T. (1978) *Ruling Passions,* Quartet.

Draper, J. (1979) 'Intermediate Care. An Offer He ought to Refuse?', *Community Care,* 19 April 1979.

Dronfield, M. W., Atkinson, M. & Langman, M. J. (1979) 'Effect of Different Operation Policies on Mortality from Bleeding Peptic Ulcer', *Lancet,* Vol. 1, pp. 1126-28.

Ettlinger, R. (1975) 'Evaluation of Suicide Prevention after Attempted Suicide', *Acta Psychiatrica Scandinavica,* Supplement 260.

Eysenck, H. J. (1952) 'The Effects of Psychotherapy: An Evaluation', *Journal of Consulting Psychology,* Vol. 16, pp. 319-24.

Eysenck, H. J. & Wilson, G. D. (1973) *The Experimental Study of Freudian Theories,* Metheun.

Fabian Society (1970) *The Fifth Social Service,* Fabian Society (*see also* Townsend, 1970).

Farmer, M. Holgate, E., Keidar, O. and Flynn, A. (1977), 'The Independent Social Work Agency: A Report of the First Year of an experiment in Social Casework', *British Journal of Social Work* Vol. 7, No. 3.

Fischer, J. (1976) *The Effectiveness of Social Casework,* Springfield, 111.: Charles C. Thomas.

Fischer, J. (1978a) *Effective Casework Practice: an Eclectic Ap-*

proach, McGraw Hill, New York.

Fischer, J. (1978b) 'Does Anything Work?', *Journal of Social Science Research,* vol. 1, no. 3, pp. 215-243.

Fitzgerald, R. (1978) 'Classification and Recording of Social Problems', *Social Science and Medicine,* Vol. 12.

Forman, J. S. and Fairbairne, E. M. (1968) *Social Casework in General Practice,* Oxford University Press.

Freud, S. (1962) *Two Short Accounts of Psychoanalysis,* translated by J. Strachey, pp. 48-71, cited by Eysenck & Wilson (1973).

Fry A. (1979) *Community Care.* 4 October, p. 6.

Geismar, L. L. & Krisberg, J. (1967) *The Forgotten Neighbourhood,* Metuchen, N. J.: Scarecrow Press.

Geismar, L. L. (1971) 'Implications of a Family Life Improvement Project', *Social Casework,* Vol. 52, No. 7, p. 465, cited by Mullen & Dumpson, *op. cit.*

Geismar, L. L. (1972) 'Thirteen Evaluative Studies', in Mullen & Dumpson, *op. cit.*

Gibbons, J. S., Butler, J., Urwin, P. and Gibbons, J. L. (1978) 'Evaluation of a Social Work Service for Self-Poisoning Patients', *British Journal of Psychiatry,* Vol. 133, pp. 111-18.

Glampson, A. and Goldberg, E. (1976) 'The Consumer's Viewpoint', *Social Work Today,* Vol. 8, No. 6.

Goldberg, E. M. (1970) *Helping the Aged,* Allen & Unwin.

Goldberg, E. M. and Fruin, D. J. (1976) 'A Case Review System', *British Journal of Social Work,* Vol. 6. No. 1.

Goldberg, E. M., *et al.* (1977) 'Towards Accountability in Social Work', *British Journal of Social Work,* Vol. 7, No. 3.

Goldberg, E. M. (1978) *Social Work since Seebohm. All Things to All Men?,* National Institute of Social Work.

Goldberg, E. M., Walker, D. & Robinson, J. (1977) 'Exploring the Task-Centred Casework Method', *Social Work Today,* Vol. 9, No. 2.

Gritter, G. W. (1978) 'Triage in the Mental Health Services', *New Zealand Medical Journal,* Vol. 88, p. 202.

Gruneberg, M. (1979) *Understanding Job Satisfaction,* Macmillan.

Guy's Health District (1979) *Effects of a Prolonged Social Workers' Strike on the Health Visiting Service.*

Hall, P. (1976) *Reforming the Welfare,* Heinemann.

Harris, N. & Palmer, E. (1976) 'How Do Social Workers Spend their Time?', *Community Care,* No. 111, 19 May 1978.

Hassall, C. & Stilwell, J. (1976) 'A Study of the Work of Social

Workers', unpublished study for the Worcester Development Project.

Hassall, C. & Stilwell, J. (1978) *Worcester Development Project: The Work of the Community Psychiatric Nursing Service,* unpublished.

Hassall, C. (1979) Personal communication.

Heasman, K. (1962) *Evangelicals in Action,* Bles.

Heywood, J. and Allen, B. (1971) *Financial Help in Social Work,* University of Stirling.

Holling, H. E. (1944) 'Prevention of Sea-Sickness by Drugs', *Lancet,* Vol. 1, p. 127.

Hollis, F. (1968) *Typologies of Casework Treatment,* Columbia, cited by Baird, P., 1976.

Home Office (1969) *The Sentence of the Court,* HMSO.

Hutton, B. (1978) Personal Communication.

Jehu, D., Hardiker, P., Yelloly, M. and Shaw, M. (1972) *Behaviour Modification in Social Work,* Wiley.

Johnson, Paul (1977) *Enemies of Society*, Weidenfeld & Nicolson.

Jones, D.I.R. (1977) Self-poisoning with Drugs: the Past Twenty Years in Sheffield, *British Medical Journal,* Vol. 1, pp. 28-9.

Jones, W. C. & Borgatta, E. F. (1972) 'Methodology of evaluation' *in* Mullen & Dumpson (op. cit.).

Joseph, K. & Sumption, J. (1979) *Equality,* Murray.

Kühl, P. H. (1969) *The Family Centre Project,* Danish National Institute of Social Research, Copenhagen, cited by Mullen & Dumpson (*op. cit.*).

Kuhn, T. (1969) *The Structure of Scientific Revolution,* University of Chicago Press.

Lait, J. M. (1979a) 'The unnecessary profession', *Community Care,* 5 April 1979.

Lait, J. M. (1979b) 'Less worse is better than better', *Community Care,* 14 June 1979.

Lait, J. M. (1979c) 'By their absence shall ye know them', *World Medicine,* 17 January 1979.

Lait, R. F. (1968) *Evidence to Seebohm Committee,* Ministry of Housing and Local Government Archives.

Latiry, J. (1978) *Development of Case Review System,* Strathclyde Regional Council.

Le Mesurier (1949) Untitled, in Timms N. (1964).

Lowinger, P. and Dobie, S. (1969) 'What Makes the Placebo Work?', *Archives of General Psychiatry,* Vol. 20, pp. 84-8.

Mackintosh, J. M. (1951) *Report of the Committee on Social Workers in the Mental Health Services,* Cmnd 8260, HMSO.

Mayer, J. and Rosenblatt, A. (1964) 'Sources of Stress Amongst Student Practitioners of Social Work', *Journal of Education for Social Work,* vol. 10.

Mayer, J. and Timms, N. (1970) *The Client Speaks,* Routledge and Kegan Paul.

Marin, R. C. (1969) 'A Comprehensive Program for Multi-Problem Families. Report on a Four-Year Controlled Experiment', Puerto Rico, cited by Mullen & Dumpson (*op. cit.*).

Marks, I. M., Hodgson, R. and Rachman, S. (1975) 'Treatment of Obsessive-Compulsive Neurosis by *in vivo* Exposure', *British Journal of Psychiatry,* Vol. 127, pp. 349-64.

McCabe, A. R., Seligman, A., Pyrke, M., Berkowitz, L., Kogan, L. & Pettiford, P. (1967) *The Pursuit of Promise,* Community Service Society, New York, cited by Mullen & Dumpson (*op. cit.*).

Mead, A. (1973) *Collaboration Between Health and Personal Social Services.* University of Sussex.

Medical Research Council (1965) 'Clinical Trial of the Treatment of Depressive Illness', *British Medical Journal,* Vol. 1, p. 881.

Meyer, H. J., Borgatta, E. F. & Jones, W. C. (1969) *Girls at Vocational High: an experiment in Social Work intervention,* Sage Foundation, New York.

Meyer, C. H. (1972) *Practice on microsystem level in* Mullen & Dumpson (*op. cit.*).

Miller, C. & Scott, T. (1979) 'Tilting at Windmills', *Community Care,* no. 259.

Mills, C. W. (1966) *The Sociological Imagination,* Oxford University Press.

Morgan, P. (1978) *Delinquent Fantasies,* Temple Smith.

Morgan, P. (1979) Personal Communication.

Mullen, E. J., Chazin, R. M. & Feldstein, R. M. (1970) *Preventing Chronic Dependency.* Community Service Society, New York, cited by Kullen & Dumpson (*op. cit.*).

Mullen, E. J. & Dumpson, J. R. (eds) (1972) *Evaluation of Social Intervention,* Jossey-Bass.

NACRO (In press) *Intermediate treatment; the Hammersmith Teenage Project.* London. NACRO.

Newman, J. H. (1923) *The Idea of a University,* Longmans Green.

Oliver, J. E., & Buchanan, A. H. (1979) 'Generations of maltreated children and multi-agency care in one kindred', *British journal of Psychiatry,* Vol. 135, pp. 289-303.

Oppenheimer, P. (1978) 'File on Four', BBC production, 12 December 1978.

Page, A. (1979) 'On the Strike', *Community Care,* 25 April 1979.

Park, L. C. and Covi, L. (1965) 'Non-blind Placebo Trial', *Archives of General Psychiatry*, Vol. 12, pp. 336-45.

Parker, J. (1965) *Local Health and Welfare Services*, Allen & Unwin'.

Parkinson, C. N. (1958) *Parkinson's Law*, Murray.

Parloff, M. B., Waskow, I. E. & Wolf, B. E. (1978) in Garfield, S. and Bergin, A. E. (eds), *Handbook of Psychotherapy and Behaviour Change,* 2nd edition, Wiley, New York.

Parry, N. and Parry, J. (1976) *The Rise of the Medical Profession*: *a Study of Collective Social Mobility*, Croom Helm.

Parsloe, P. (1977) 'How training may unfit people', *Social Work Today*, Vol. 4, 20 September 1977.

Parsloe, P. (1978) *Social Service Teams, The Practitioners' View,* HMSO.

Payne, M. (1977) 'An apprenticeship model of social work education', *Social Work Today*, Vol. 9, No. 5.

Pinker, R. (1979) Personal Communication.

Pins, A. M. (1963) *Who Does Social Work, When and Why?*, Council for Social Work Education, U.S.A.

Popper, K. (1945) *The Open Society and its Enemies,* Routledge & Kegan Paul.

Popper, K. (1959) *The Logic of Scientific Discovery,* Hutchinson.

Pratt, J. P. & Thomas, W. L. (1937) 'Endocrine Treatment of Menopausal Phenomena', *Journal of the American Medical Association*, Vol. 109, pp. 1875-7.

Prentice, R. C. (1978) *Concepts of Effectiveness and Inferred Worth in Social Services Resource Allocation,* Durham University Business School.

Prentice, R. C. (1979) *A prospect into the 1980s for corporate planning in local government,* University College, Swansea, Occasional Paper No. 1

Prins, H. (1975) 'Motivation in Social Work', *Social Work Today,* Vol. 5.

Rankine, W. (1978) in *News of the World,* 23 April 1978, p. 4.

Ratoff *et al.* (1973) 'Seebohm and the National Health Service', *British Medical Journal,* 19 May 1973.

Registrar-General of Scotland (1977) *Annual Report,* Part 1, HMSO.

Reid, W. J. and Epstein, L. (1972) *Task-Centred Casework,* Columbia University Press.

Reid W. J. and Shyne A. W. (1969) *Brief and Extended Casework,* Columbia University Press.

Residential Care Association (1977) Report of the AGM.

Reynolds, D. (1978) 'Treatments under Suspended Sentence', *Community Care,* 31 May 1978.

Richan, W. C. & Mendelsohn, A. R. (1973) 'Social Work: The Un-loved Profession', *New Viewpoints,* New York.

Rosenhahn, D. L. (1973) 'On Being Sane in Insane Places', *Science,* Vol. 179, pp. 250-8.

Rutherford, D. (1977) 'Personality in social work students', *Social Work Today,* Vol. 8 (20), 22 February 1977, p. 9.

Rutter, M., Maughan, B., Mortimore, P. & Ouston, J. (1979) *Fifteen Thousand Hours: Secondary Schools and Their Effects on Children,* Open Books.

Ryan, T. M. R. (1967) 'Child Guidance', *Social Work,* Vol. 24, No. 3.

Sainsbury, E. (1977) *Personal Social Services,* Pitman.

Sainsbury, P., Bart, A. & Jenkins J. (in press) *Suicide Trends in Europe: A Study of the Decline in Suicide in England and Wales and the Increases Elsewhere,* World Health Organisation, Copenhagen.

Schwarz, E. E. & Sample, W. C. (1970) *Organisation and Utilisation of Public Service Personnel,* School of Social Service Admini-stration, Chicago, cited by Mullen & Dumpson (*op. cit.*).

Seagrave, J. R. (1978) 'The Brutal Realities of Dealing with Need', *Municipal and Public Services Journal,* Vol. 86, No. 1

Seebohm, F. (1968) *Report on the Local Authority and Allied Personal Social Services,* HMSO, Comnd. 3703.

Seldon, A. (1976) *The Impact of the Implementation of the Child-ren and Young Persons Act. 1969, On Obtaining Residential Accommodation for Children in Trouble,* MSc. dissertation, Brunel University.

Seldon, A. (1978) *Charge,* Temple Smith.

Serota, B. (1970) *Family Health and Social Services in the 70's,* National Institute of Social Work.

Shapiro, A. K. & Morris, L. A. (1978) 'The Placebo Effect in Medical and Psychological Therapies', in Bergin and Lambert, (*op. cit.*).

Shaw, I. (1976) 'Consumer Opinion and Social Policy', *Journal of Social Policy,* Vol. 5, pt. 1.

Sheldon, B. (1978) 'Theory and Practice in Social Work: a Re-examination of a Tenuous Relationship', *British Journal of*

Social Work, Vol. 8, pp. 1-22.

Sheldon, B. (1979) 'Not Proven : Social Work Effectiveness' *Community Care,* 14 January 1979, (and subsequent correspondence).

Sherline, D. M. & Davidson, R. M. (1978) 'Adolescent Pregnancy: The Jackson, Mississippi, Experience', *American Journal of Obstetrics and Gynaecology,* Vol. 132, No. 3, pp. 245-5.

Simpkin, M. (1979) *Trapped within Welfare,* Macmillan.

Sinfield, A. (1970) *Which way for Social Work,* Fabian Society.

Sloane, R., Staples, F., Cristol, A., Yorkston, N., & Whipple, K. (1975) *Psychotherapy versus Behaviour Therapy,* Cambridge, Mass.: Harvard University Press.

Smith, M. (1953) *Professional Education for Social Work,* National Institute of Social Work.

Smith, M. J. (1965) *Professional Education for Social Work: an historical account,* Allen & Unwin, 1965.

Stevenson, N. O. (1973) *Claimant or Client,* Allen & Unwin.

Strupp, H. H. & Hadley, S. W. (1979) 'Specific versus nonspecific factors in psychotherapy; a controlled study of outcome, *Archives of General Psychiatry,* Vol. 36, No. 10, 1125-36.

Surrey Social Services Department (1979) *'Woodborough: a Study of Observation and Assessment',* Surrey County Council.

Sutherland, S. (1976) *Breakdown,* Weidenfeld & Nicolson.

Sutton, C. (1979) 'Editorial', *Behavioural Social Work,* Vol. 1, No. 1.

Tilbury, C. (1977) 'A Mammoth Task', *Social Work Today,* Vol. 9, No. 5.

Timms, N. (1964) *Psychiatric Social Work in Great Britain, 1939-1962,* Routledge & Kegan Paul.

Timms, N. & Timms, R. (1977) *Perspectives in Social Work,* Routledge & Kegan Paul.

Timms, N. and Watson, D. (1978) *Philosophy in Social Work,* Routledge & Kegan Paul.

Tonge, W. L., James, D. S. & Hillam, S. M. (1975) *Families without Hope: A Controlled Study of 33 Problem Families,* Royal College of Psychiatrists, London.

Townsend, P. (1970) *Objectives of the New Social Service,* Fabian Society.

Truax, B. B. and Carkhuff, R. R. (1967) *Towards Effective Counselling and Psychotherapy,* Aldine.

Turner, J. (1979) 'Comment', *New Society,* Vol. 48, No. 886.

Tutt, N. (1979) 'Compulsory Intervention: Who Needs It?' paper read to the Association of Reporters to Children's Panels, Annual Study Conference, 30 March — 1 April 1970.

United Community Services of Greater Vancouver (1968) *Area Development Project Monographs.* Vancouver. Cited by Mullen & Dumpson (op. cit.).

Vinar, D. (1969) 'Dependence on a Placebo: A Case Report', *British Journal of Psychiatry,* Vol. 115, pp. 1189-90.

Walker, W. L. (1972) *'Using Research Findings for Macrosystem Intervention'* in Mullen & Dumpson (*op. cit.*).

Warburton, W. (1978) *Case Review System in Action,* Cambridgeshire County Council.

Wasserman, H. (1964) 'Essay', *Social Work (USA),* Vol. 15.

Woodroofe, K. (1962) *From Charity to Social work,* Routledge & Kegan Paul.

Wootton, B. (1959) *Social Science and Social Pathology,* Allen & Unwin.

Yelloly, M. (1979) *Independent Evaluation of 25 placements,* Kent Special Family Placement Project, Kent Social Services Department.

Young, R. (1979) Personal Communication.

Younghusband, E. (1947) *Report on the Social Workers,* Constable.

Younghusband, E. (1959) *Report of the Working Party on Social workers in the Local Authority Health and Welfare Services,* HMSO.

Younghusband, E. (1966) *New Development in Casework,* National Institute of Social Work.

Younghusband, E. (1978) *Social Work in Britain 1950-1975,* two vols, Allen & Unwin.

Index